IMAGES
of America

Cleveland's Ohio City Neighborhood

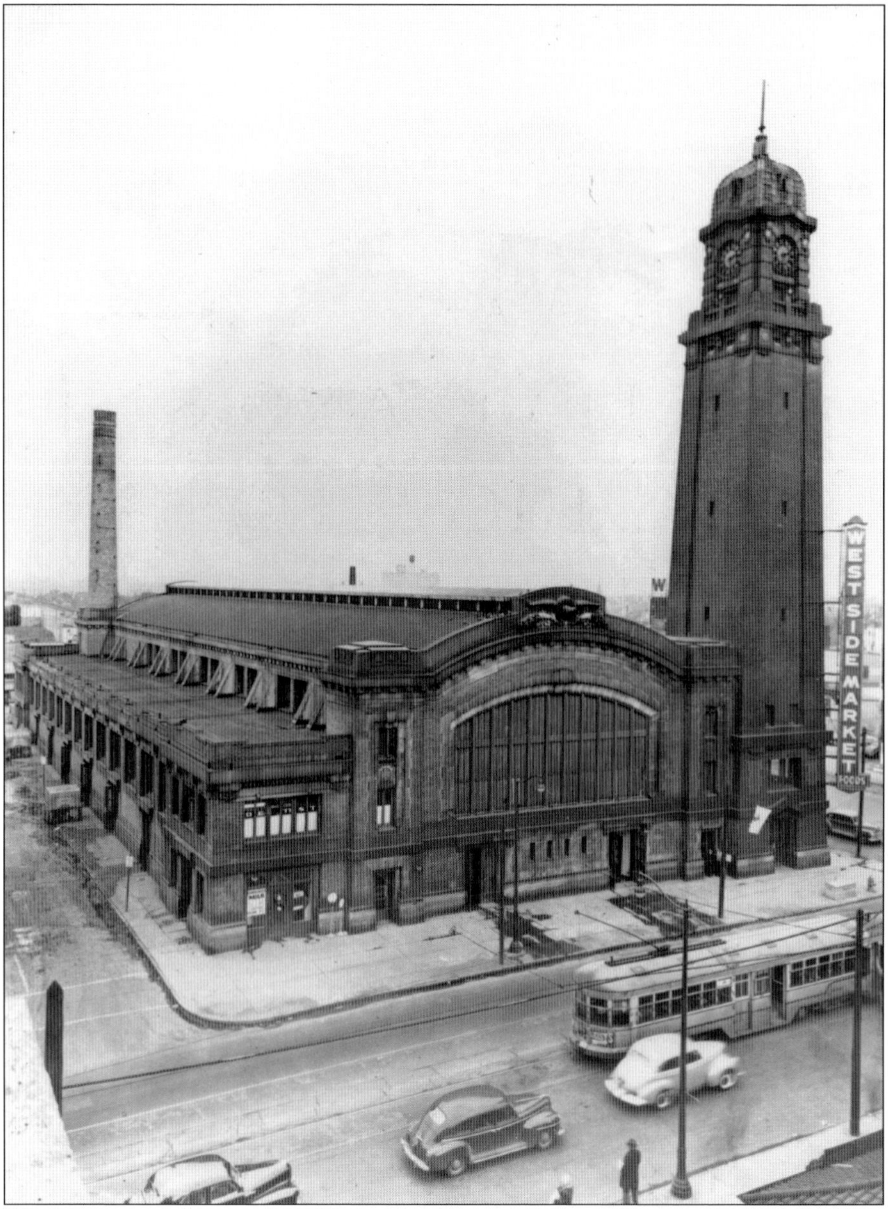

Cornerstone of Community. The West Side Market has anchored Ohio City's commercial heart since 1912. Designed by architects Hubbell and Benes, with its distinctive clock tower and vaulted interior, the building exemplifies Cleveland's grand civic vision. Captured here in 1950, the market stands proudly at the historic intersection of West Twenty-Fifth Street and Lorain Avenue, where trolleys and automobiles bring shoppers to this bustling landmark, just as it continues to serve the community today. (Cleveland Public Library Photograph Collection.)

On the Cover: Market Day Bustle. Shoppers crowd the produce arcade in 1927, where vendors displayed fresh fruits and vegetables along the market's exterior. Originally operating from curbside stands, produce sellers gained permanent shelter when the city constructed covered walkways, expanding the market's capacity to 236 total vendor stalls. (Cleveland Public Library Photograph Collection.)

IMAGES
of America

CLEVELAND'S OHIO CITY NEIGHBORHOOD

Thomas Kaschalk

ARCADIA
PUBLISHING

ISBN 978-1-4671-6284-5
Hardback ISBN: 978-1-5402-9953-6

Published by Arcadia Publishing
Charleston, South Carolina

Printed in the United States of America

Library of Congress Control Number: 2025937161

For all general information, please contact Arcadia Publishing:
Telephone 843-853-2070
Fax 843-853-0044
E-mail sales@arcadiapublishing.com

Visit us on the Internet at www.arcadiapublishing.com

To my beloved wife, Natalie, whose unwavering support and shared passion for Cleveland's history made this book possible. Your love guides every page.

Contents

Acknowledgments

This book would not have been possible without the generous support and expertise of many individuals and organizations.

I am deeply grateful to the dedicated team at the Cleveland Public Library Photograph Collection department, whose tireless efforts to explore the archives and provide invaluable images have enriched this work. Special thanks to Melissa Carr from the library's archive department, whose assistance in uncovering touching photographs of the neighborhood's historic library added a unique dimension to this book. Your collective commitment to preserving Cleveland's visual and cultural history is truly appreciated.

I also extend my sincere thanks to Elizabeth Piwkowski at Cleveland State University and the Cleveland Memory Project (clevelandmemory.org). The extensive digital archives of the Cleveland Memory Project were essential to my research, offering a wealth of historical images and documents.

Special thanks to Jim Dubelko, a retired municipal lawyer and researcher at the Center for Public History and Digital Humanities at Cleveland State University. Jim's past research and contributions of historical images were invaluable to this project, helping to illuminate Ohio City's vibrant history.

I am also deeply appreciative of Chuck Mocsiran, chief archivist for the City of Cleveland, and Dr. Judith Cetina, Cuyahoga County archivist. Your guidance, mentorship, and passion for preserving the region's historical records have significantly deepened my understanding of Cleveland's past. A heartfelt thank you goes to the group of friends who joined me to review and discuss the image selections for this book: Tony Brancatelli, Gail Glamm, John and Tina Fillinger, and Carl and Mary Brancatelli. Your thoughtful feedback, insights, and shared enthusiasm for Cleveland's history were invaluable during this process.

Finally, I am especially grateful to my family and friends whose unwavering support has sustained me throughout this endeavor. A heartfelt thank you to Brian Passell—your encouragement, friendship, and thoughtful perspective continue to shape both my writing and my personal journey.

To all who contributed in ways both large and small, I offer my heartfelt thanks.

INTRODUCTION

Ohio City's story is one of resilience and transformation—an urban center shaped by its proximity to the river, where wealthy industrialists and working-class laborers lived in close proximity, contributing to a diverse and dynamic melting pot. As one of Cleveland's oldest neighborhoods, it has witnessed the rise of industry, waves of immigration, economic booms and busts, and a renewed appreciation for its historic character. Once a separate municipality rivaling Cleveland, Ohio City has been shaped by the people who lived, worked, and built businesses there. Today, its historic streets, iconic landmarks, and cultural institutions tell the tale of a neighborhood that has not only endured but evolved to meet the changing needs of its community.

Located on the western bank of the Cuyahoga River, Ohio City's origins can be traced to 1818, when Josiah Barber and Richard Lord envisioned a thriving community. Officially incorporated in 1836, just days before Cleveland's incorporation, Ohio City was an independent municipality with its own government, economy, and identity. The two cities immediately became rivals, vying for economic dominance. This tension culminated in the infamous "Battle of the Bridge" in 1836. The dispute arose when Cleveland built a bridge connecting the east and west sides, diverting traffic away from Ohio City's commercial district. In response, Ohio City residents attempted to destroy the bridge with axes and crowbars. Though the conflict was resolved without lasting violence, it signaled the growing dominance of Cleveland, which ultimately annexed Ohio City in 1854. The merger brought significant infrastructure improvements, including the construction of the Kentucky Street Reservoir, which provided clean water to the growing city. Bridges like the Superior Viaduct further connected Ohio City to downtown Cleveland, facilitating trade and transportation.

By the mid-19th century, Ohio City had become a hub for shipbuilding, manufacturing, and brewing, fueled by its proximity to the Cuyahoga River and Lake Erie. Breweries such as Leisy, Schlather, and Gehring flourished, establishing a strong German influence in the neighborhood. The West Side Market, established in 1840 and expanded into its iconic structure in 1912, became the commercial heart of the community, offering fresh produce, meats, and baked goods to generations of residents. The market remains one of the city's most recognizable landmarks, drawing shoppers from across Cleveland.

Ohio City's development was deeply intertwined with immigration. German, Irish, and Hungarian settlers built homes, businesses, and churches, many of which still stand as architectural landmarks. St. John's Episcopal Church, founded in 1836, is the oldest consecrated building in Cuyahoga County and played a role in the Underground Railroad. St. Patrick's and St. Malachi's churches served the Irish Catholic community, while Trinity Evangelical Lutheran Church and St. Mary's catered to German immigrants. At the same time, wealthier residents built stately homes along Franklin Boulevard, creating a striking contrast between the grand mansions of industrialists and the modest cottages of factory workers. As the decades passed, new waves of immigrants, including Appalachian and Puerto Rican families, found a home in Ohio City, adding to its diverse cultural tapestry.

Despite its economic and cultural vibrancy, Ohio City faced significant challenges throughout the 20th century. The Great Depression hit the neighborhood hard, with institutions like the Martin de Porres House of Hospitality providing essential relief. World War II spurred industrial growth, but the suburban boom of the 1950s and 1960s drew longtime residents away from the urban core, leaving behind aging homes and vacant storefronts.

As the neighborhood's population declined, many historic buildings fell into disrepair. Absentee landlords neglected properties, and once-proud homes were subdivided into overcrowded rental units. Crime became a growing concern, with incidents of theft, assault, and vandalism making some residents feel unsafe. The neighborhood's reputation suffered despite the continued operation of anchors like the West Side Market and St. Ignatius High School. At the same time, new groups arrived in Ohio City, including Appalachian and Puerto Rican families seeking affordable housing and economic opportunity. While their presence added to the neighborhood's cultural diversity, tensions sometimes emerged as different communities navigated the challenges of a changing urban landscape.

By the 1970s, a renewed appreciation for preserving Ohio City's architectural heritage and efforts were underway to save key landmarks, while community activists worked to address issues of housing, crime, and economic decline. Commercial revival followed as restaurants like Heck's and Ohio City Tavern attracted diners back to the neighborhood. Young professionals and artists, drawn to the neighborhood's historic charm and affordability, began moving in, marking the early stages of gentrification. Former industrial buildings were repurposed into residential lofts, attracting new residents and businesses to the area. The 1988 opening of Great Lakes Brewing Company in a historic Market Street building sparked a craft brewing renaissance that reconnected Ohio City with its brewing heritage.

This transformation would accelerate in the coming decades, bringing both revitalization and displacement concerns. The neighborhood's designation as a historic district helped protect its architectural legacy, while investments in local businesses, restaurants, and breweries revitalized its commercial corridors. Yet, with growth comes challenges. The rapid influx of new residents and businesses has sparked debates over gentrification, affordability, and community identity. Longtime residents worry about rising property values pushing out families who have called Ohio City home for generations. Tensions between preservation and development remain, as new construction projects seek to balance modern living with the neighborhood's historic charm. The very factors that have made Ohio City a desirable place to live—walkability, historic character, and a strong sense of community—now raise questions about how to manage growth while maintaining inclusivity.

The photographs in this book tell Ohio City's story through its buildings, streets, and people. From the imposing clock tower of the West Side Market to modest worker cottages, from bustling commercial corridors to intimate residential streets, these images document both change and continuity in one of Cleveland's most distinctive neighborhoods. They capture the architectural diversity that defines the area, from restored Victorian mansions and stately brick townhomes to humble cottages and apartment buildings—each reflecting the layers of history and transformation that have shaped Ohio City over the decades.

As Ohio City continues to evolve, these photographs remind us of the value of preserving our built heritage while adapting it for new generations. They show how a neighborhood can honor its past while embracing its future—a lesson as relevant today as when Josiah Barber and Richard Lord first laid out streets on the west bank of the Cuyahoga nearly two centuries ago.

One

Establishing Ohio City

Pre-1836–1854

Before it was Ohio City, the land west of the Cuyahoga River was part of the Connecticut Western Reserve. Surveyed in 1796, the west side remained "Indian country" until 1805, when Indigenous peoples ceded the land. In 1818, the township of Brooklyn was organized, encompassing what would later become Ohio City. Early paths like Detroit and Pearl Streets became vital routes for settlers.

Josiah Barber, a Connecticut native, arrived in 1818 and partnered with his brother-in-law, Richard Lord, to develop an urban settlement rather than farmland. By 1835, they laid out streets and sold village lots, with early development centered around a public square that would evolve into Franklin Circle. Economic expansion played a critical role in Ohio City's growth. The construction of the Ohio-Erie Canal and a land speculation boom in the 1830s brought investment and new residents. Key industries emerged, including shipbuilding and iron manufacturing, with the Cuyahoga Steam Furnace Company employing over 100 workers by 1834. As the community grew, so did its institutions; churches like St. John's Episcopal and early Methodist and Presbyterian congregations were founded to serve the population.

The "City of Ohio" was officially incorporated on March 3, 1836, just two days before Cleveland, sparking a rivalry. The competition intensified with Cleveland's construction of the Columbus Street Bridge in 1836. The bridge redirected trade away from Ohio City, prompting residents to dismantle parts of it in what became known as the "Bridge War." The conflict peaked on October 31, 1836, when Ohio City residents clashed with Clevelanders, resulting in several injuries before the county sheriff intervened. The courts ultimately ruled to keep both bridges open, easing immediate tensions but cementing the rivalry.

Proposals for Ohio City's annexation to Cleveland began in 1845 but were defeated until unity proved advantageous. Cleveland's need for a reservoir spurred Ohio City to vote for annexation, and the cities merged on June 5, 1854. The *Cleveland Leader* commemorated the merger, noting, "The narrow, serpentine Cuyahoga no longer divides a people that are of one interest, one in aim, and one in destiny."

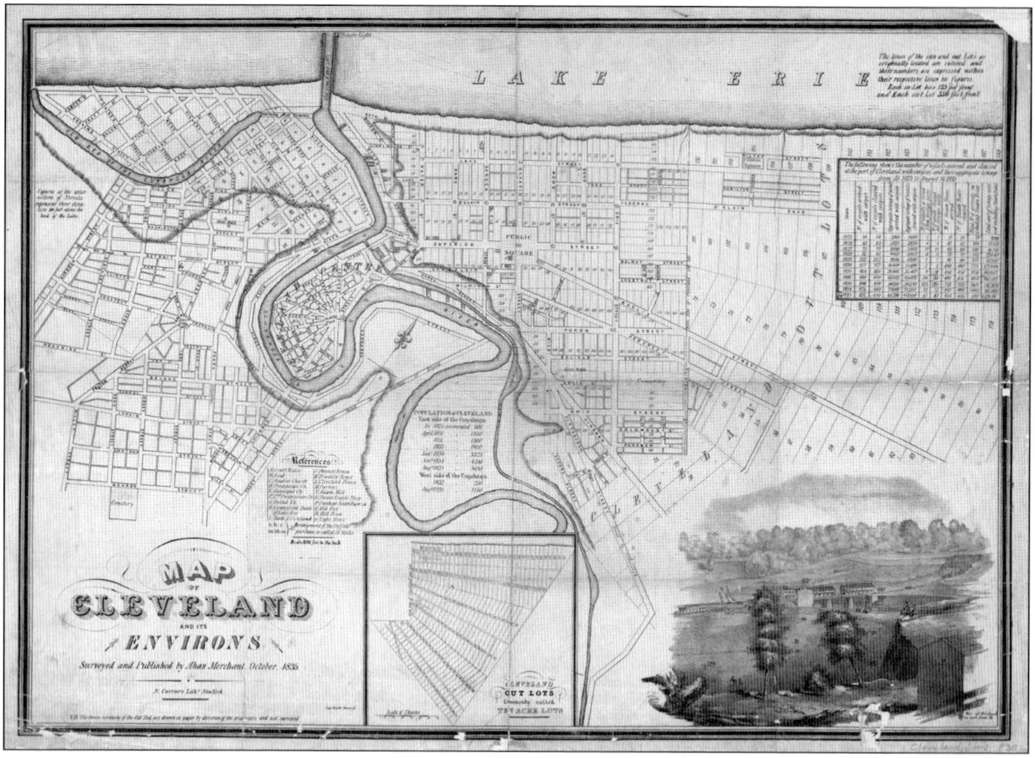

CLEVELAND AND ENVIRONS, 1835. This 1835 map, created by Cuyahoga County surveyor Ahaz Merchant, predates the incorporation of both Cleveland and Ohio City. The illustration in the lower right corner shows the Columbus Street Bridge. The map highlights the area's early development, with streets beginning to shape the community. (Michael Schwartz Library Special Collections, Cleveland State University.)

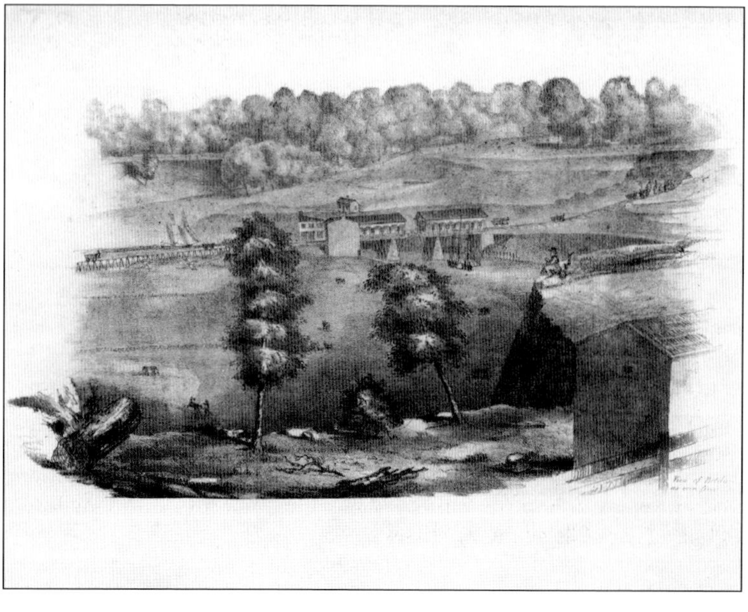

COLUMBUS STREET BRIDGE, MID-19TH CENTURY. This illustration depicts the Columbus Street Bridge over the Cuyahoga River, built around 1835–1836, as it appeared during the contentious "Battle of the Bridge" between Ohio City and Cleveland residents. The bridge is covered, with a central drawbridge to allow boats to pass. (Cleveland Public Library Photograph Collection.)

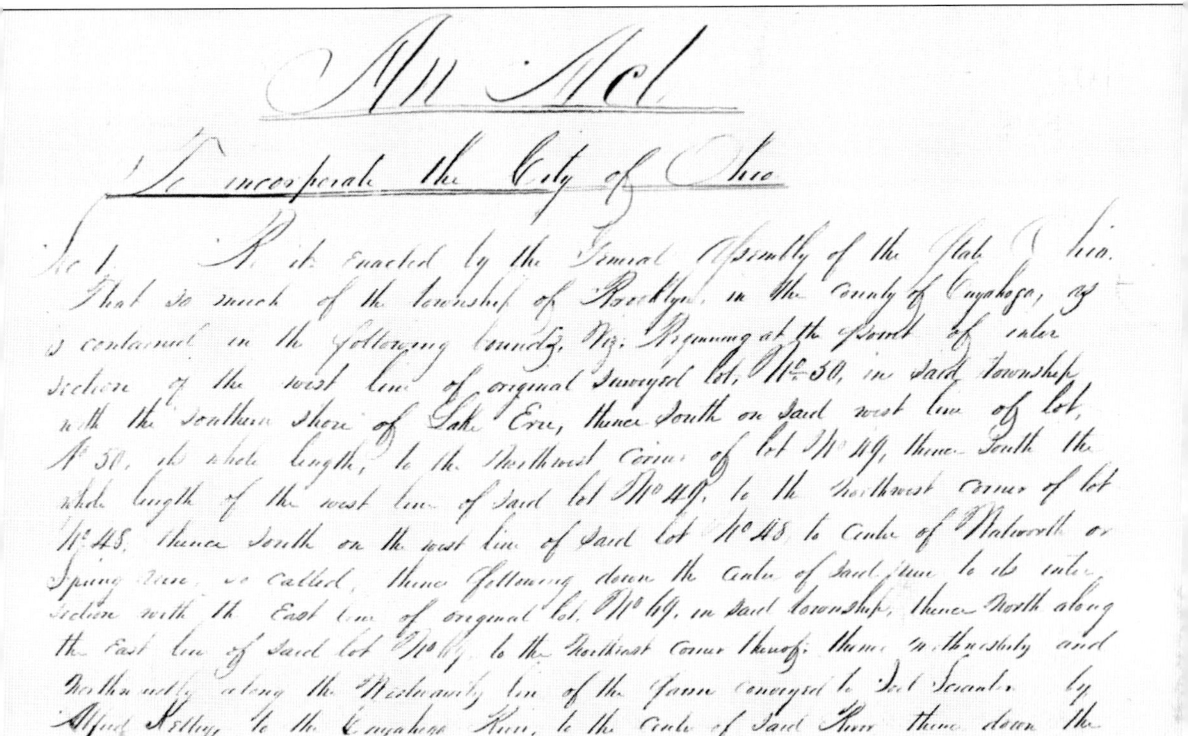

An Act

To incorporate the City of Ohio

Sec 1. Be it Enacted by the General Assembly of the State of Ohio. That so much of the township of Brooklyn, in the County of Cuyahoga, as is contained in the following bounds, viz: Beginning at the point of intersection of the west line of original surveyed lot No. 50, in said township, with the southern shore of Lake Erie, thence South on said west line of lot No 50, the whole length, to the Northwest Corner of lot No 49, thence South the whole length of the west line of said lot No 49, to the Northwest corner of lot No 48, thence South on the west line of said lot No 48 to Centre of Walworth or Spring Run, so called, thence following down the Centre of said Run to its intersection with the East line of original lot No 49, in said township, thence North along the East line of said lot No 49, to the Northeast Corner thereof, thence Northeasterly and Northwesterly along the Westwardly line of the farm conveyed to [illegible] Scranton by Alfred Kelley, to the Cuyahoga River, to the Centre of said River thence down the Centre of said River, to the Extreme Northerly End of the West Pier of the present harbor, thence Northerly in Lake Erie on the line of the townships of Brooklyn and Cleveland, to the North line of the township of Brooklyn, to a point due North from the place of beginning, thence South to said place of beginning, shall be, and hereby is declared to be a City, and the inhabitants thereof are created a body Corporate & politic, by the Name and Style of the "City of Ohio," and by that Name, shall be capable of contracting and being contracted with, of suing and being sued, pleading and being impleaded, answering and being answered unto, in all Courts & places, and in all matters whatsoever, with power of purchasing, receiving, holding, occupying and conveying real and personal Estate, and may have a Corporate Seal, and change the same at pleasure, and shall be competent to have and exercise all the rights and privileges, and be subject to all the duties and obligations appertaining to a Municipal Corporation.

Incorporation Proclamation of the City of Ohio. This historic document marks the incorporation of the City of Ohio on March 3, 1836. Before incorporation, the City of Ohio was part of Brooklyn Township, founded in 1818. Josiah Barber, a prominent landowner and visionary developer, was elected as the city's first mayor, while his brother-in-law and business partner, Richard Lord, served as the president of the city council. Barber served only one term but laid the foundation for Ohio City's early growth. Tragically, he passed away in 1842. The council proceedings, preserved here, embody the spirit of early civic engagement and the aspirations of a frontier town evolving into a thriving urban community. (The City of Cleveland Archives.)

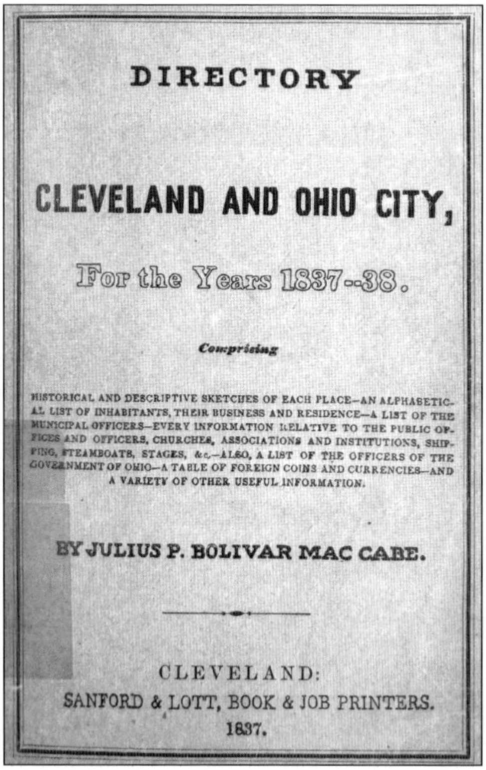
DIRECTORY

CLEVELAND AND OHIO CITY,

For the Years 1837–38.

Comprising

HISTORICAL AND DESCRIPTIVE SKETCHES OF EACH PLACE—AN ALPHABETICAL LIST OF INHABITANTS, THEIR BUSINESS AND RESIDENCE—A LIST OF THE MUNICIPAL OFFICERS—EVERY INFORMATION RELATIVE TO THE PUBLIC OFFICES AND OFFICERS, CHURCHES, ASSOCIATIONS AND INSTITUTIONS, SHIPPING, STEAMBOATS, STAGES, &c.—ALSO, A LIST OF THE OFFICERS OF THE GOVERNMENT OF OHIO—A TABLE OF FOREIGN COINS AND CURRENCIES—AND A VARIETY OF OTHER USEFUL INFORMATION.

BY JULIUS P. BOLIVAR MAC CABE.

CLEVELAND:
SANFORD & LOTT, BOOK & JOB PRINTERS.
1837.

PIONEERS IN PRINT. These pages from the 1837 City of Cleveland and Ohio City Directory showcase advertisements from businesses in Ohio City, offering a glimpse into the bustling trade environment of the time. This inaugural directory recorded a population of over 4,000 in Cleveland and 2,400 in Ohio City, reflecting the rapid growth and ambition of the region. The municipal government of Ohio City included a mayor, 12 councilmen, a recorder, a marshal, a city treasurer, and a fire department, illustrating the early framework of civic organization. Published by Julius B. MacCabe, the directory also featured the City of Cleveland's charter, a history of Cleveland, and the names of original lot owners in Cleveland, making it an invaluable snapshot of a frontier town transforming into an urban hub. (All, the Cuyahoga County Archives.)

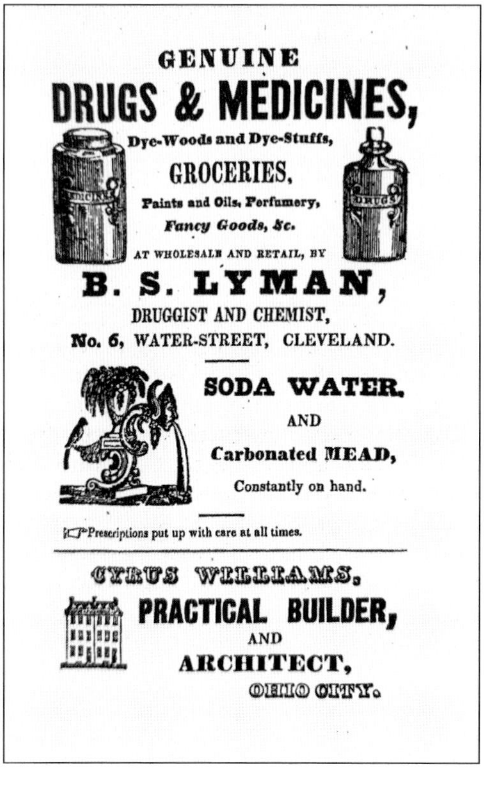

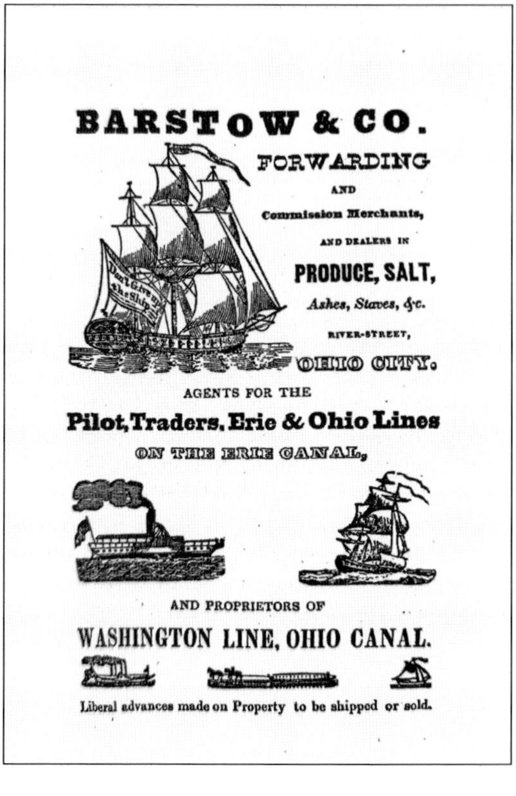

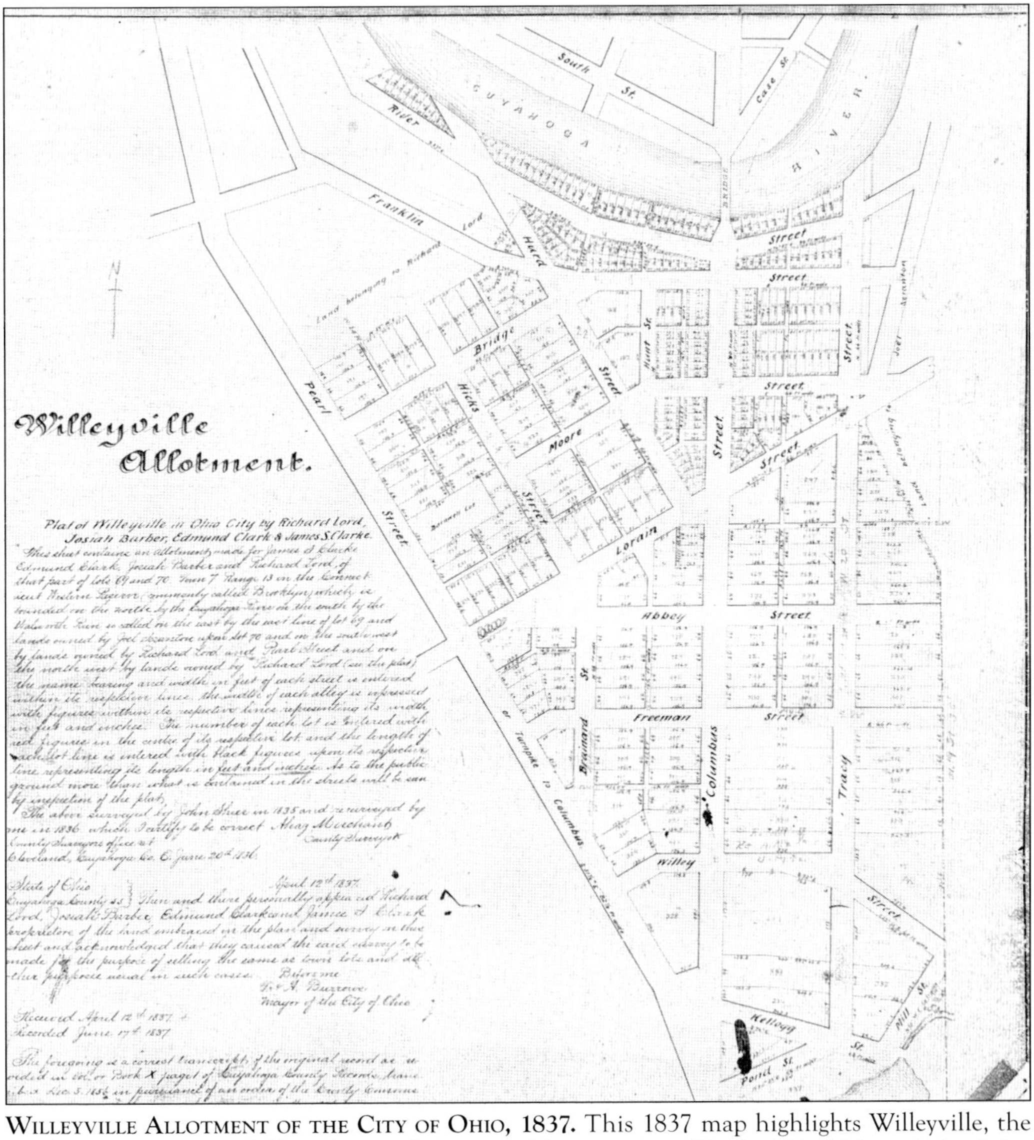

WILLEYVILLE ALLOTMENT OF THE CITY OF OHIO, 1837. This 1837 map highlights Willeyville, the southeastern section of Ohio City, and the site of the notorious "Bridge War." Named after John W. Willey, Cleveland's first mayor (1836–1838), Willeyville was part of an ambitious development project by Willey and his partner, James S. Clark. Together, they constructed a drawbridge at Columbus Road, aiming to connect Ohio City with Cleveland and funnel traffic toward their business districts, including Cleveland Centre. Willey, a lawyer and lawmaker, drafted Cleveland's original charter and was a key figure in early city governance. The bridge's strategic location sparked fierce competition with Ohio City's established routes, leading to the infamous Bridge War, a dramatic standoff that underscored the rivalry between the two communities vying for economic dominance. (The Cuyahoga County Archives.)

Oct. 7, 1853

At a meeting of the Commissioners of Cuyahoga County held pursuant to adjournment at the Auditors office in the City of Cleveland on the 7th day of October 1853, for the purpose of considering the matter of the petition of the City of Ohio for the annexation of territory to said City --- Present Diodate Clark, John Welch & Jason Bradley, Commissioners --

On the final hearing of the Case, it was ordered by the Commissioners, that the prayer of the petitioners be granted, and that the territory as ascribed in the petition be annexed to the City of Ohio

Oct. 8, 1853 - Adjourned Sine Die

Charles Winslow

Clerk to Commissioners

County Commissioner Journal Entries. These two images, transcribed by the US Works Progress Administration (WPA) around 1940, document critical milestones from the original *Cuyahoga County Commissioner Journal*. The October 1853 entry details Cleveland's petition for the annexation of the City of Ohio, marking a pivotal moment in the unification of the two municipalities. This petition was approved by the Clerk of Commissioners, setting the stage for the eventual incorporation of Ohio City into Cleveland. The 1854 entry highlights the establishment of Brooklyn Township, formalizing its separation from the City of Ohio. These journal entries reflect the dynamic political and administrative landscape of the mid-19th century as Cleveland expanded westward, reshaping municipal boundaries and fostering the area's integration and growth. (Both, the Cuyahoga County Archives.)

At a Special meeting of the Commissioners of Cuyahoga County held at the Auditors office in Cleveland June 26, 1854

Present Melancton Barnett, Jason Bradley & John Welch Commissioners -

The following business was transacted - to wit:

In the matter of the petition of the Citizens of the township of Brooklyn presented to the Commissioners at their March Session 1853 to be set off from the City of Ohio into a separate twonship, it was ordered by the Commissioners that so much of said twonship of Brooklyn as was not included in the original limits of the City of Ohio, and the territory recently annexed to the said City of Ohio by the Commissioners of the County of Cuyahoga, be & the same is hereby set off and shall form a separate township, which said township shall be called and known by the name of the township of Brooklyn -

Adj. Sine Die

Chas. Winslow

MAYOR OF TWO CITIES. William Bainbridge Castle (1814–1872), born in Essex, Vermont, was the last mayor of Ohio City (1853–1854) and later served as Cleveland's 14th mayor (1855–1856) after annexation. A member of the Whig Party, Castle was interred at Monroe Street Cemetery before being reburied at Lake View Cemetery. His leadership marked a pivotal period in Ohio City's history. This image is from *A History of Cleveland, Ohio*, published by the S.J. Clarke Publishing Company in 1910.

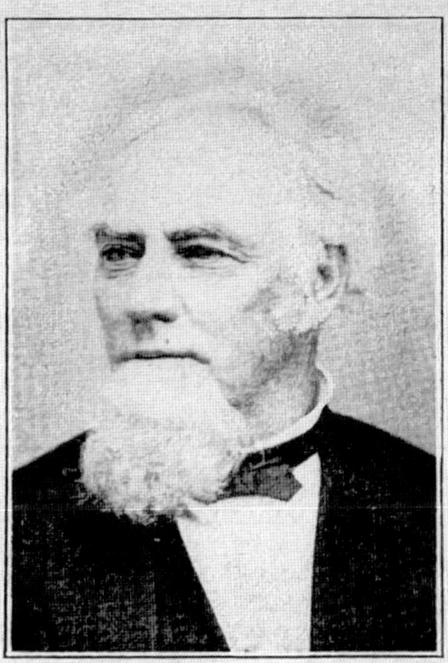

William B. Castle

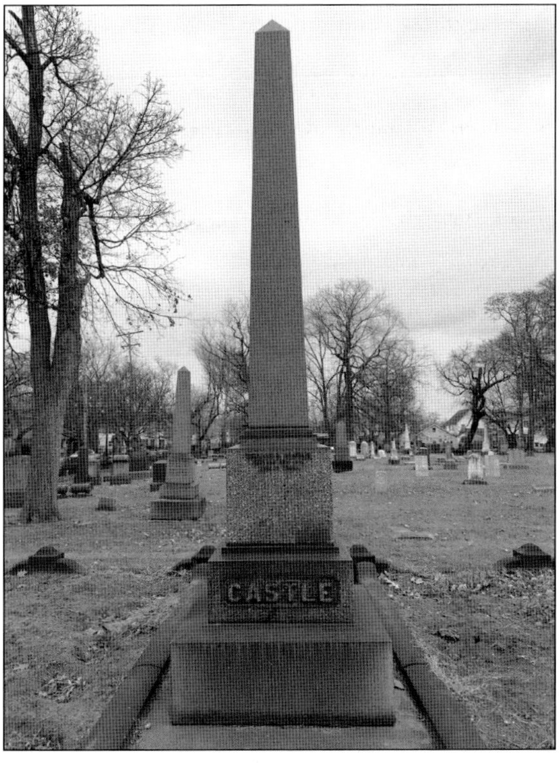

THE CASTLE PLOT. Located at Monroe Street Cemetery, this family plot remains intact despite several reinterments. William Bainbridge Castle, Cleveland's 17th mayor, was moved to Lake View Cemetery in 1888 along with his wife Mary D. and children George N. and Mary F. His father, Jonathan Castle, died of cholera in 1834 and was originally buried at Ohio City's Abbey and Lorain grounds before being reinterred at Monroe in 1837. (Author's collection.)

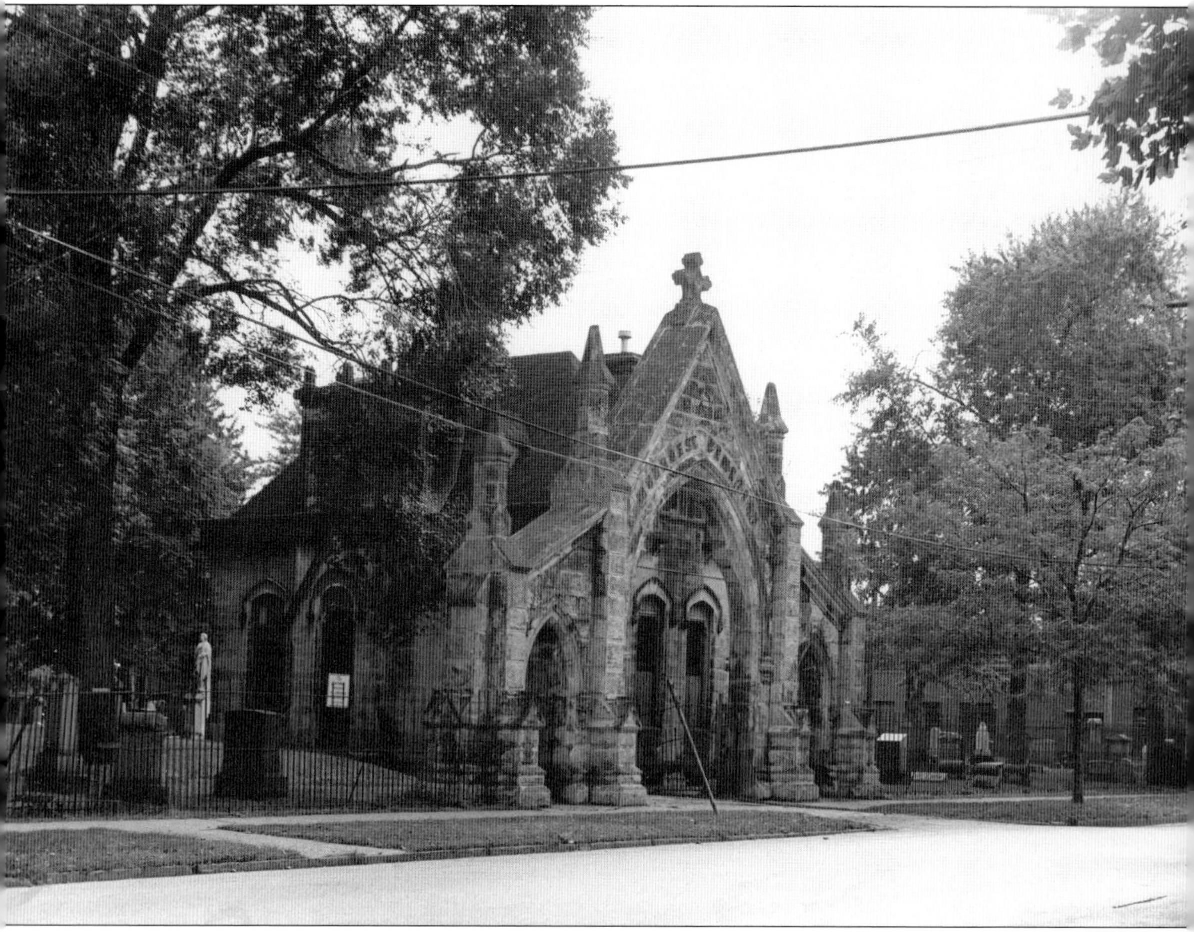

Gateway to History. Monroe Street Cemetery stands as one of Ohio City's most enduring landmarks. Established in 1836 when pioneers Josiah Barber and Richard Lord sold land to Brooklyn Township for a public burial ground, the cemetery reflected the growing community's need for a dignified final resting place. The ornate Gothic Revival stone archway and gatehouse, added in 1874, demonstrate the prosperity and civic pride of post–Civil War Cleveland. Originally serving Ohio City's diverse population, from wealthy merchants to immigrant laborers, the cemetery became Cleveland's primary west-side burial ground after the 1854 annexation. Notable interments included early settlers, Civil War veterans, and prominent business leaders. Today, this 13.63-acre site contains over 31,400 burials and serves as an outdoor museum of Victorian-era funerary art. Designated a Cleveland Historic Landmark in 1973, Monroe Street Cemetery provides a tangible link to Ohio City's rich heritage through its monuments, iron fencing, and mature landscape. (Cleveland Public Library Photograph Collection.)

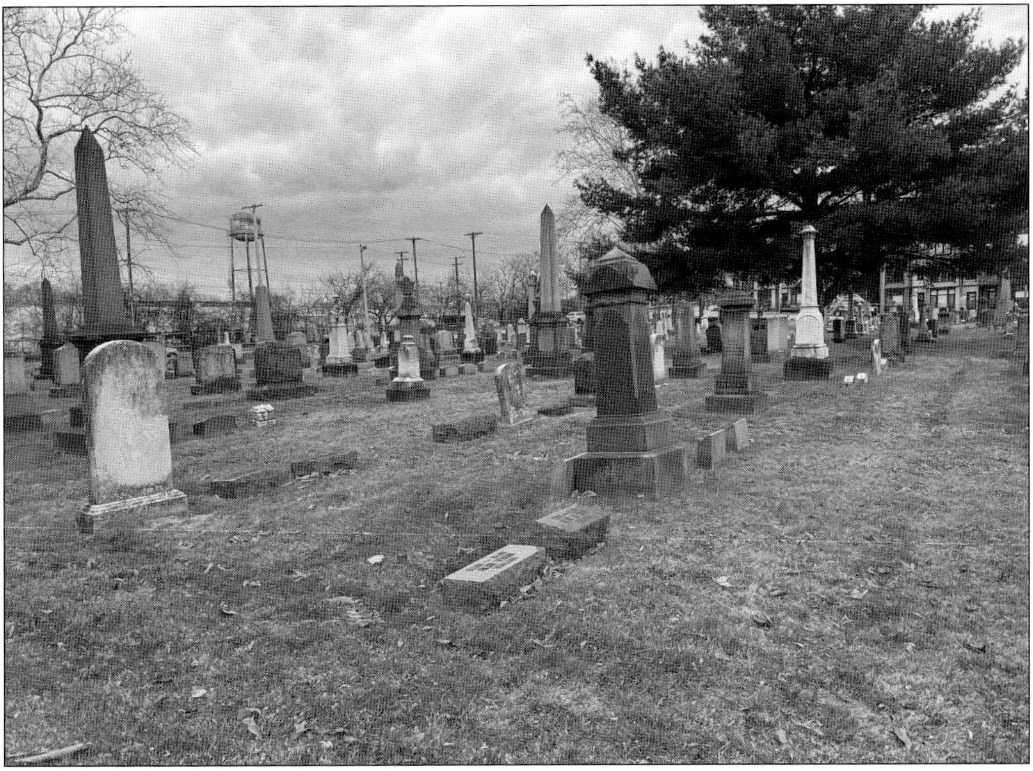

SACRED GROUND, WILLET STREET CEMETERY. Cleveland's oldest Jewish cemetery was established in 1840 when the Israelitic Society purchased an acre from Ohio City pioneer Josiah Barber for $100. This 1.6-acre burial ground at Fulton and Monroe streets became jointly owned by Anshe Chesed and Tifereth Israel congregations. Many of Cleveland's prominent Jewish pioneers, including Simson Thorman, the city's first permanent Jewish resident, are buried here. (Author's collection.)

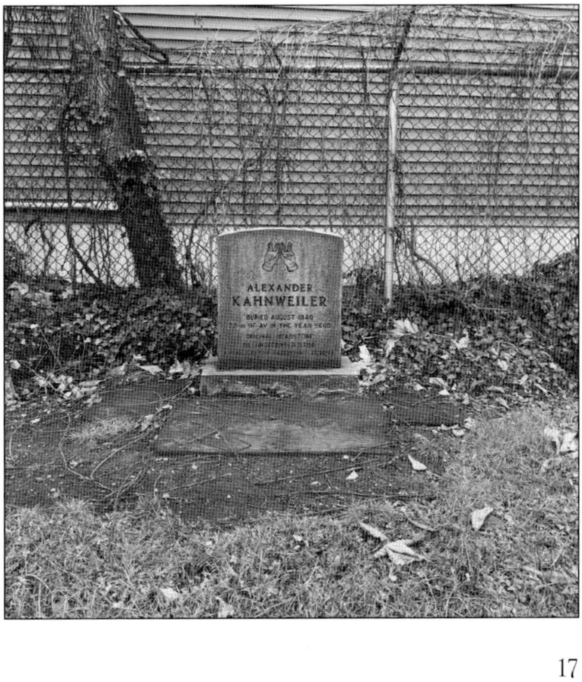

A COMMUNITY'S FIRST LOSS. Alexander Kahnweiler became the first burial in Cleveland's new Jewish cemetery on August 7, 1840. A young Bavarian immigrant working as a peddler, Kahnweiler's death united the small Jewish community. His burial on the eve of Tisha B'Av inspired the founding members to later name their congregation Anshe Chesed—"people of loving kindness." (Author's collection.)

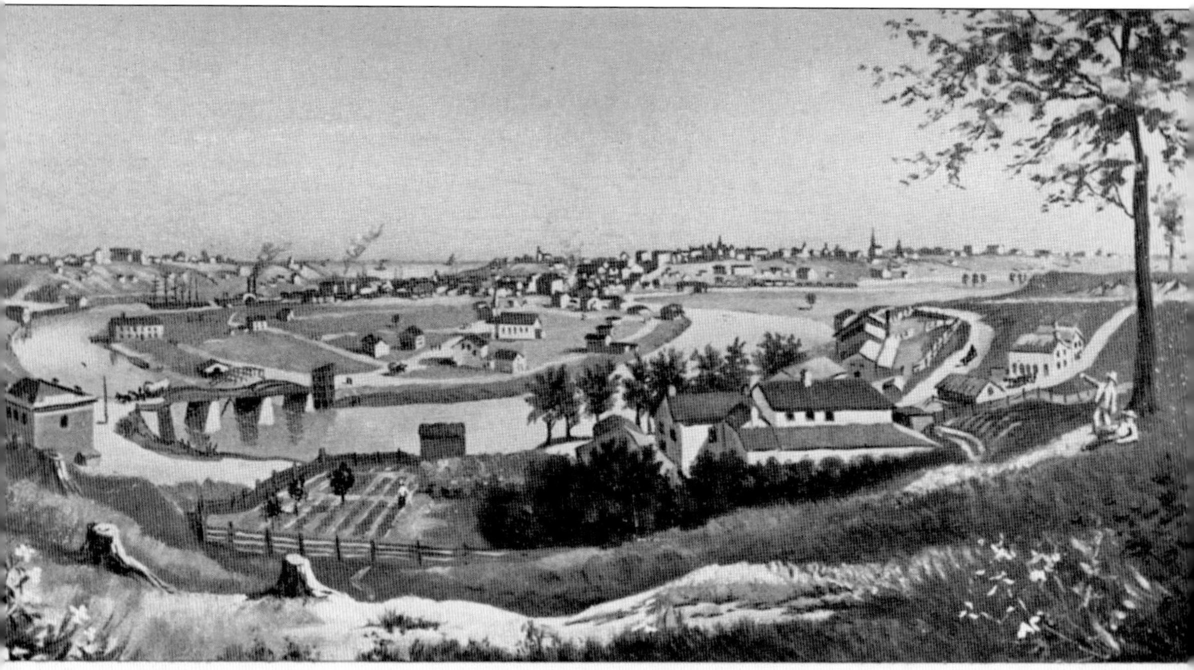

CLEVELAND AND OHIO CITY, 1851.
(From Scranton Heights).

CITIES ON THE CUSP. This 1851 wood engraving captures Cleveland and Ohio City's history, just three years before their merger. The view from Scranton Heights was a high point of land owned by Joel Scranton. A pioneering entrepreneur, Scranton arrived in Cleveland in 1819, and his foresight led to the 1833 purchase of the west bank flats and surrounding heights, later known as "Scranton's Flats." The engraving reveals Ohio City's pastoral scenes of wooded hills and open meadows, which are on the cusp of residential and industrial transformation. The 1854 merger would set Ohio City on a path from independent municipality to an integral Cleveland neighborhood, reshaped by immigration and the industrial boom of the late 19th century. Today, the area is part of the vibrant Tremont neighborhood, adjacent to Ohio City, with Scranton Road remaining a prominent roadway connecting the rich history of the past to the thriving community of the present. (Michael Schwartz Library Special Collections, Cleveland State University.)

Two

Bridging Two Cities

Building Early Ohio City

The annexation of Ohio City to Cleveland in 1854 marked the start of a pivotal era in infrastructure development, uniting the once-rival communities. One of the first major projects after annexation was the Kentucky Street Reservoir, completed in 1856. Located on Ohio City's higher elevation, the reservoir became part of Cleveland's first waterworks system, providing clean water for the city's growing population. This early achievement underscored the importance of the annexation and set the stage for further modernization.

Bridges became critical to connecting Ohio City with downtown Cleveland. The Superior Viaduct, completed in 1878, was the first high-level bridge to span the Cuyahoga River, ending Ohio City's geographic isolation. Eliminating the need for steep climbs through the Flats allowed for the uninterrupted flow of goods and people. The Viaduct reinforced Ohio City's integration into Cleveland's economy and solidified its role as a vital gateway to the west side. The Central Viaduct, completed in 1888, added another key crossing, further linking the neighborhood to downtown and expanding its transportation options.

The development of early streetcar systems also helped bridge the two communities. The West Side Railroad Company, established in 1863, was the first to serve Ohio City. Its route climbed from the Flats up the Detroit Street hill to what is now West Thirty-Eighth Street (then known as Kentucky Street), turned south to Lorain Avenue, and continued east to Market Square at West Twenty-Fifth Street (formerly Pearl Street). The streetcar system not only improved mobility but also helped shape the city's urban development, bringing shoppers and workers into Ohio City's bustling business corridors. By 1880, the streetcars began using the Superior Viaduct, streamlining travel between Ohio City and downtown Cleveland.

The era of infrastructure growth culminated with the construction of the Lorain-Carnegie Bridge in the early 1930s. This Art Deco masterpiece connects Ohio City to downtown Cleveland via Lorain Avenue, featuring the iconic Guardians of Traffic. These massive stone sculptures, now the inspiration for Cleveland's baseball team, symbolize the city's industrial and urban progress. Crossing the bridge, with its Guardians standing watch, reflects the enduring connection between Ohio City and Cleveland.

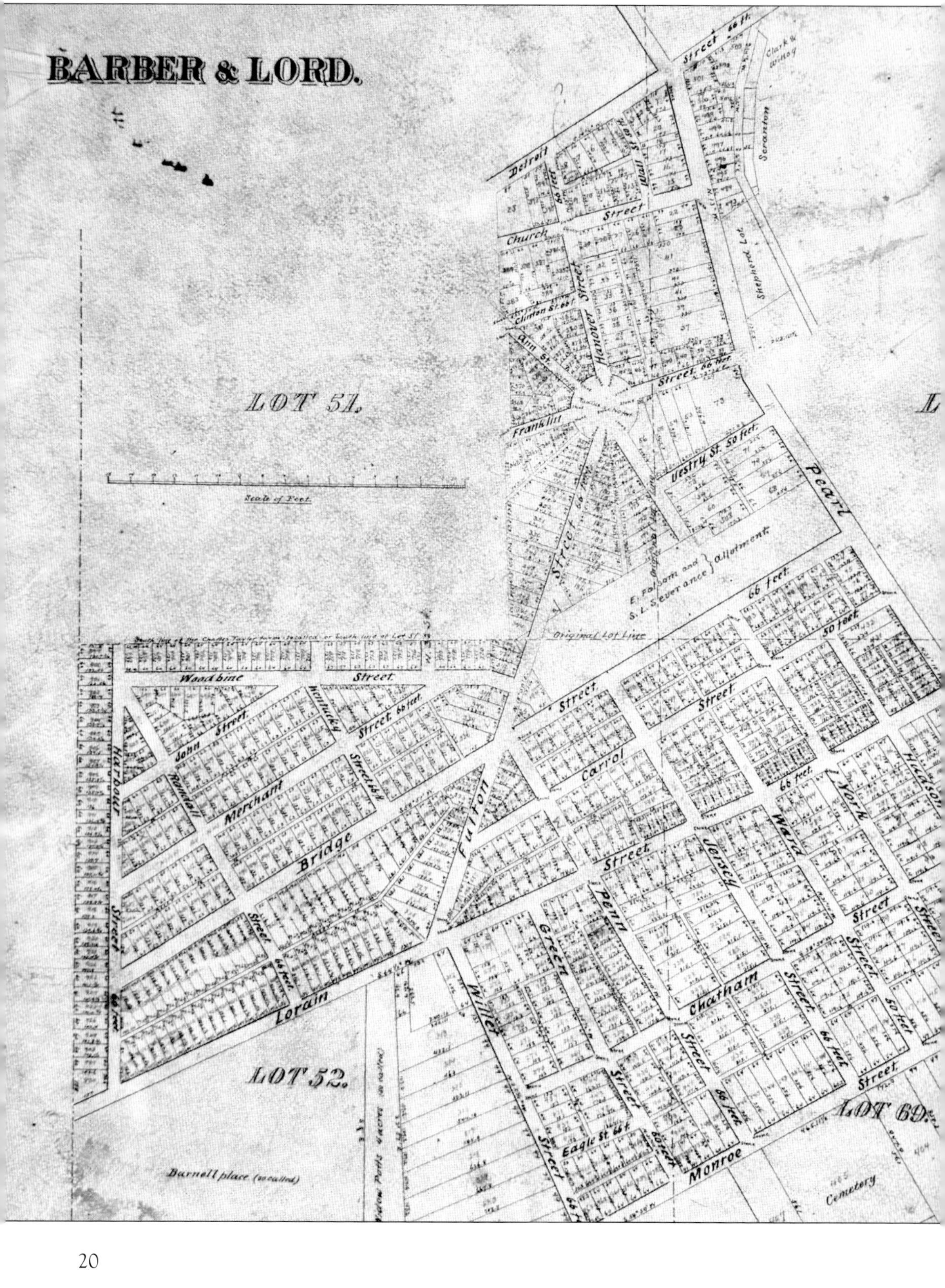
BARBER & LORD.
LOT 51.
LOT 52.
LOT 69.
Scale of Feet.
Original Lot Line
E. Folsom and S. L. Severance Allotment.
Detroit
Church
Clinton St.
Hanover Street
Wall St.
Ann St.
Franklin
Vestry St. 50 feet.
Pearl
Shepherd Lot
Scranton
Woodbine
Street
Kentucky
John Street
Harbour
Randall
Merchant
Bridge
Fulton
Carrol
Street
Jersey
Ward
York
Hickson
Penn
Green
Willet
Lorain
Chatham
Eagle St.
Monroe
Cemetery
Barnell place (so called)

Blueprint for a City. This map, transcribed in 1856 from the original 1840 plat by Josiah Barber and Richard Lord, outlines the foundation of what remains the heart of Ohio City today. The boundaries stretch from Detroit Street to the north, Pearl Street (now West Twenty-Fifth Street) to the east, Monroe Street to the south, and Harbour Street (now West Forty-Fourth Street) to the west. Notably, Franklin Circle was envisioned as the centerpiece of the community, designed to serve as a central gathering point for civic and social life. This early planning reflected Barber and Lord's ambition to establish Ohio City as a vibrant, residential urban community. The radial design with Franklin Circle as the hub and the mix of wide avenues and spokes of smaller residential streets demonstrated sophisticated urban planning. (The Cuyahoga County Archives)

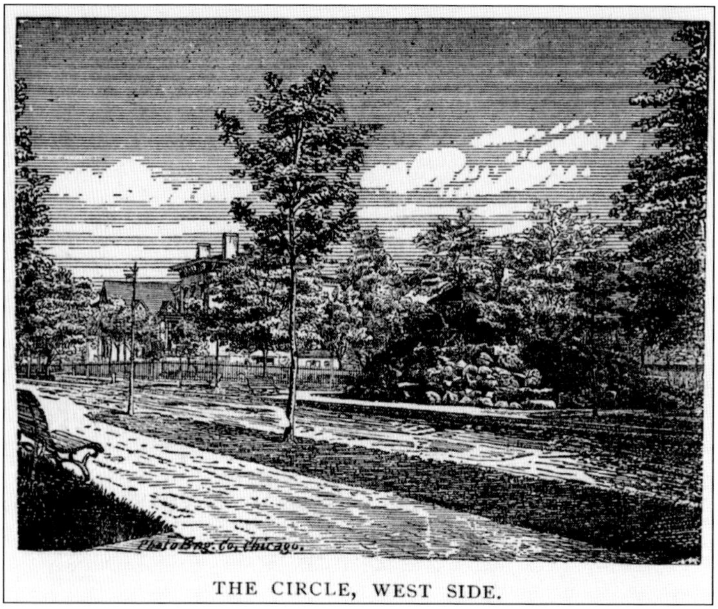

OHIO CITY'S ELEGANT HEART. This 1876 engraving captures Franklin Circle during its heyday as a fashionable public park. Originally surveyed in 1836 as a marketplace, the Circle was transformed in 1857 with ornamental fencing, a fountain, and a pavilion. The landscaped grounds attracted wealthy residents, whose mansions once graced this unique radial-plan setting. (Michael Schwartz Library Special Collections, Cleveland State University.)

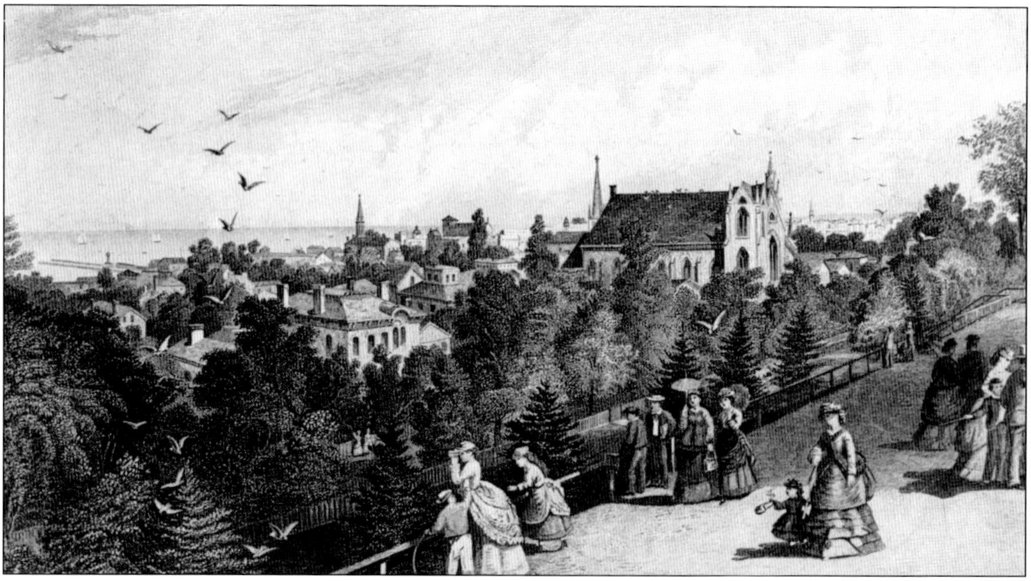

HEIGHTS OF LEISURE. This c. 1870 view of the Kentucky Street Reservoir showcases one of Ohio City's most elegant gathering spots. Built atop a six-acre mound as part of Cleveland's first waterworks system, its graveled path surrounding a six-million-gallon reservoir became a fashionable promenade. St. John's Episcopal Church spire provides a scenic backdrop. (Michael Schwartz Library Special Collections, Cleveland State University.)

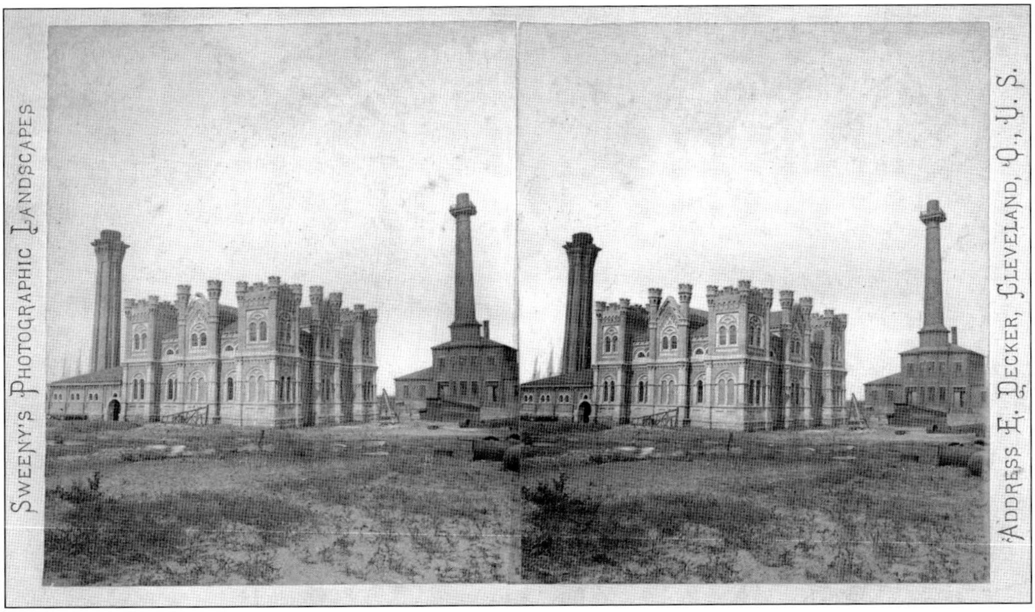

WATERS OF PROGRESS. This stereograph image captures Cleveland's first public waterworks system, constructed between 1853 and 1856 under engineer Theodore Scowden's direction. Responding to the city's rapid growth, the system included a six-million-gallon reservoir, a pump station, and a water intake in Lake Erie. A large fountain in Public Square, fed by the reservoir, celebrated the system's completion and marked the official launch of the Cleveland Water Department. (Cleveland Public Library Photograph Collection.)

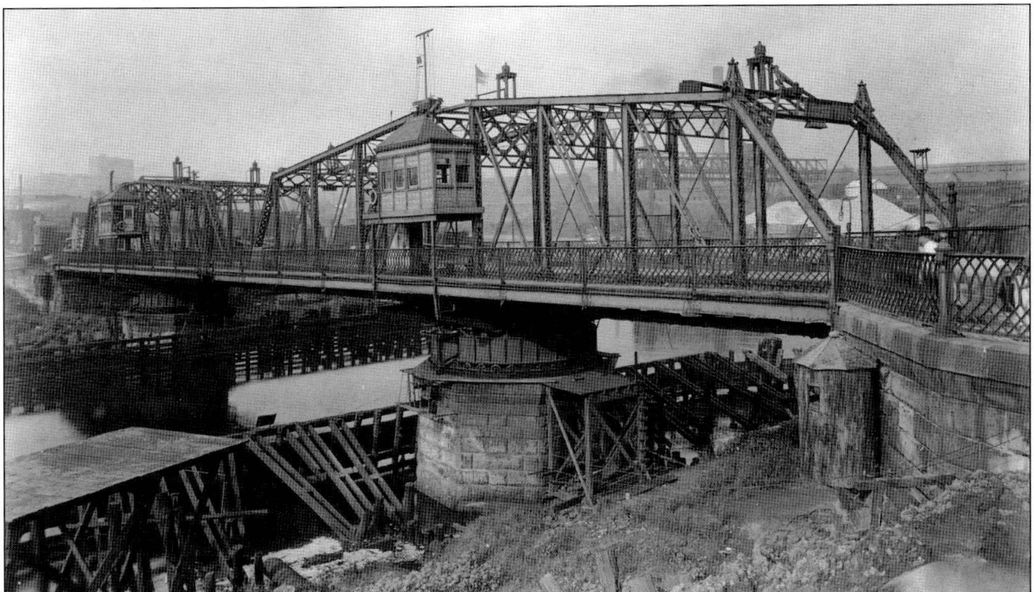

BRIDGE OF PROGRESS. This 1912 image shows the Columbus Street Bridge, rebuilt in 1895 as the world's first double swing bridge. Powered by two 25-horsepower dynamos, it represented cutting-edge engineering of the era. Connecting Ohio City and Cleveland, the bridge replaced earlier versions, including the one at the center of the infamous Bridge War during the cities' rivalry in the 1830s. (Cleveland Public Library Photograph Collection.)

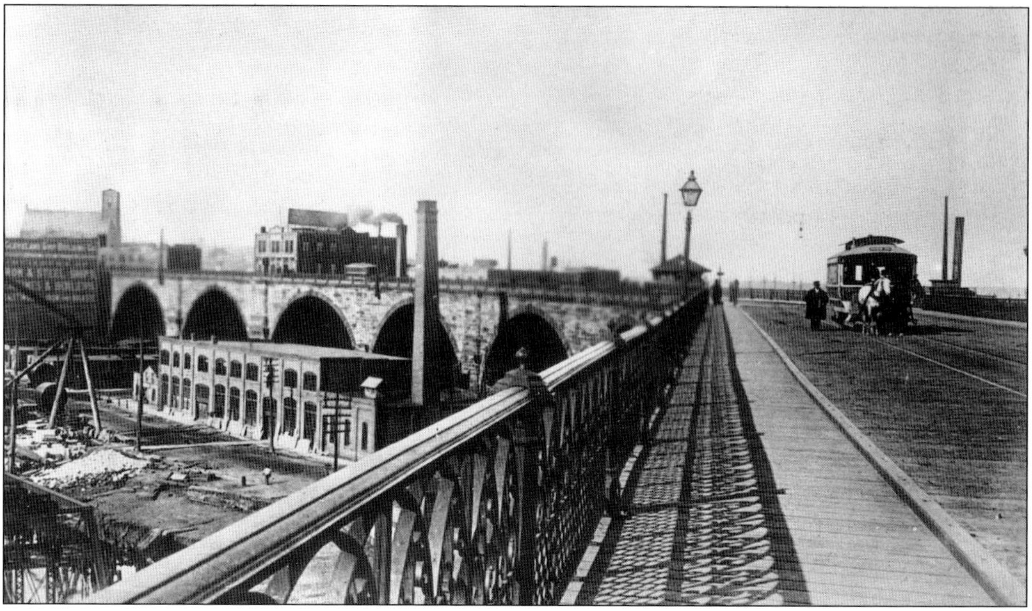

Spanning the Industrial Age. The Superior Viaduct, Cleveland's first high-level bridge, was a transformative structure connecting the city's east and west sides when it opened in 1878. This innovative bridge featured grand sandstone arches and a 332-foot pivoting center span to accommodate river traffic, as seen in these views. One image captures a horse-drawn streetcar approaching the center, illustrating its vital role in transriver commuting. Another shows the bridge from the east bank in 1896, highlighting its architectural and engineering significance. The viaduct reduced interruptions caused by river crossings, symbolizing Cleveland's urban and industrial progress. Although replaced by the Detroit–Superior Bridge in 1917, the Superior Viaduct remains a landmark of the city's transformative growth. (Cleveland Public Library Photograph Collection.)

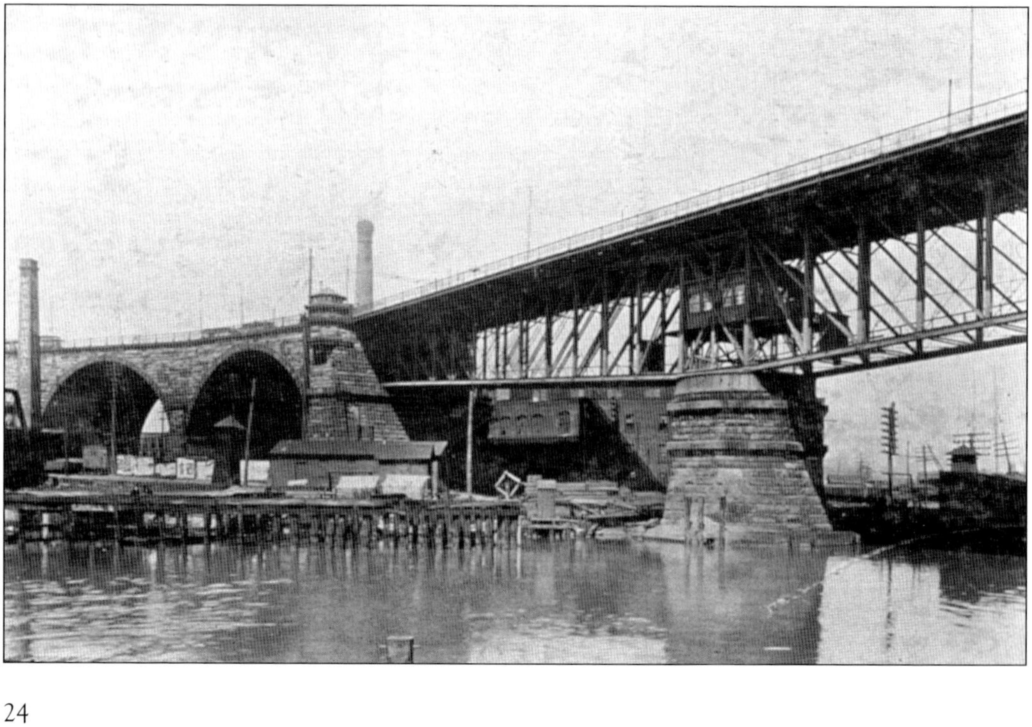

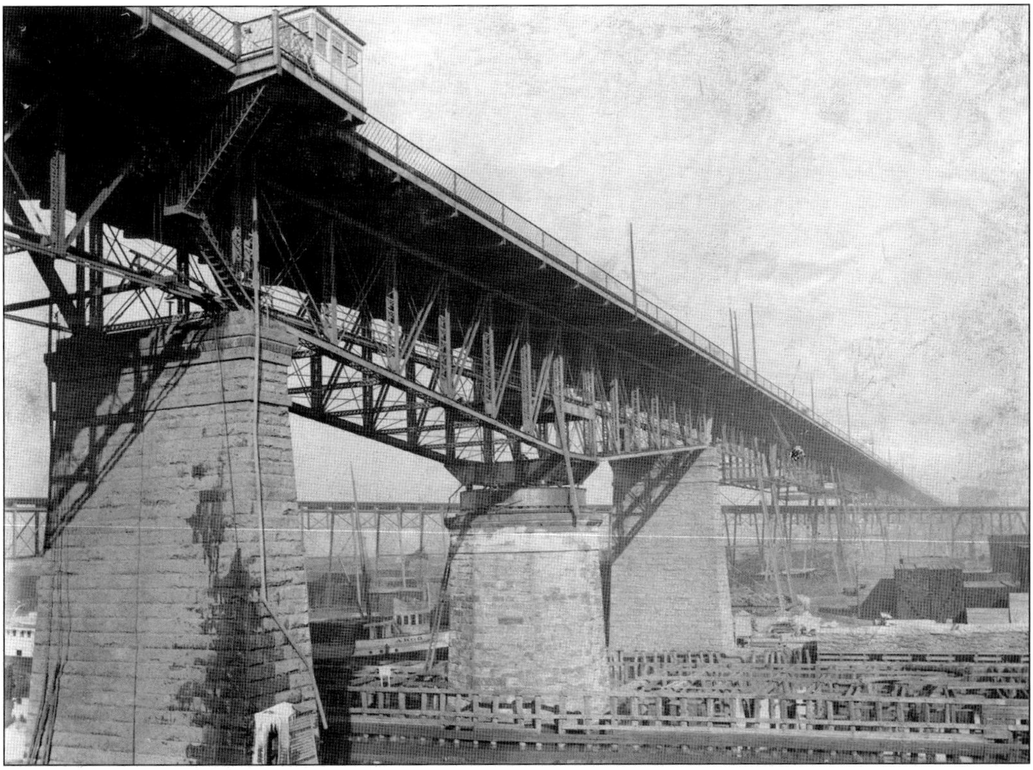

Iron and Tragedy. The Central Viaduct, captured here in 1895, served as Cleveland's second high-level bridge when it opened in December 1888. Rising 101 feet above the Cuyahoga River, this iron structure featured an innovative pivoting center span for river traffic. Just months after this photograph was taken, the bridge became the site of Cleveland's worst transit disaster when a streetcar plunged into the frigid river, claiming 17 lives. (Courtesy Cleveland Public Library Photograph Collection.)

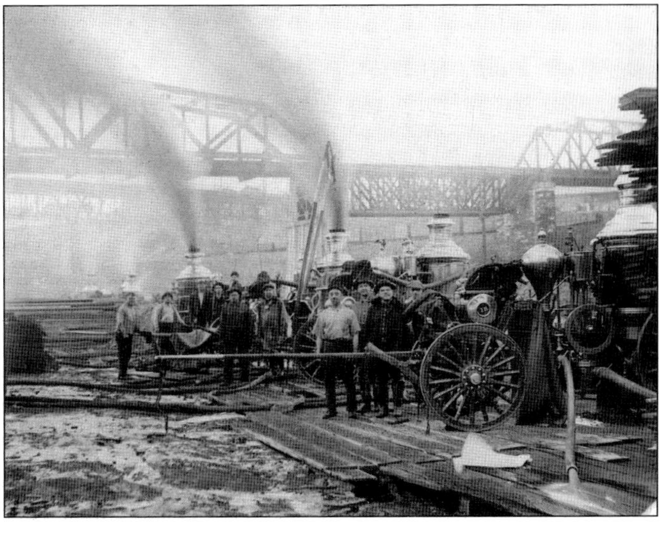

Bridge over Troubled Waters. This 1914 photograph shows workers inspecting the Central Viaduct after a fire in nearby lumber yards forced its closure for over a year. Constructed in 1888, the viaduct's stilt design and steel spans connected Jennings Avenue (now West Fourteenth Street) to Central Avenue (now Carnegie Avenue). Despite its innovative design, the bridge faced numerous challenges before being dismantled in 1941. (Cleveland Public Library Photograph Collection.)

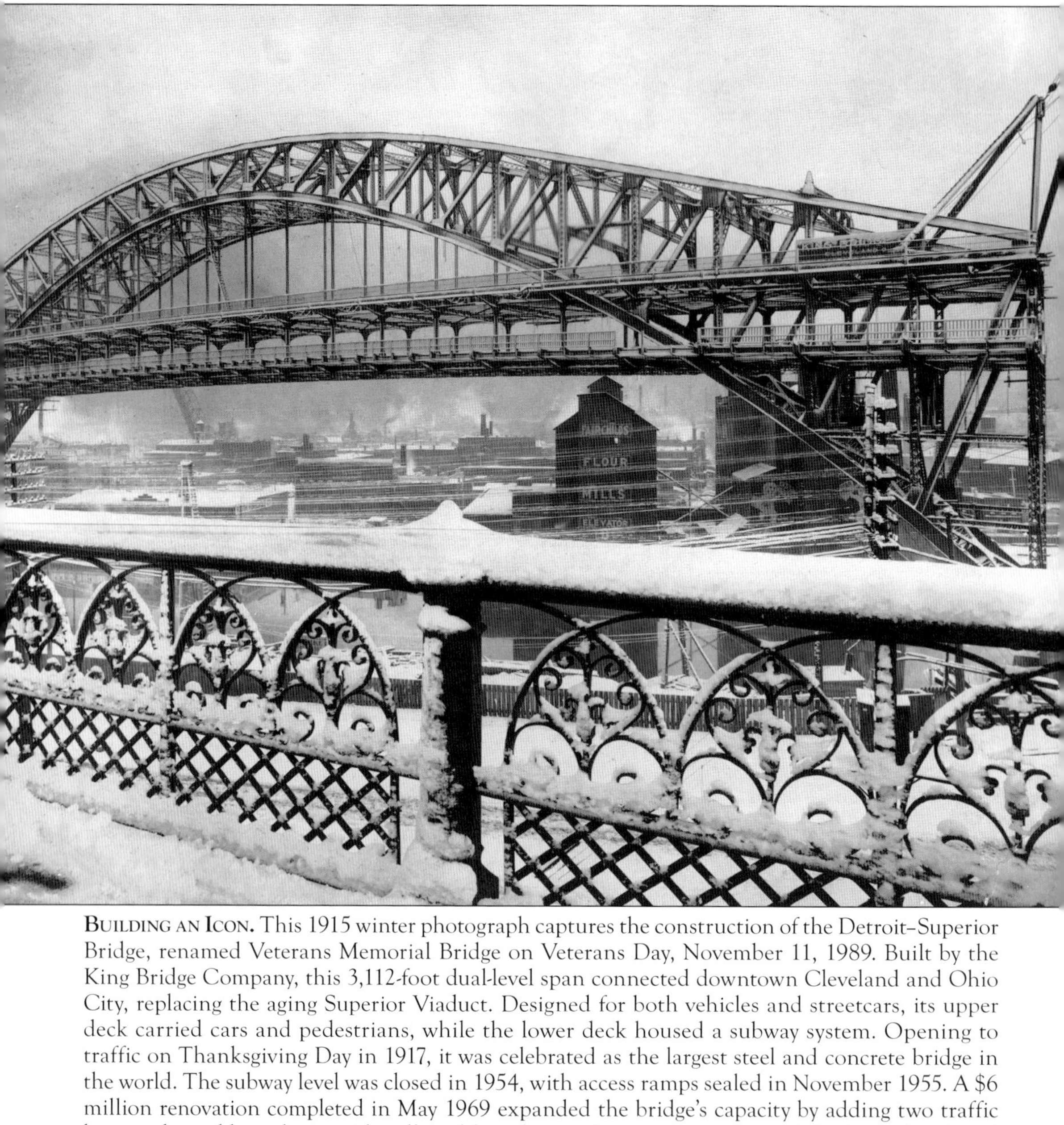

Building an Icon. This 1915 winter photograph captures the construction of the Detroit–Superior Bridge, renamed Veterans Memorial Bridge on Veterans Day, November 11, 1989. Built by the King Bridge Company, this 3,112-foot dual-level span connected downtown Cleveland and Ohio City, replacing the aging Superior Viaduct. Designed for both vehicles and streetcars, its upper deck carried cars and pedestrians, while the lower deck housed a subway system. Opening to traffic on Thanksgiving Day in 1917, it was celebrated as the largest steel and concrete bridge in the world. The subway level was closed in 1954, with access ramps sealed in November 1955. A $6 million renovation completed in May 1969 expanded the bridge's capacity by adding two traffic lanes, achieved by reducing sidewalk width and extending new lanes beyond the bridge's original structure. Listed in the National Register of Historic Places in 1976, the bridge remains an iconic Cleveland landmark. Today, the unused subway level occasionally reopens for tours, allowing visitors to explore a unique part of the city's transportation history. (Cleveland Public Library Photograph Collection.)

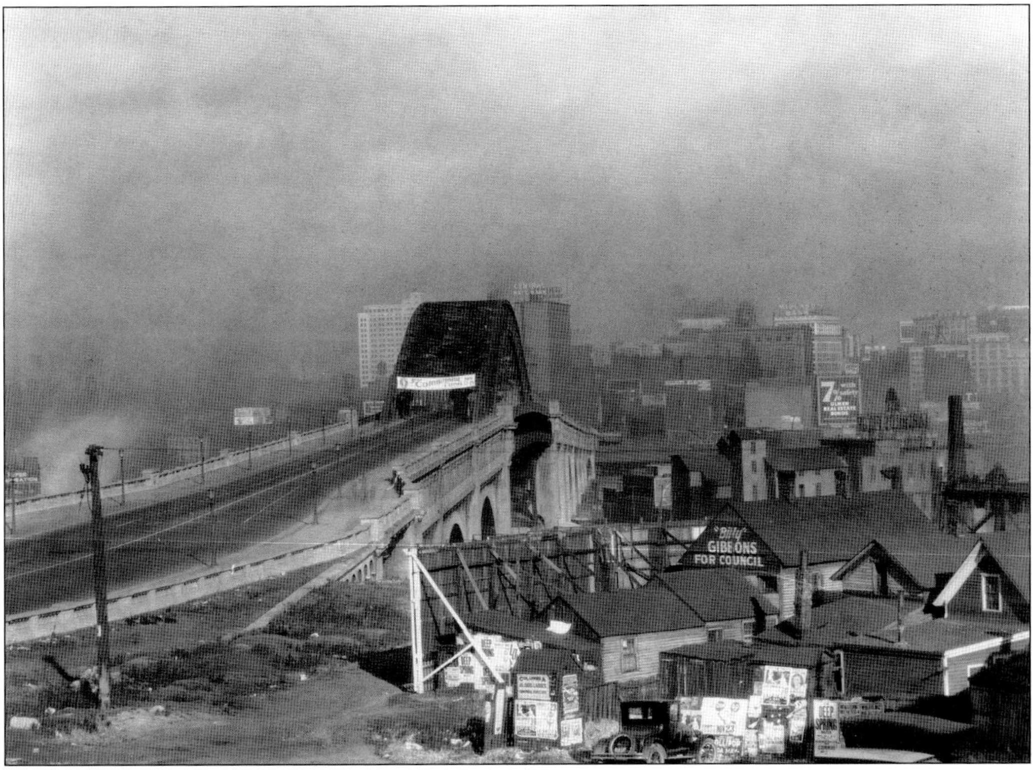

A Glimpse of Cleveland's Industrial Era, 1924. The view from Irishtown Bend in Ohio City looks east toward downtown Cleveland. Below, pollution rises from the Flats, reflecting the industrialization of the time. A sign reading "Billy Gibbons for Council" and a banner promoting the community fund hang prominently, adding a glimpse of local civic life to the scene. (Cleveland Public Library Photograph Collection.)

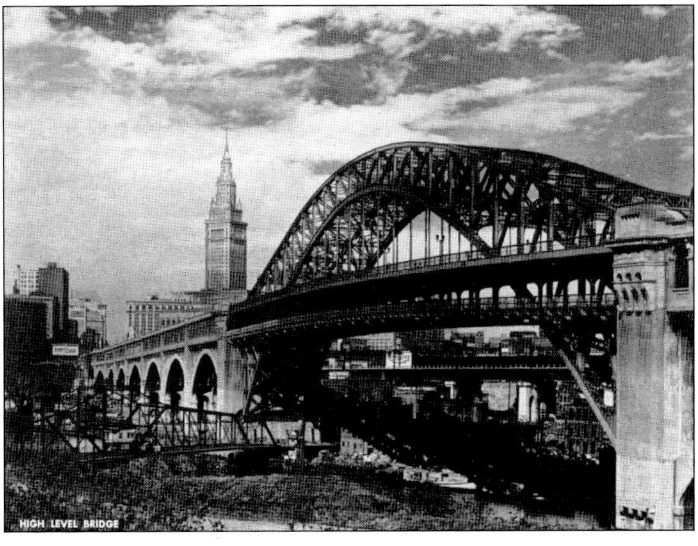

Cleveland's Dual Landmarks, c. 1928. This image highlights the central arch of the Detroit–Superior Bridge, framed by the iconic Terminal Tower in the background. Completed in 1927, Terminal Tower was the tallest building in North America outside New York City until 1964 and the second-tallest in the world upon its debut. This view symbolizes Cleveland's ambition and rapid growth in the early 20th century. (Cleveland Public Library Photograph Collection.)

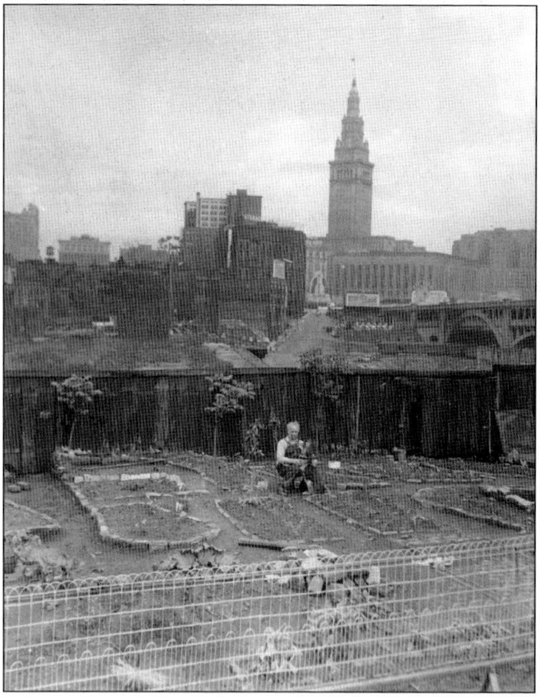

Flowers in the Dust. This 1938 image features John Rein, who cultivated a thriving garden on the remnants of the Superior Viaduct. Starting his efforts two years earlier, Rein successfully grew blooming flowers despite the dust and grime from nearby industries. The view looks east toward the Terminal Tower against Cleveland's industrial backdrop. (Cleveland Public Library Photograph Collection.)

Bridge Subway Transit, 1918. Commuters board a train at the Detroit–Superior Bridge's lower-level subway station, heading toward Lorain Avenue. The bridge's innovative dual-deck design served both automobiles above and streetcar passengers below, providing efficient public transit between downtown and Ohio City. (Michael Schwartz Library Special Collections, Cleveland State University.)

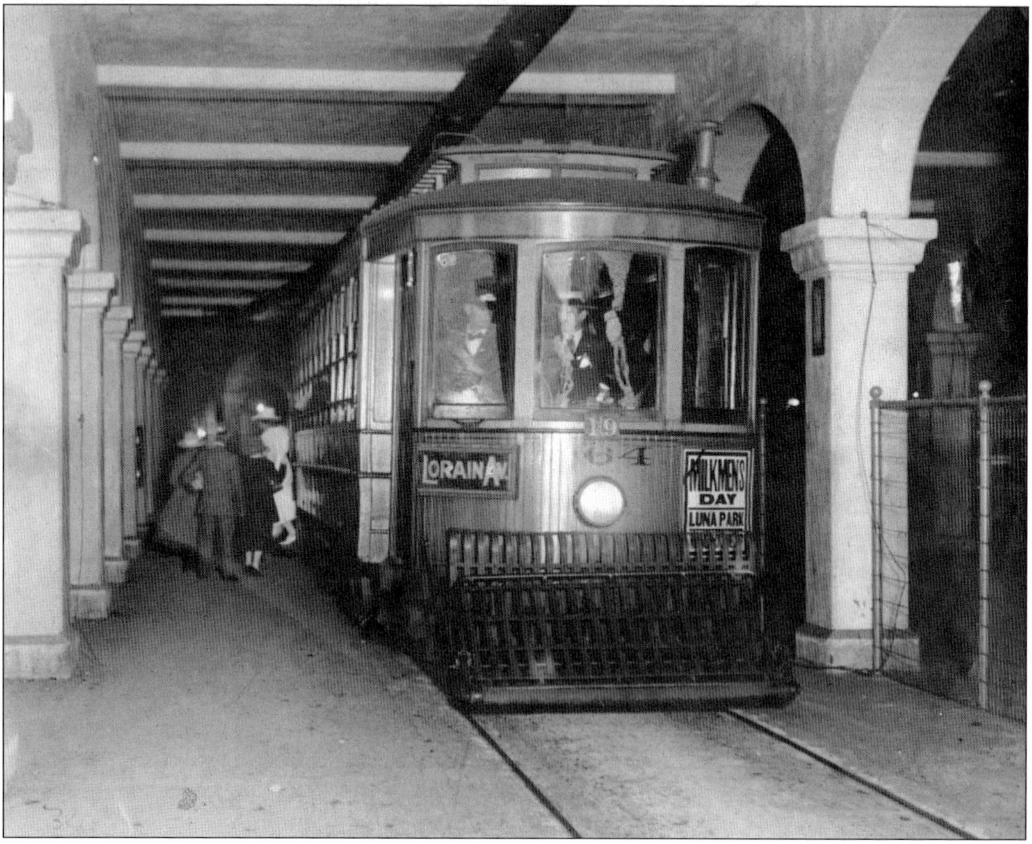

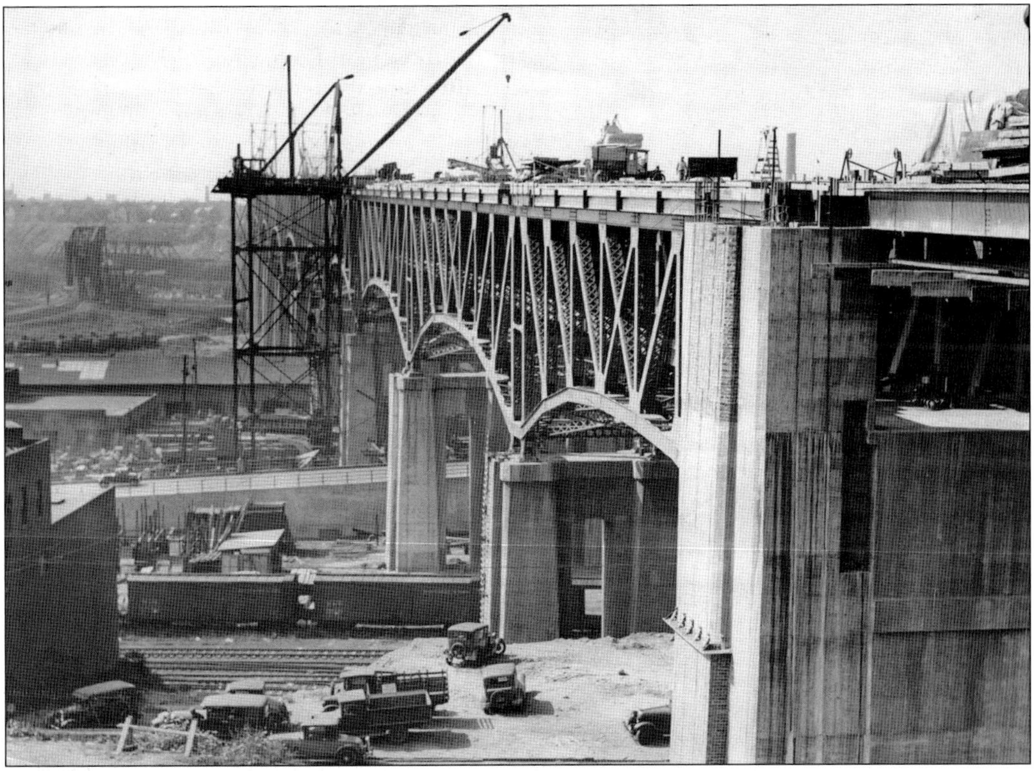

LORAIN-CARNEGIE, A MONUMENT IN PROGRESS, 1931. The Lorain-Carnegie Bridge, a 4,490-foot-long Art Deco truss bridge linking Cleveland's west and east sides, is pictured under construction. Opened in 1932, its design included a lower deck for rapid transit, though it was never used. The bridge was later renamed the Hope Memorial Bridge in the 1980s to honor local stonemasons and the Hope family. (Cleveland Public Library Photograph Collection.)

OHIO CITY'S GATEWAY, 1972. Vehicles drive across the Lorain-Carnegie Bridge, approaching the iconic Guardians of Traffic. These towering Art Deco statues symbolize the progress of transportation and have become a Cleveland landmark. The Guardians also inspired the name of Cleveland's Major League Baseball team, reflecting their enduring significance in the city's identity and cultural history. (Cleveland Public Library Photograph Collection.)

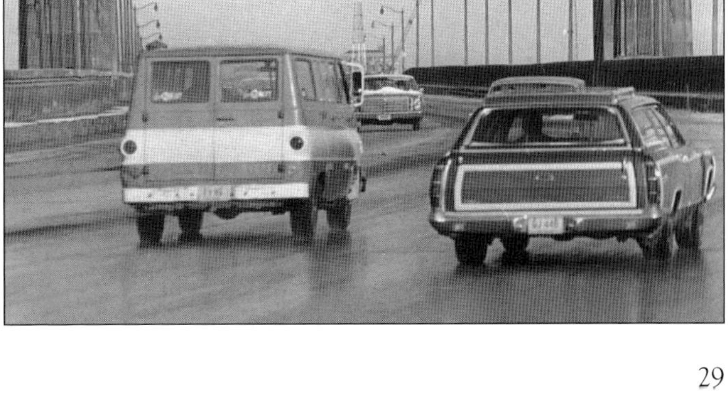

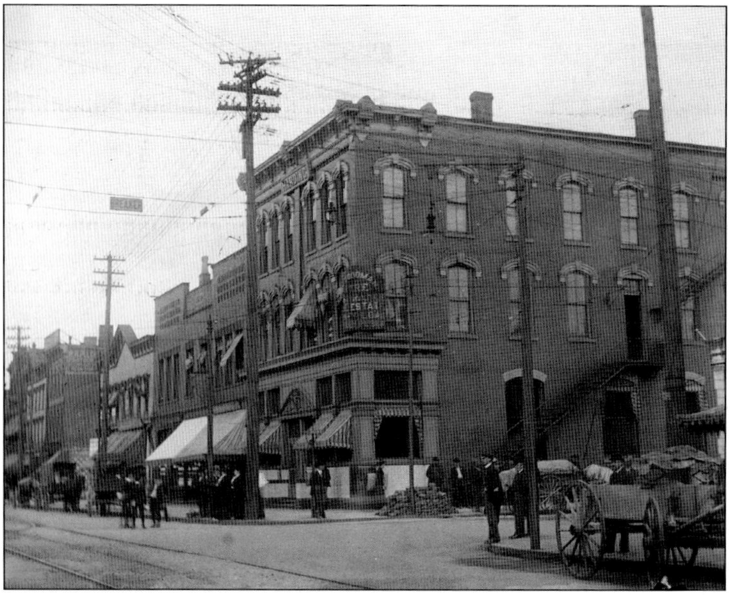

The Heartbeat of Ohio City, 1902. This bustling view from the corner of West Twenty-Fifth Street and Lorain Avenue captures the vibrant commercial district of the era. Horse-drawn carts and wagons line the street, with the Harding Building, home to Goodman Fire Insurance and Real Estate Company, prominently visible on the right. A snapshot of Cleveland's dynamic early-20th-century commerce. (Cleveland Public Library Photograph Collection.)

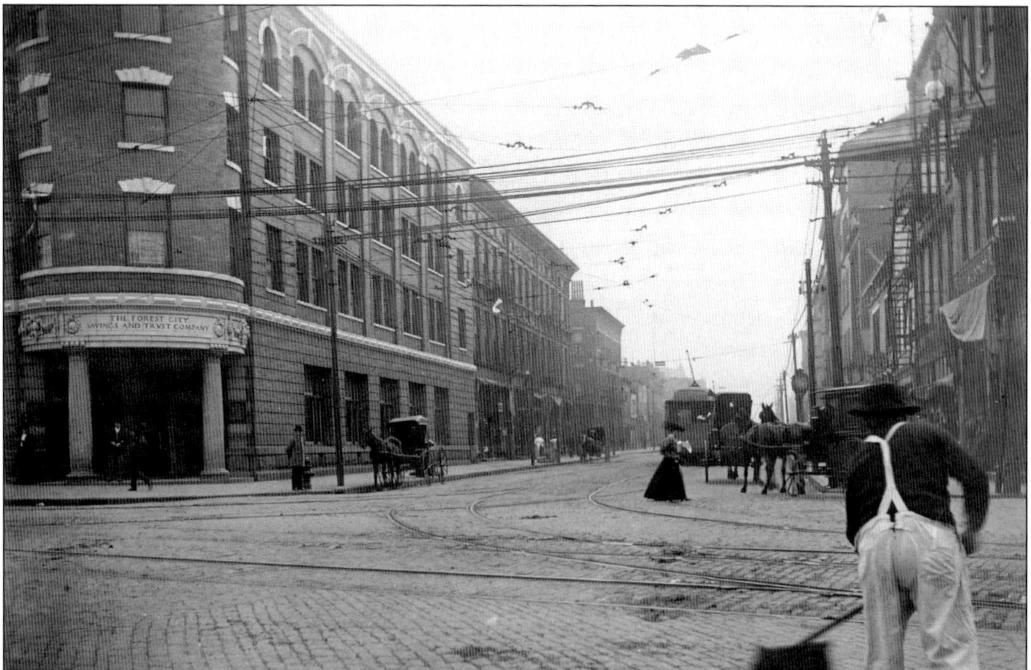

Banking on Progress: Streetcar Access in Ohio City, 1909. Looking west from the intersection of Detroit Avenue and West Twenty-Fifth Street, this image highlights the historic Forest City Savings and Trust Building, constructed in 1904. Still standing today and listed in the National Register of Historic Places, this landmark once provided access to the streetcar line below ground. (Cleveland Public Library Photograph Collection.)

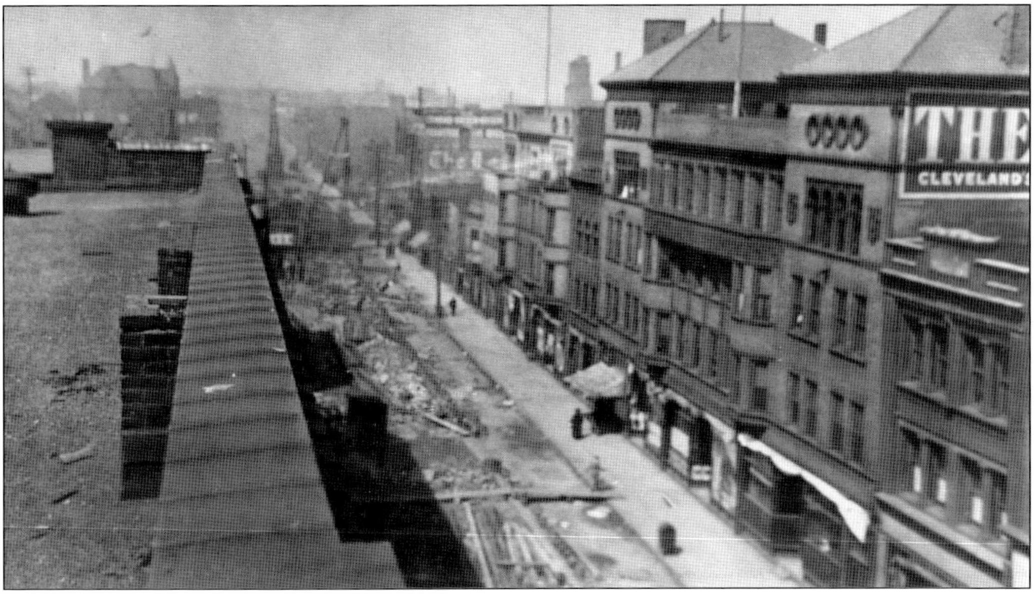

Detroit Avenue's Bridge to Progress, 1917. Photographed from atop the Forest City Bank on June 11, 1917, this westward view of Detroit Avenue captures a city in transition. Construction materials for the Detroit–Superior Bridge line the thoroughfare, documenting a pivotal moment in Cleveland's infrastructure as the landmark span would soon connect Ohio City to downtown in dramatic new fashion. (The Cuyahoga County Archives.)

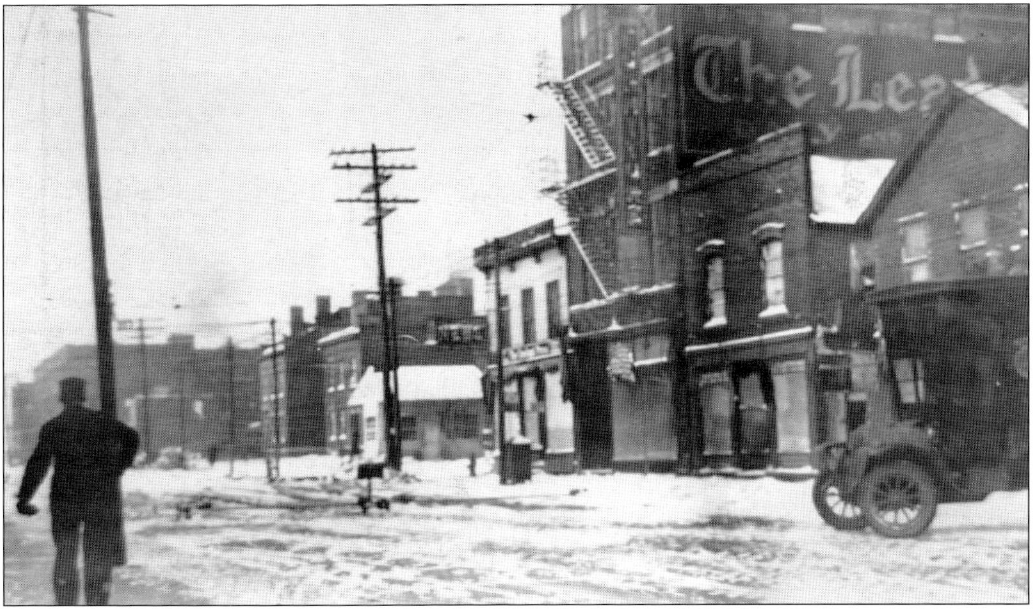

Winter Grit on Detroit Avenue, 1917. Captured on February 5, 1917, this gritty streetscape shows Detroit Avenue at West Twenty-Eighth Street looking northwest. A solitary pedestrian and automobile navigate the industrial-era thoroughfare, where soot and winter weather create a stark urban scene typical of Cleveland's early-20th-century commercial corridors. (The Cuyahoga County Archives.)

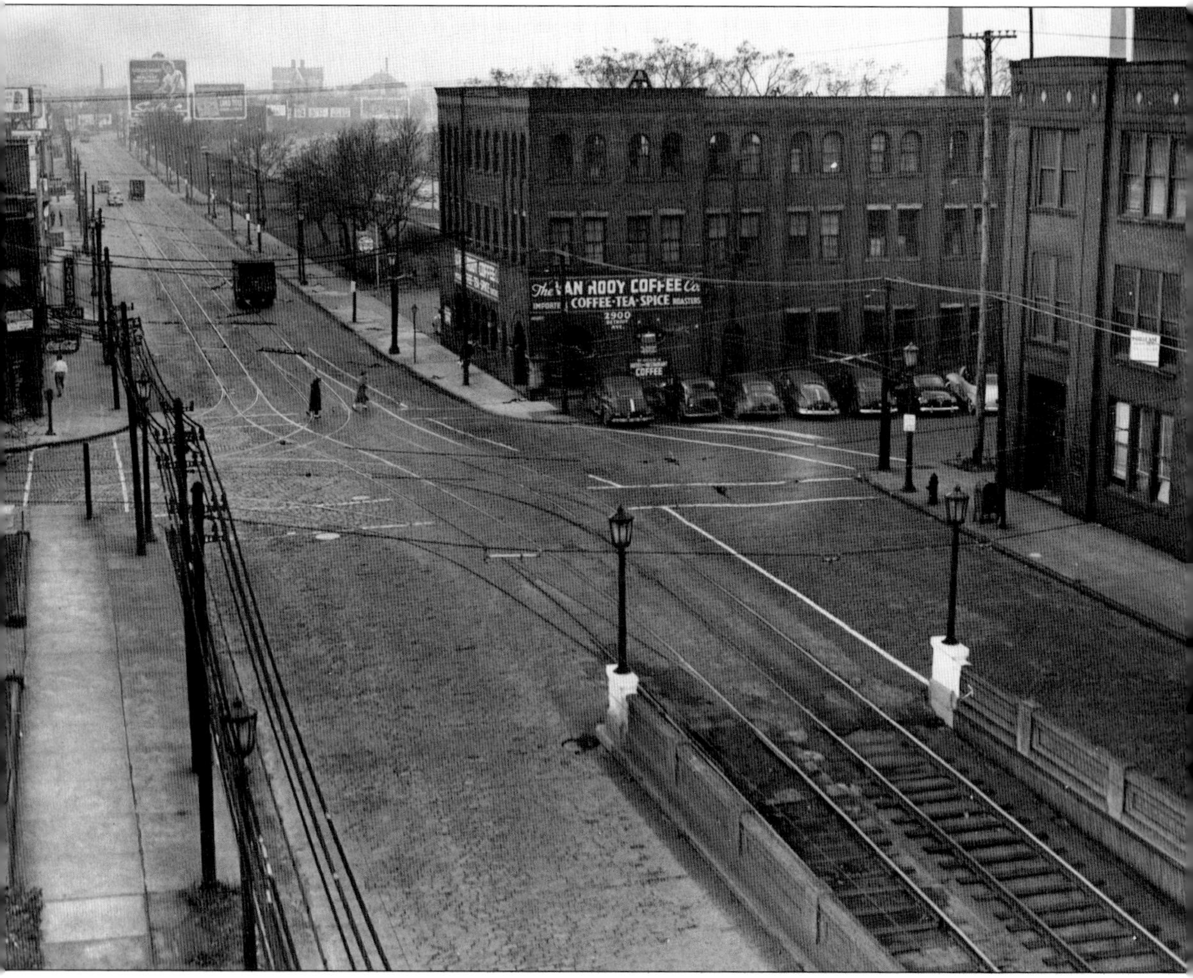

The Westside Connection. This 1949 view captures Detroit Avenue looking west from West Twenty-Ninth Street, showcasing the west side transit corridor. Once a major streetcar line, this area connected Ohio City to neighborhoods farther west, serving as a vital artery for Cleveland's urban mobility. The street was flanked by thriving storefronts and small businesses, reflecting the neighborhood's vibrancy. Among the notable buildings still standing is the Van Rooy Coffee Company Building, a three-story, 38,000-square-foot Romanesque Revival structure. Originally constructed for the Cleveland Steel Range Company, it later housed Thompson Products, the precursor to TRW Inc., before becoming home to the Van Rooy Coffee Co. from 1935 to 2003. The building was known for its iconic coffee-can mural, while the aroma of roasted coffee permeated the neighborhood. Now listed in the National Register of Historic Places, the building has been repurposed, contributing to the area's ongoing revitalization. Today, the intersection remains lively, anchored by small businesses, including Saucy Brew Works at the southeast corner of West Twenty-Ninth and Detroit. (Cleveland Public Library Photograph Collection.)

Three

Faith and Foundations

Churches of Ohio City

As Ohio City expanded in the late 19th and early 20th centuries, so too did its spiritual landscape. Religious institutions not only provided places of worship but also shaped the social, cultural, and educational lives of immigrant populations. Churches anchored neighborhoods, offering solace, support, and a sense of belonging to diverse communities.

St. John's Episcopal Church, built between 1836 and 1838, stands as a cornerstone of Ohio City's religious history. Located on Church Avenue, it is the oldest consecrated building in Cuyahoga County. Its Gothic Revival architecture and role as a stop on the Underground Railroad earned it the nickname "Station Hope."

Irish Catholic immigrants established two major parishes that became iconic landmarks. St. Patrick's Church, founded in 1853, was the first Catholic parish west of the Cuyahoga River. Its Gothic Revival structure, completed in the 1870s, served as a spiritual and cultural hub for the Irish community. St. Malachi Church, founded in 1865 near the Flats, became another anchor for Irish families, particularly those living in Irishtown Bend and The Angle. Both churches symbolized resilience and cultural pride amid the challenges of immigrant life.

German immigrants also shaped Ohio City's spiritual identity. St. Mary's Church, established in 1865, became a spiritual home for German Catholics and supported nearby St. Ignatius College and High School for over a century. For German Protestants, Trinity Evangelical Lutheran Church, founded in 1853, was equally vital. In 1873, the congregation completed its Victorian Gothic church on Lorain Avenue, featuring a 175-foot steeple that remains a neighborhood landmark. Trinity adapted to Ohio City's evolving demographics, eventually incorporating English, Spanish, and even Kirundi services.

Hungarian Catholics joined the spiritual mosaic with St. Emeric's Church, established in 1904 near the West Side Market. Protestant congregations like Franklin Circle Christian Church and Franklin Boulevard Methodist Church emphasized education, charity, and community engagement.

By the 1930s, Ohio City's skyline was defined by church spires, symbols of faith and resilience. These institutions shaped the neighborhood's identity and left a legacy that continues to inspire.

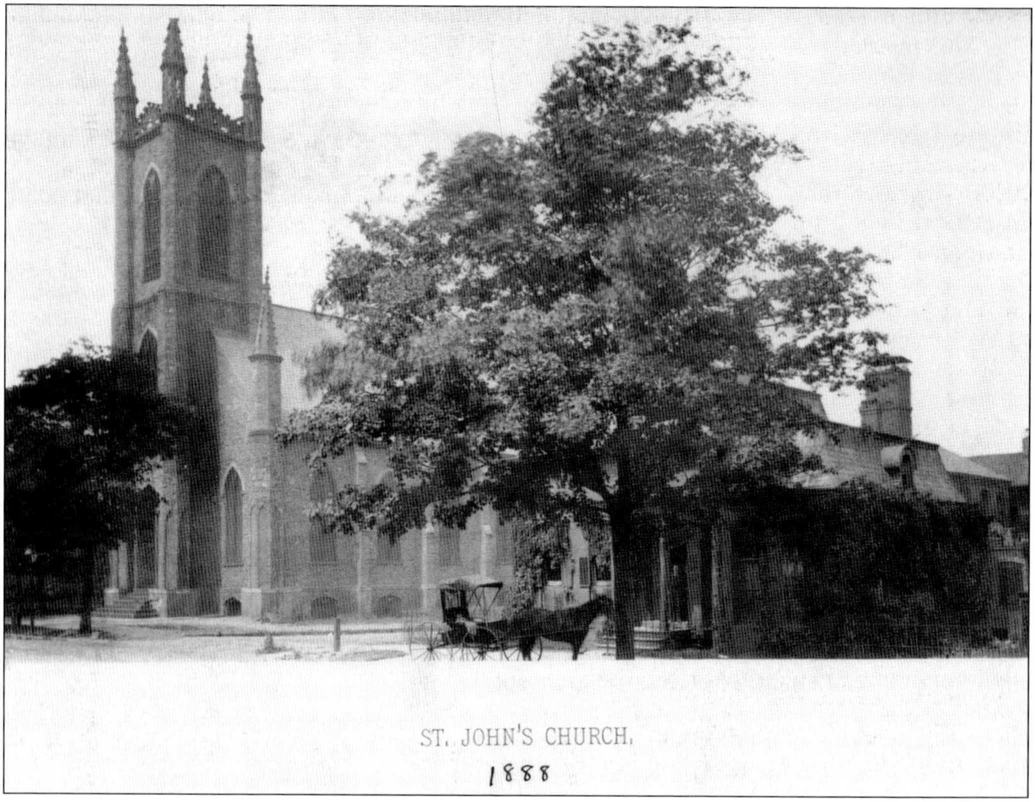

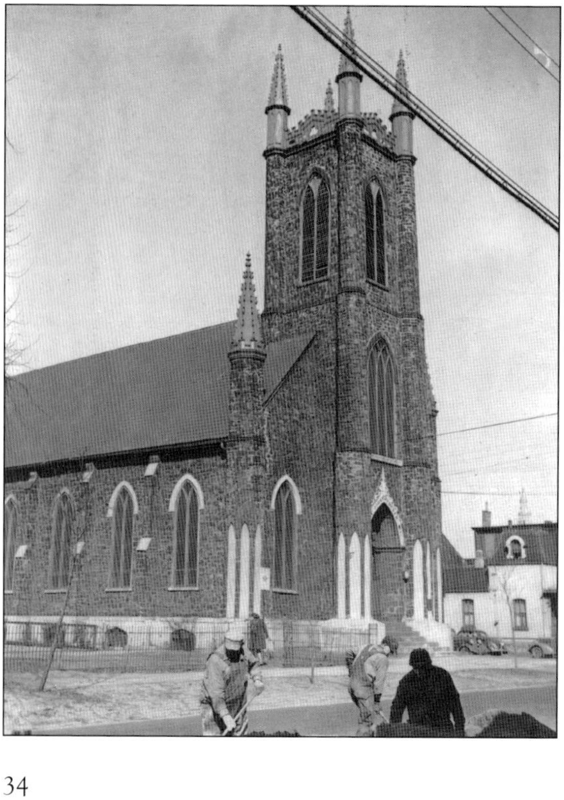

Sacred Refuge. These images from 1888 (above) and 1946 (left) capture the historic St. John's Episcopal Church, the oldest consecrated building in Cuyahoga County. Located at 2600 Church Avenue, the Gothic Revival structure was designed by Hezekiah Eldredge and completed in 1838. Originally described as an "ornament" to Ohio City, the church played a significant role as Station Hope on the Underground Railroad, providing refuge to escaping slaves. Over the years, the building endured fires in the 1880s and tornado damage in 1953, leading to the loss of some architectural features like its original pinnacles. By the 1980s, a $100,000 restoration was required to address structural issues. The building ultimately closed in December 2007. Today, St. John's stands as a resilient symbol of both Cleveland's architectural heritage and its commitment to social justice. (Both, Cleveland Public Library Photograph Collection.)

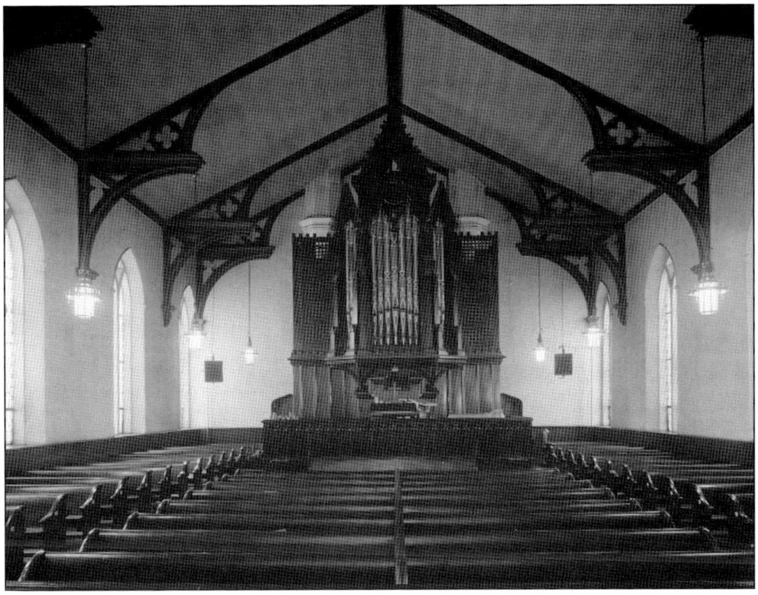

Beyond the Altar. This 1965 interior view of St. John's highlights renovations after an 1880s fire and redecorations in the 1920s. The basement, later adapted for classrooms, hosted the Head Start program and, in the 1970s, became home to Russell Means's Cleveland American Indian Center. (Photograph by Martin Linsey, Historic American Buildings Survey [HABS], the Library of Congress.)

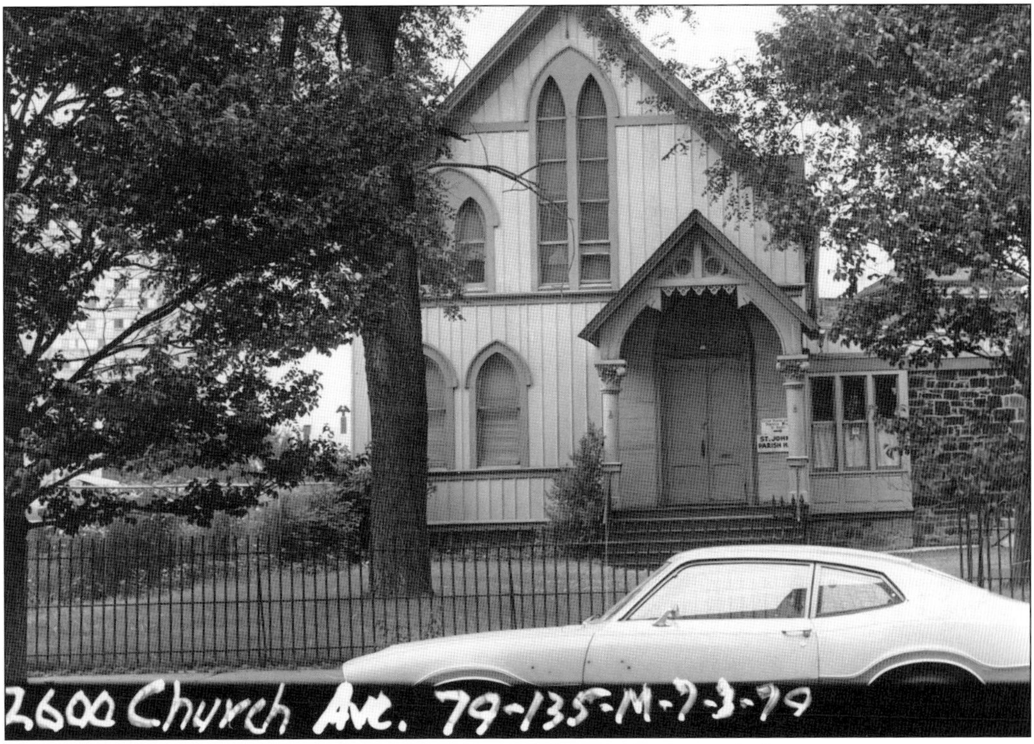

Historic Parish Life. St. John's Episcopal Parish House has served the congregation since its construction around 1875. Standing west of the historic church building, this brick structure has undergone several renovations while maintaining its original character. It continues to anchor this corner of Church Street despite surrounding industrial development. (Cleveland Public Library Photograph Collection.)

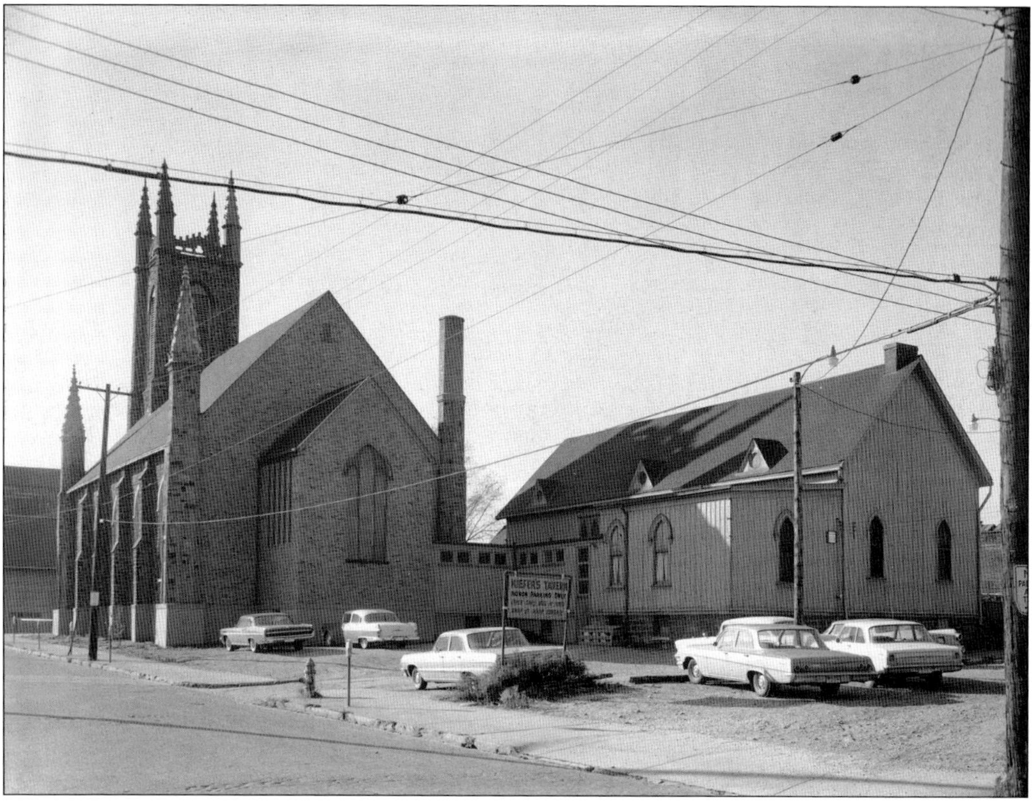

Landmark Through Time. This 1965 view of St. John's Episcopal Church and its adjoining 1875 Parish House depicts the historic complex adapting to mid-century needs. While parking lots, including Kiefer's commercial space, reflect urban changes, the church's north and east facades maintain their architectural integrity. This streetscape, largely unchanged today, demonstrates Ohio City's successful preservation of its religious landmarks. (Photograph by Martin Linsey, Historic American Buildings Survey [HABS], the Library of Congress.)

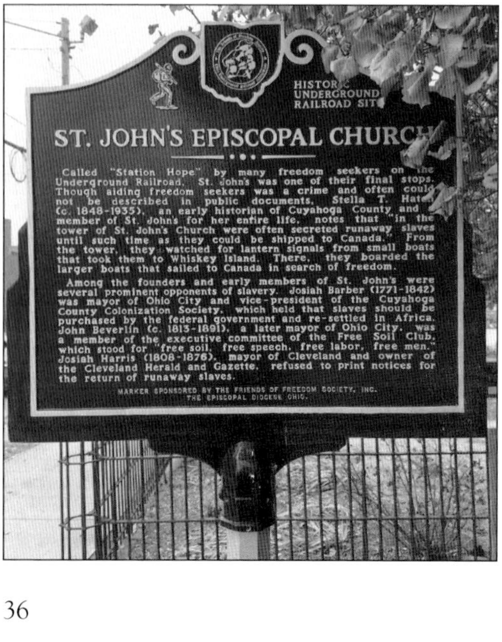

History's Sacred Station. This historic marker honors St. John's role as a critical site on the Underground Railroad, serving as the last stop for freedom seekers before crossing into Canada. Established in 1836, the church stands as Cleveland's oldest consecrated building and a testament to its abolitionist history. (Author's collection.)

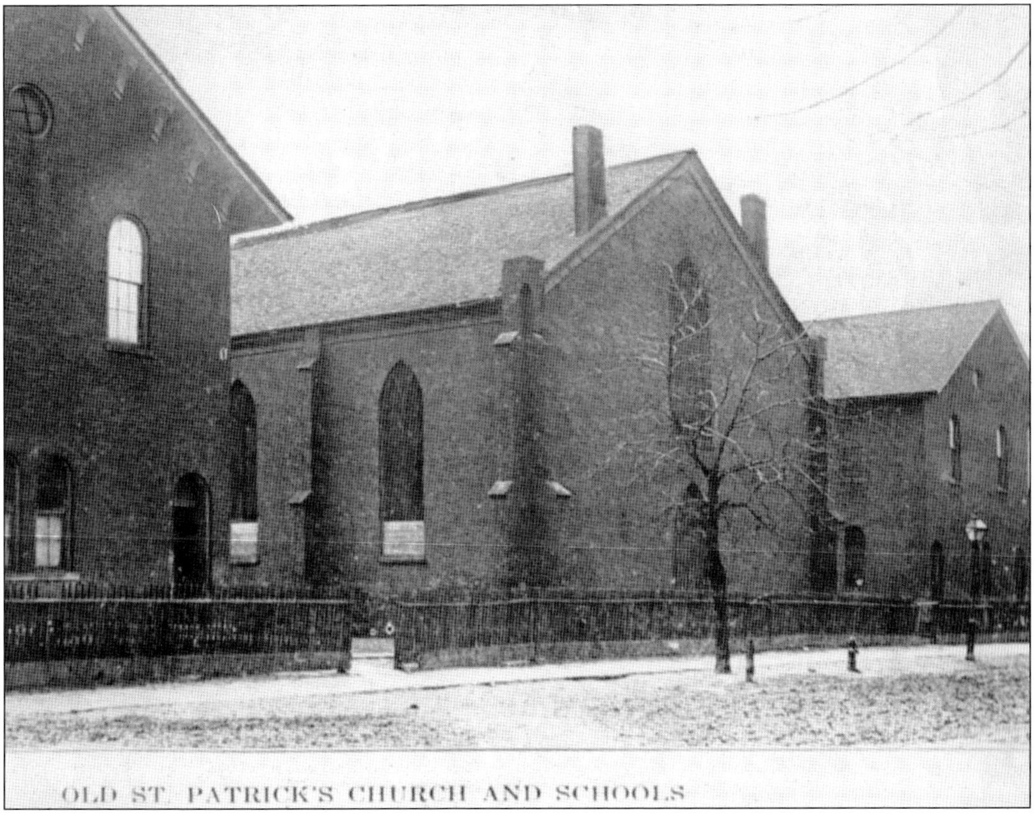

Parish Perseveres. A snowy scene from 1925 captures St. Patrick Church and School on Bridge Avenue. Established in 1853, the parish began construction of this iconic church in 1871, but financial challenges extended its completion until 1889. By 1925, the adjacent school had grown to educate over 900 students, cementing St. Patrick's role as a cornerstone of faith and learning in Ohio City. (Michael Schwartz Library Special Collections, Cleveland State University.)

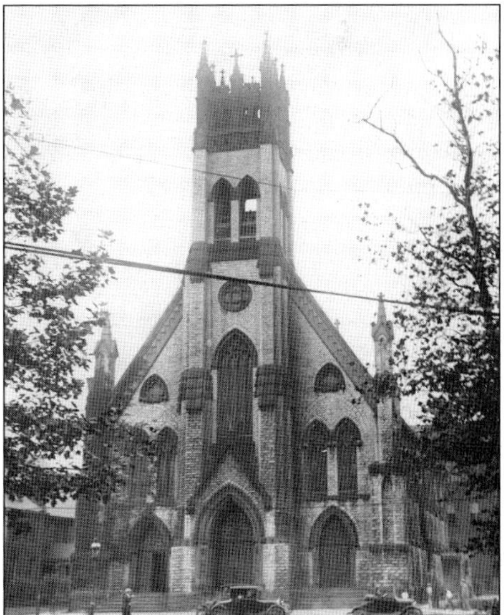

Irish Gothic Legacy. This 1928 view of St. Patrick Church on Bridge Avenue showcases its Gothic Revival architecture, highlighted by its towering spire and intricate stonework. The church still stands as a testament to the craftsmanship and dedication of its Irish Catholic parishioners, who labored for decades to complete the structure, making it a prominent and enduring landmark of Ohio City. (Michael Schwartz Library Special Collections, Cleveland State University.)

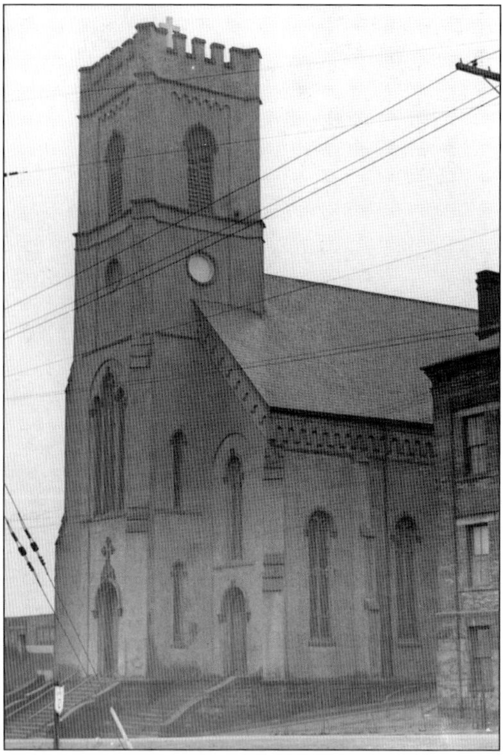

St. Malachi Church, 1934. The original St. Malachi Church at Washington Avenue and West Twenty-Fifth Street was dedicated in 1871. It was a Gothic-style landmark with a spire topped by an illuminated cross that guided sailors on Lake Erie. Although the spire was lost to a storm in 1876 and the original church was destroyed by fire in 1943, the parish was rebuilt and continues to thrive today. (Cleveland Public Library Photograph Collection.)

St. Malachi in Flames. The devastating fire on December 23, 1943, consumed much of St. Malachi Church's Gothic-style structure. Likely caused by a boiler explosion, the blaze destroyed its beautiful interior and steeple. The parish community rallied, laying the foundation for the Romanesque-style church that rose from the ruins years later. (Cleveland Public Library Photograph Collection.)

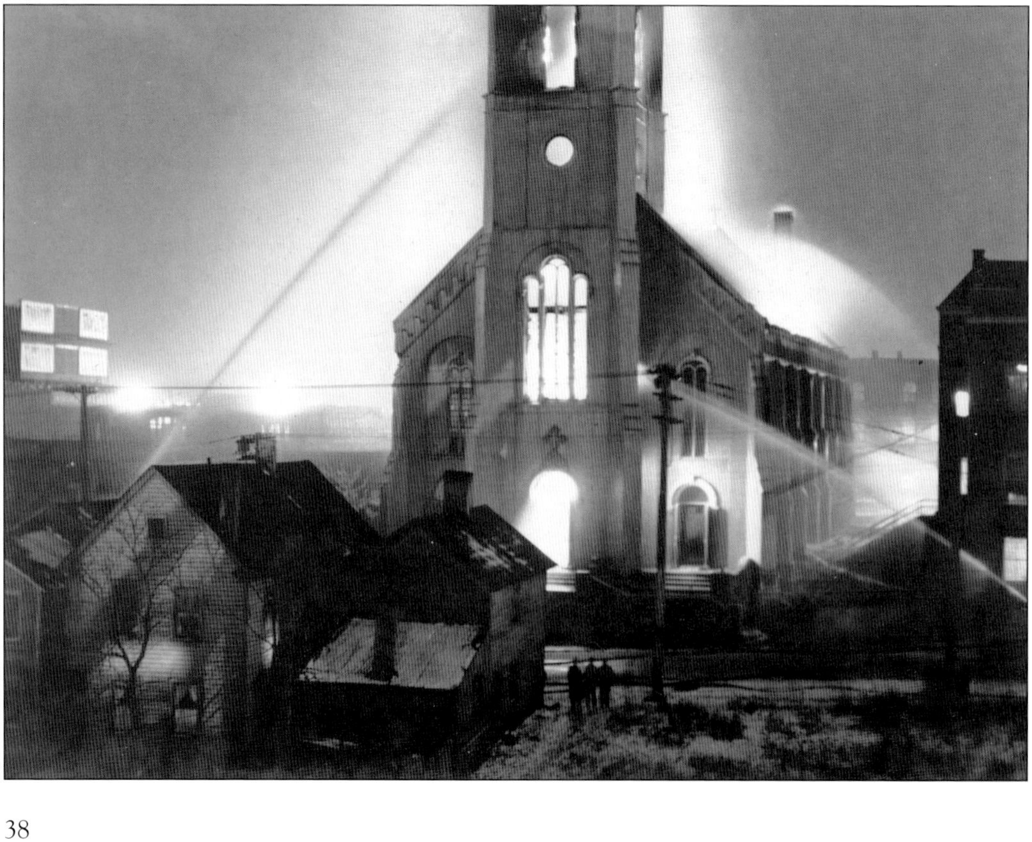

From Ruins to Renewal. The first image reveals the destruction of St. Malachi Church's interior after the fire, with the charred framework and collapsed ceiling showing the scale of devastation. Despite the loss, the parish persevered, transforming tragedy into renewal. The image below presents the beautifully rebuilt interior, completed in 1947. Featuring Romanesque design elements by architect George W. Stickle, the church includes multi-colored Tennessee crab-orchard stone, decorative buttresses, and lancet windows. Restored statues and the original baptismal font were integrated, honoring the past while embracing a new chapter. The rebuilt sanctuary reflects the parish's enduring commitment to faith and community. (Both, Michael Schwartz Library Special Collections, Cleveland State University.)

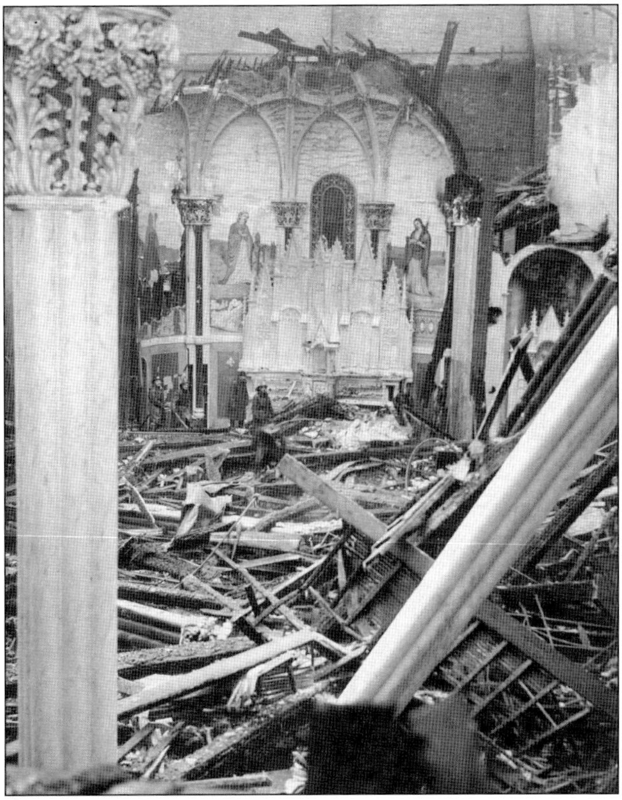

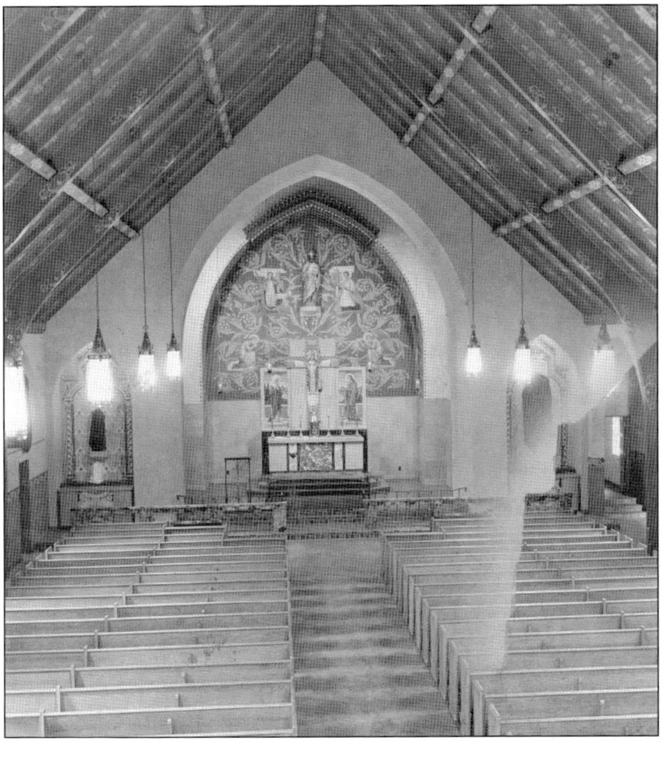

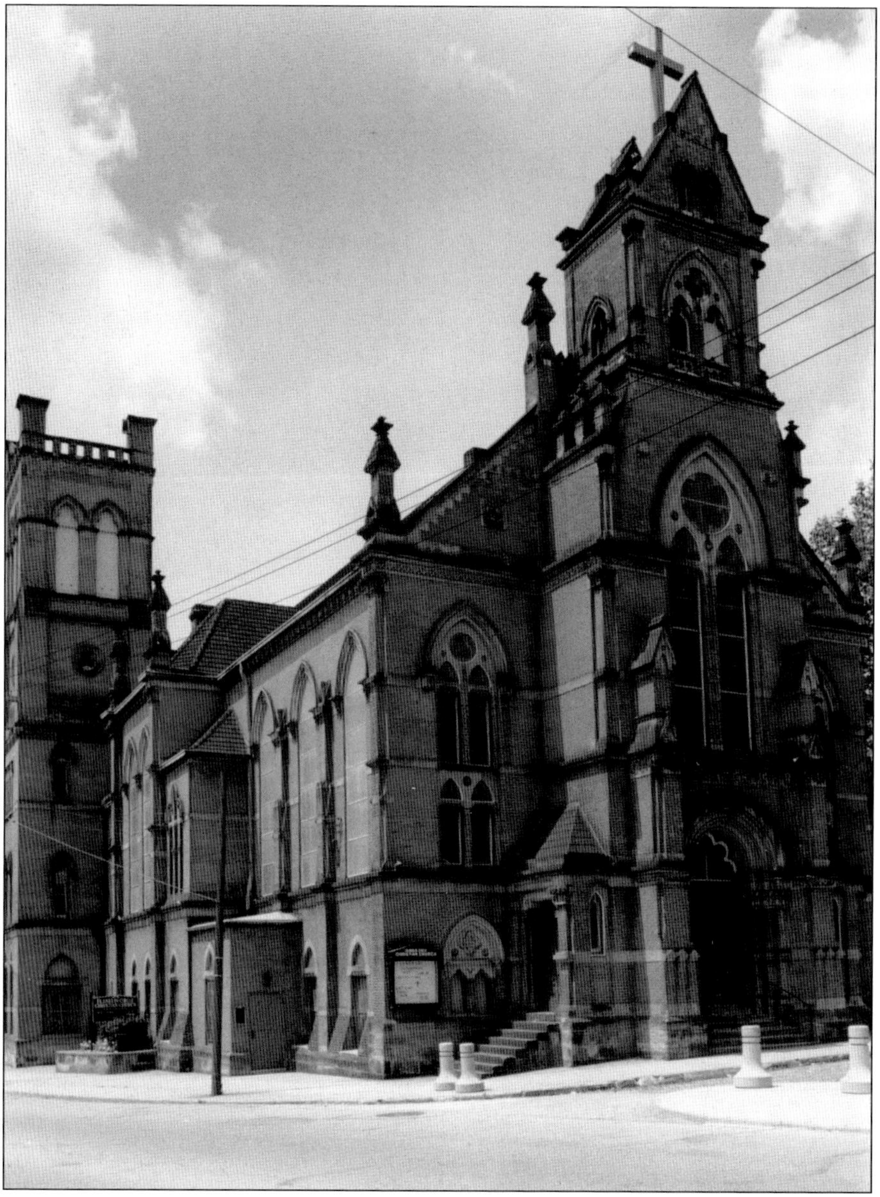

A Legacy of Faith and Activism. Standing at the heart of Franklin Circle, Franklin Circle Christian Church is an enduring landmark and a testament to Ohio City's history. Built in 1874 by prominent Cleveland architects Cudell and Richardson, the Victorian Gothic structure replaced the original humble meeting place affectionately known as "God's Barn." Its striking design, complete with pointed arches and intricate detailing, reflects the architectural ambition of its era. For nearly 150 years, the church has been more than a house of worship. It has served as a vital center for community engagement and social activism on Cleveland's near west side, addressing issues like housing, hunger, and social justice. Its prominent location on Franklin Circle underscores its role as a beacon of hope and a gathering place for generations. Today, Franklin Circle Christian Church continues its legacy, adapting to modern challenges while preserving its historic charm, making it a cherished part of Ohio City's vibrant cultural tapestry. (Michael Schwartz Library Special Collections, Cleveland State University.)

Pres. James A. Garfield. This vintage portrait of Pres. James A. Garfield reflects his later years, but his connection to Franklin Circle Christian Church began in his youth. Garfield, a future US president, served as pastor at the church in 1857 while also leading Hiram College. His early leadership in the Disciples of Christ movement exemplifies the church's historic role in fostering education and faith. (The Library of Congress.)

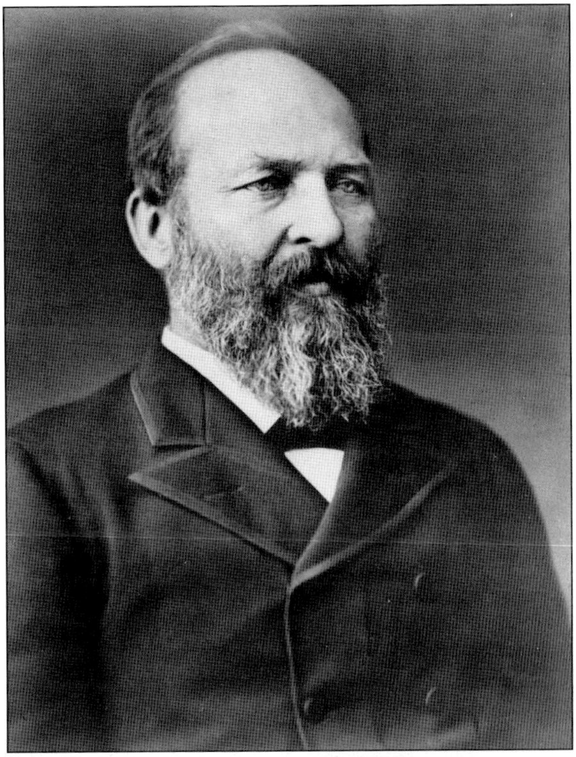

Raising the Banner. This April 1962 image of Franklin Circle Christian Church, featuring a banner reading "What is Real Religion," underscores the church's long-standing commitment to inclusivity and social outreach. Known for addressing the community's pressing issues, the church continues to serve its diverse neighbors through programs supporting education, social justice, and aid for the less fortunate. (Cleveland Public Library Photograph Collection.)

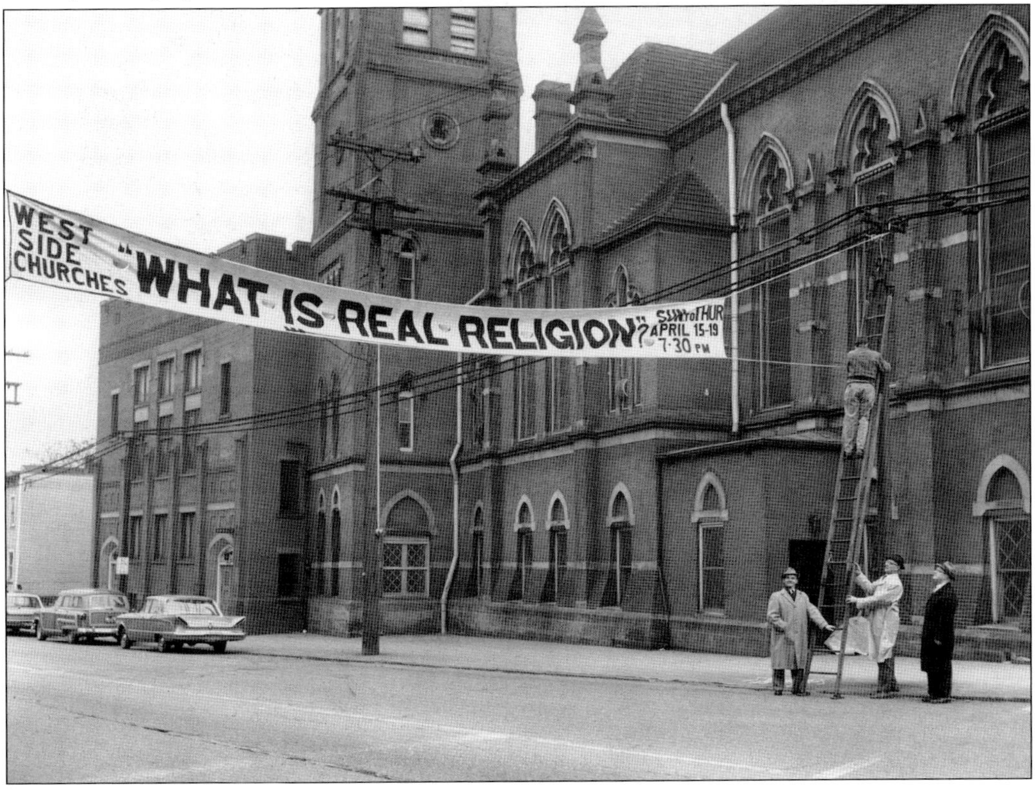

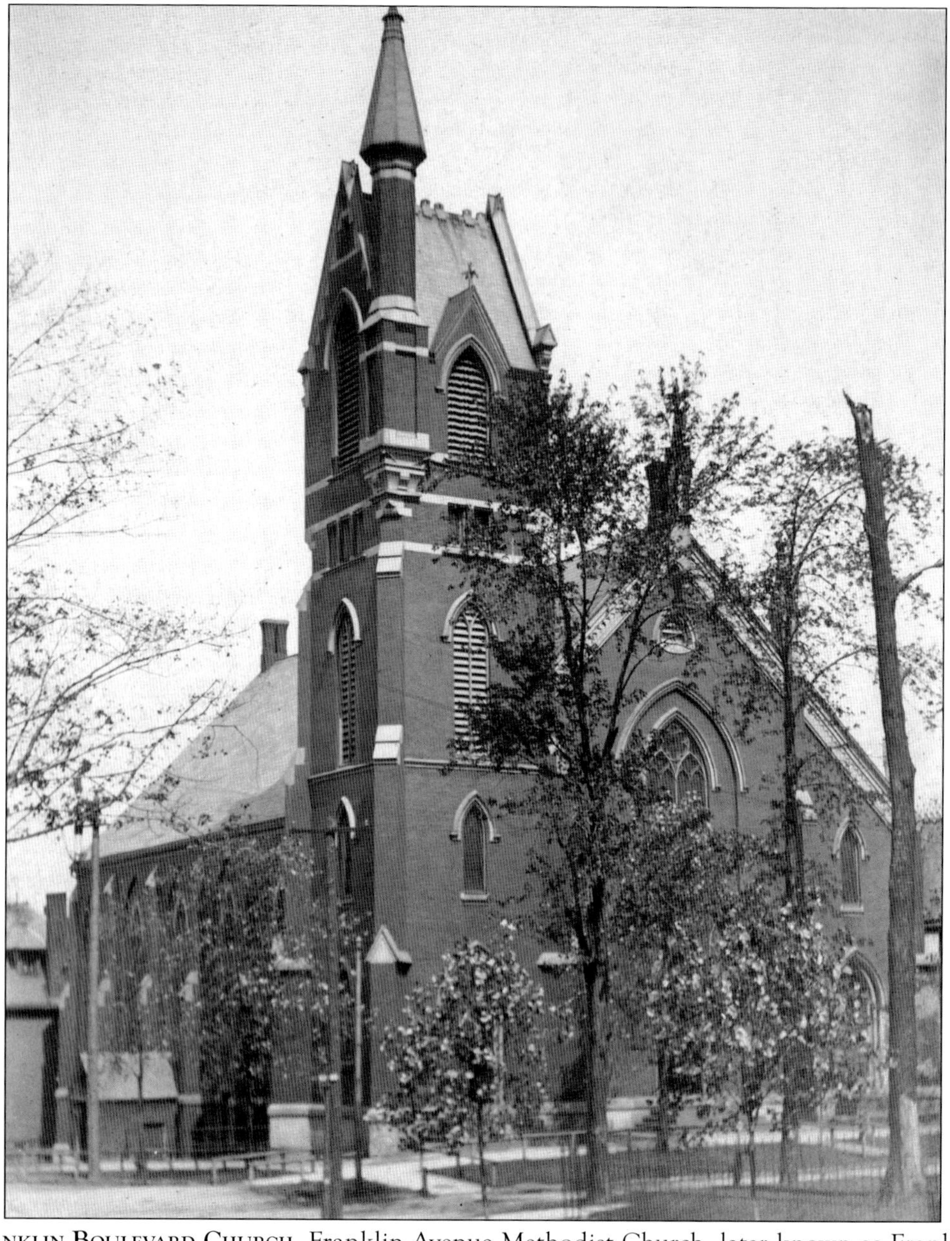

Franklin Boulevard Church. Franklin Avenue Methodist Church, later known as Franklin Boulevard Methodist Church, was established in 1867 and dedicated in 1870. The church was located at Franklin and Duane Street (West Thirty-Second Street). A towering landmark in Ohio City, the church was renowned for its architecture and its two-ton Liberty Bell replica. The bell once crashed through two floors to the basement and was rehung in time to celebrate the armistice ending World War I. For decades, the church served as a spiritual and social hub across the west side. Tragically, in March 1947, a devastating fire completely destroyed the church. Ultimately, the congregation joined with St. Paul's German Methodist Episcopal Church later that year to form Wesley Methodist Church, continuing their mission in a new home. Though the original building is gone, its legacy endures as a testament to the resilience and unity of its congregation. (The Ketteringham Collection, Cleveland Public Library.)

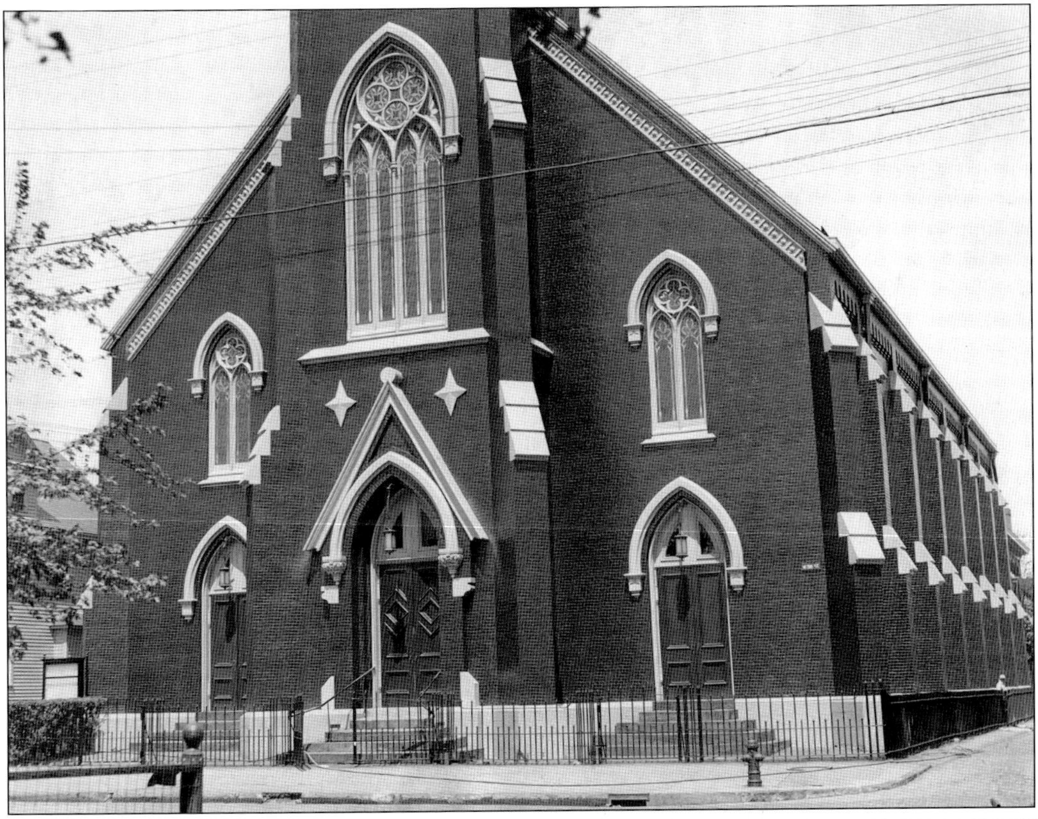

Trinity Evangelical Lutheran Church, 1932 (above) and 1960s (right). These two views of Trinity Evangelical Lutheran Church, located at West Thirtieth Street and Lorain Avenue, showcase its historical significance and architectural beauty. The 1932 image highlights the church's red brick Victorian Gothic design, completed in 1873 by German immigrants. By the 1960s, its towering 175-foot steeple had become a spiritual and visual landmark in Ohio City. Built to serve a rapidly growing congregation, Trinity initially held services exclusively in German, reflecting the cultural heritage of its founders. Over the years, the church adapted to the neighborhood's evolving demographics, incorporating multilingual services and becoming a hub for social justice and community outreach. Today, Trinity Evangelical Lutheran Church stands as a testament to faith, resilience, and its enduring role in the Ohio City community. (Both, Michael Schwartz Library Special Collections, Cleveland State University.)

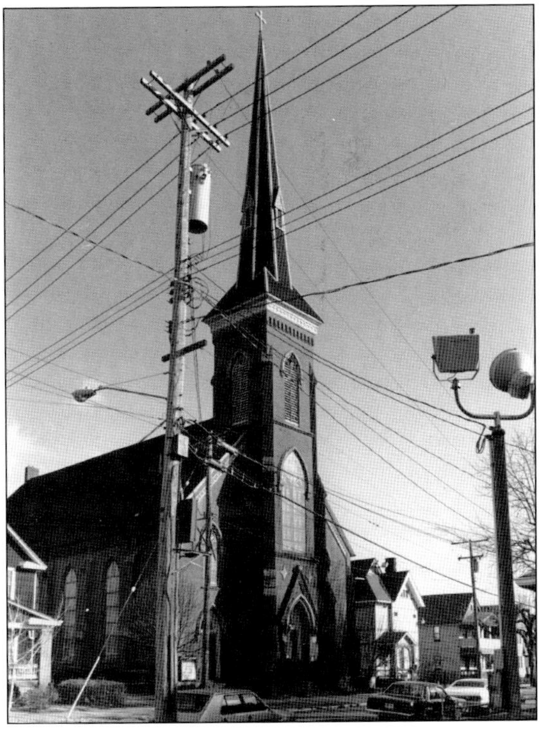

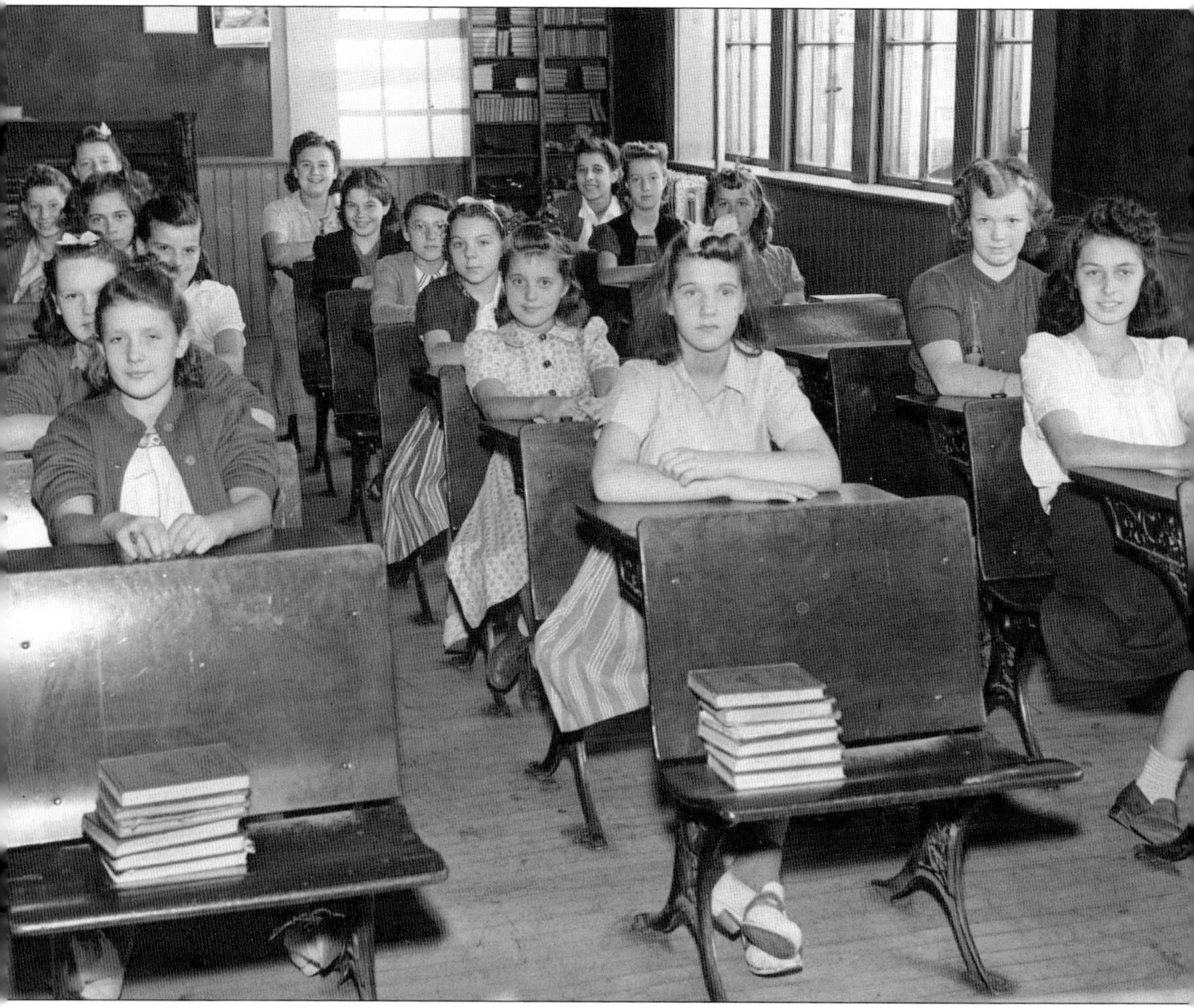

Trinity's Daughters in Class. This 1941 photograph offers a view into a classroom at Trinity Lutheran School. Established in 1853 as a mission of Zion Evangelical Lutheran Church, Trinity Evangelical Lutheran Church initially conducted services and lessons in a house that served as both a church and a school. The dedicated school building was completed in 1870, two years before the iconic church behind it, and it remained an elementary school until 1979. The classroom, featuring an all-girls class, highlights the church's deep commitment to education and the preservation of the neighborhood's German immigrant community. Early lessons were taught in German, maintaining a connection to their heritage while incorporating faith-based instruction. As Ohio City's demographics changed, the school adapted to provide inclusive education to a broader population, transitioning to English instruction while maintaining its Lutheran values. Trinity Lutheran School played a vital role in shaping generations of young minds, standing as a beacon of faith, education, and cultural identity for the Ohio City community. (Michael Schwartz Library Special Collections, Cleveland State University.)

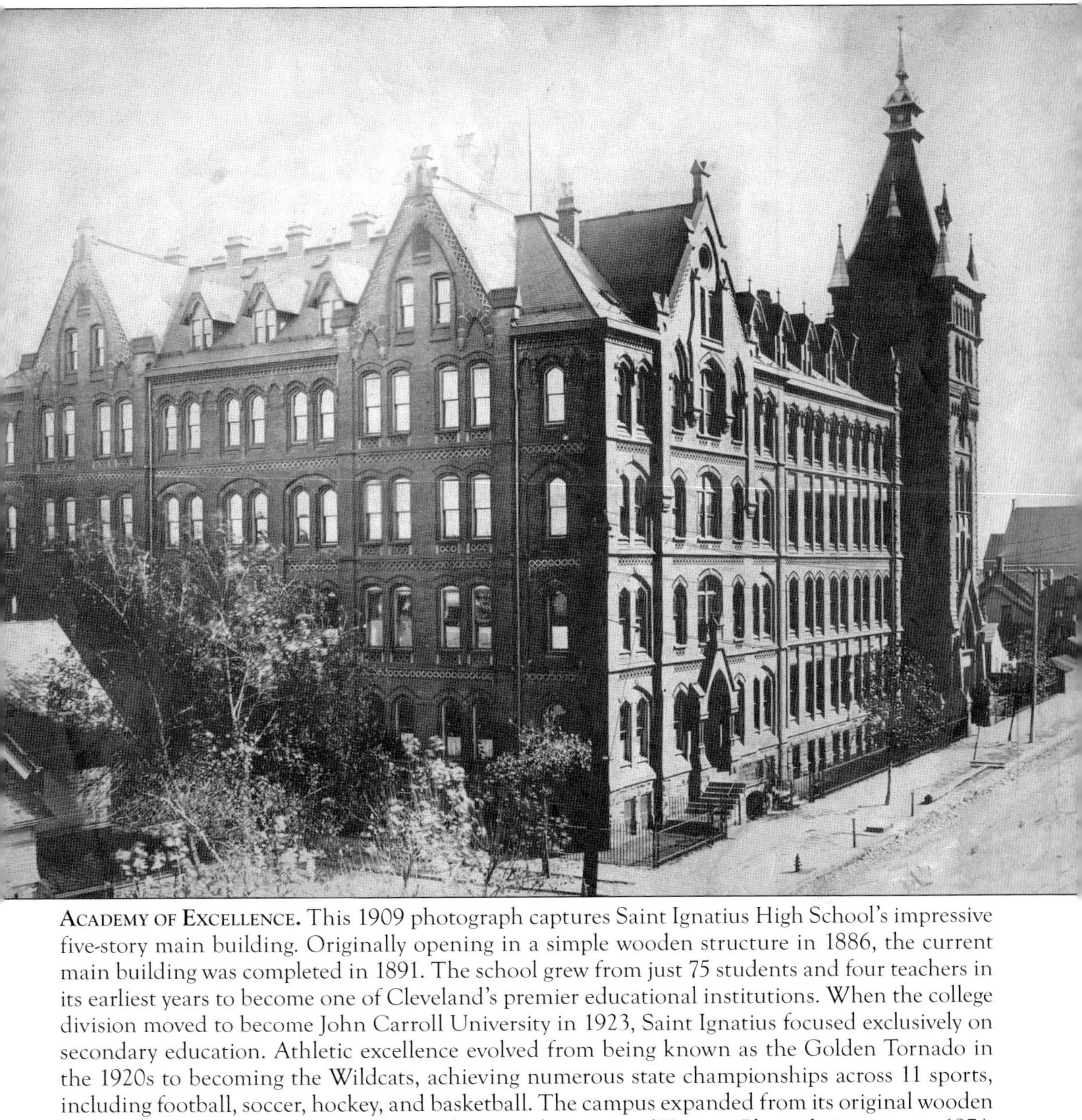

ACADEMY OF EXCELLENCE. This 1909 photograph captures Saint Ignatius High School's impressive five-story main building. Originally opening in a simple wooden structure in 1886, the current main building was completed in 1891. The school grew from just 75 students and four teachers in its earliest years to become one of Cleveland's premier educational institutions. When the college division moved to become John Carroll University in 1923, Saint Ignatius focused exclusively on secondary education. Athletic excellence evolved from being known as the Golden Tornado in the 1920s to becoming the Wildcats, achieving numerous state championships across 11 sports, including football, soccer, hockey, and basketball. The campus expanded from its original wooden structure to a 15-acre complex and gained National Register of Historic Places designation in 1974. A Blue Ribbon School recognized for academic excellence, Saint Ignatius has produced notable alumni in law, business, athletics, and public service while maintaining its Jesuit tradition of forming leaders through rigorous academics and community service, with 99 percent of students advancing to college annually. (Michael Schwartz Library Special Collections, Cleveland State University.)

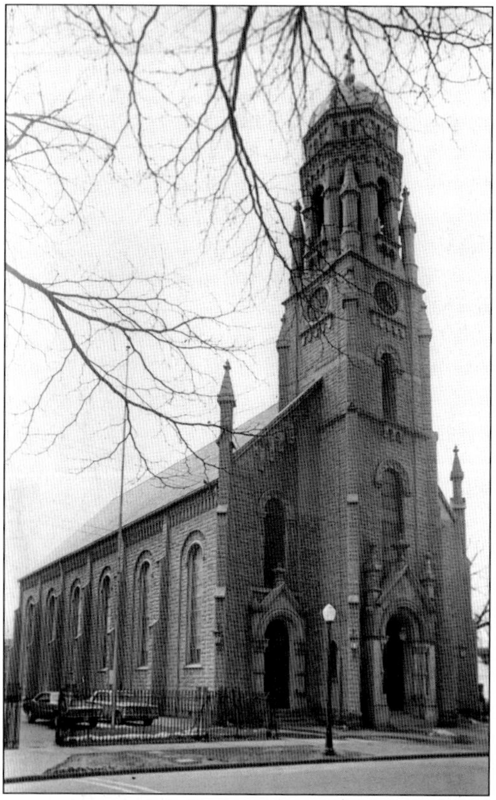

Foundations of Faith, 1968. St. Mary's Catholic Church was established in 1854 to serve German Catholics at West Thirtieth Street and Carroll Avenue. Built through parishioners' efforts, it was dedicated in 1865. Over a century later, the parish merged with St. Patrick, and the church closed in 1959. Demolished in 1968, its site became home to a science center for St. Ignatius High School. (Michael Schwartz Library Special Collections, Cleveland State University.)

Final Sanctuary. This 1968 interior view captures St. Mary's final days. The soaring vaulted ceiling, decorative altar, and architectural elements showcase the craftsmanship invested by German Catholic immigrants when building their spiritual home in 1865. Shortly after this photograph, the sanctuary fell to expansion plans. (Michael Schwartz Library Special Collections, Cleveland State University.)

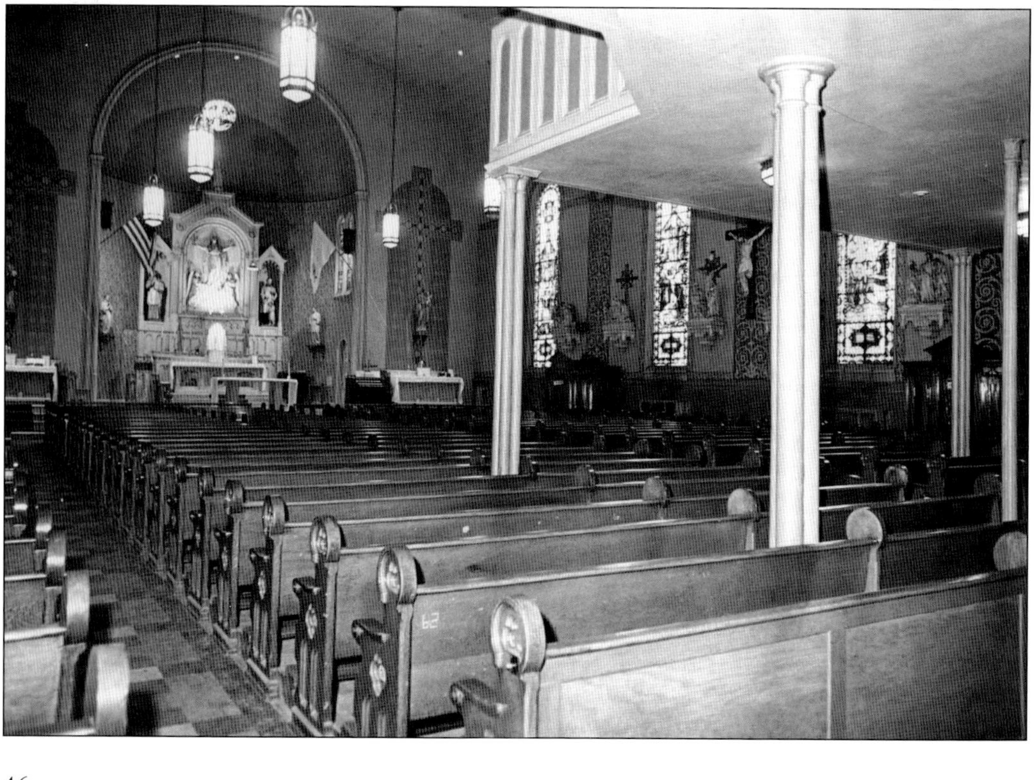

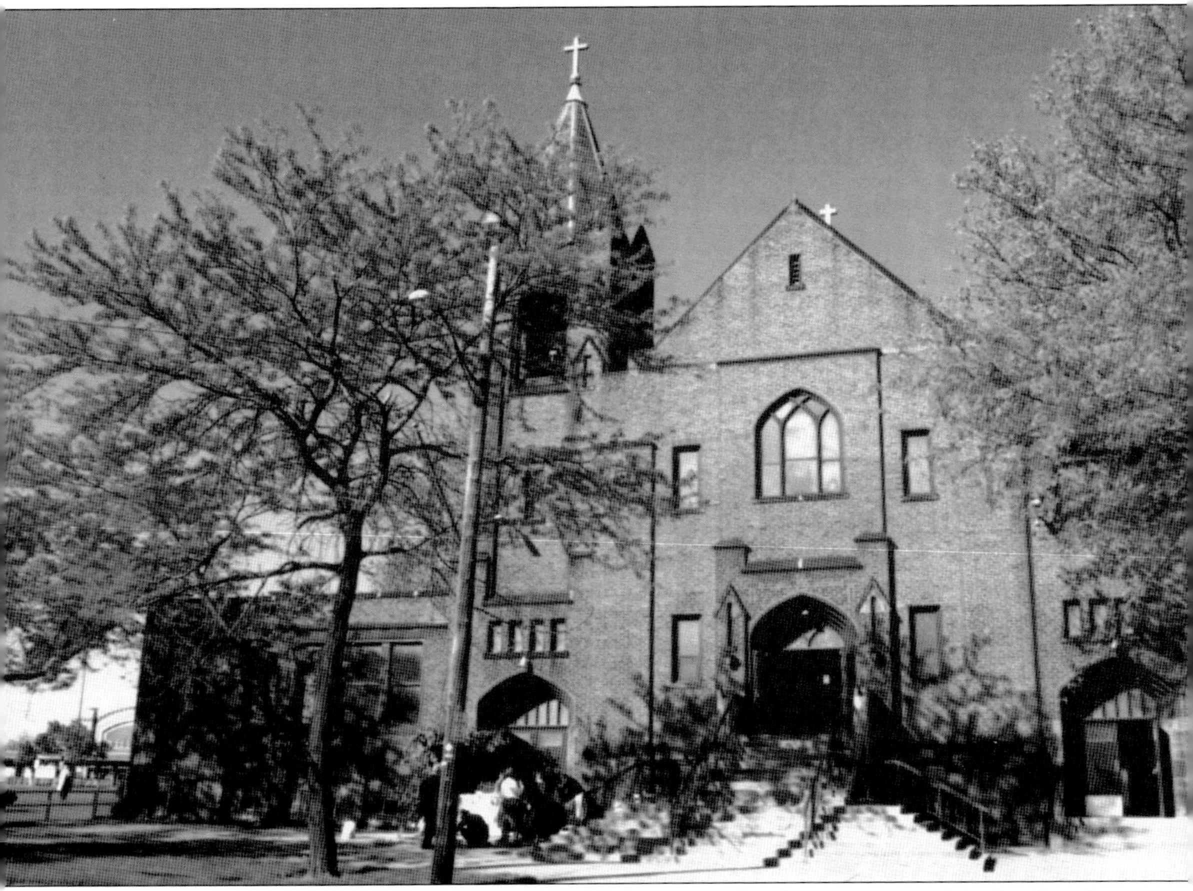

St. Emeric. St. Emeric's Catholic Church, founded in 1904, has been a spiritual and cultural anchor for Cleveland's Hungarian community. The parish emerged when Hungarian Catholics on Cleveland's west side sought a local place of worship. In 1905, Reverend Stephen Soltész dedicated a wood-frame church at Bridge Avenue and West Twenty-Fourth Street, where he also established a school staffed by Ursuline Sisters, serving over 150 children. Classes included Hungarian language, history, and geography. A fire destroyed the original church in 1915, and after another fire at their temporary home, the congregation built the current structure in 1925. The new building also housed a school taught by the Daughters of the Divine Redeemer Sisters. Over the years, St. Emeric has been a beacon of resilience, adapting to challenges while preserving Hungarian traditions. Today, the church continues to serve Hungarian-speaking Catholics, hosting bilingual services and celebrating its rich heritage. (Michael Schwartz Library Special Collections, Cleveland State University.)

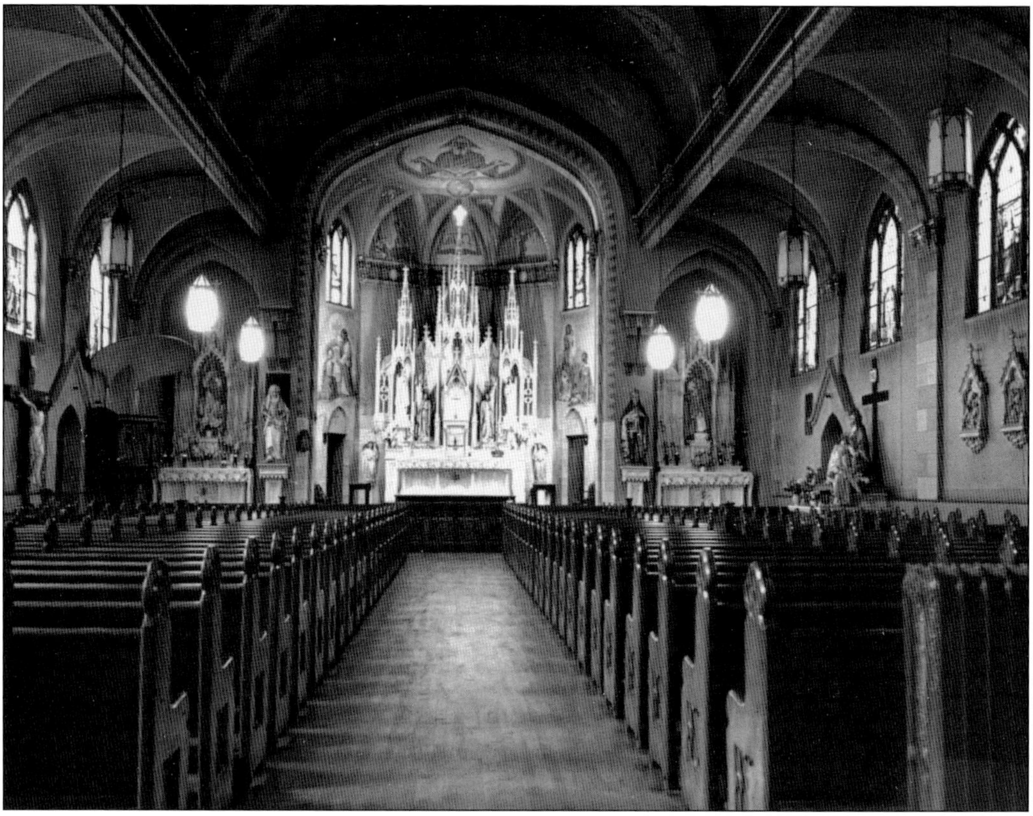

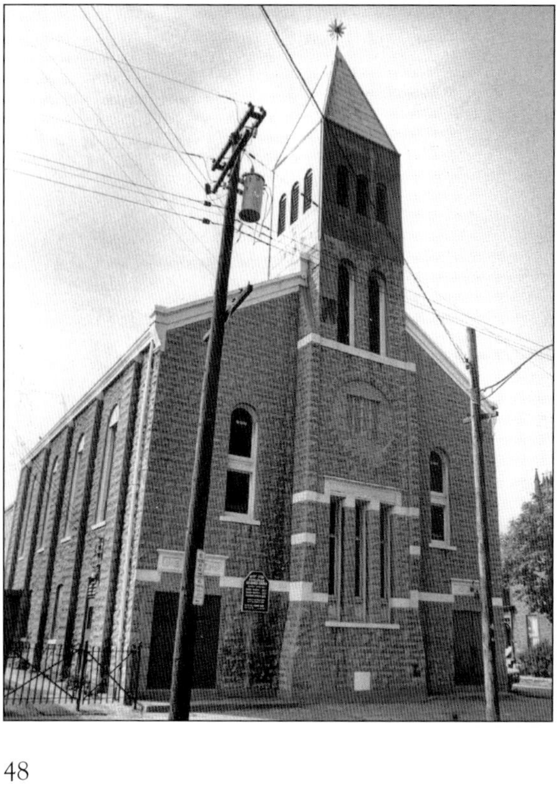

Hungarian Elegance. The interior of St. Emeric Church highlights its Gothic architecture, featuring intricate altars, vibrant stained-glass windows, and a majestic white-carved wood high altar adorned with delicate spires. Immersed in Hungarian Christian heritage, the sanctuary is adorned with murals depicting saints and historical figures. (Cleveland Catholic Diocese.)

From Hungarian to Hispanic. The church building at 1946 West Thirty-Second Street has a rich history, beginning as the West Side Hungarian Reformed Church in 1890, when Reverend Gusztáv Jurányi preached to Cleveland's Hungarian community. In 1976, the structure was purchased by San Juan Bautista Parish, Cleveland's first Roman Catholic parish dedicated to the Hispanic community, continuing its legacy of faith and cultural service. (Michael Schwartz Library Special Collections, Cleveland State University.)

Four

Commerce and Community

Brewing Heritage and Market Roots

Ohio City's commercial identity was shaped by the diverse trades and enterprises of its immigrant residents, anchored by two powerful forces: the public market that became its heart and the brewing industry that fueled its growth. In 1840, Connecticut landowners Josiah Barber and Richard Lord established an open-air market at Lorain Street and Pearl (West Twenty-Fifth) Streets, setting the foundation for what would become the West Side Market. What began as a simple "public square" with wooden market stalls evolved into a civic monument by 1912, when Mayor Newton D. Baker dedicated the stunning brick structure with its 137-foot clock tower and vaulted interior.

By 1869, considered Ohio City's "prime" year, the district had become an epicenter of commerce and industry. Bridge Street exemplified this diversity, with its brewers, machinists, blacksmiths, coopers, cabinet makers, and sailors all living and working in close proximity. German immigrants, in particular, were predominantly skilled tradesmen and established numerous successful businesses.

The brewing industry emerged as a crucial economic engine. By the turn of the century, Cleveland boasted 30 large breweries, with a significant concentration in Ohio City. The district between Market Avenue and Bridge Avenue housed several major operations, including the Gehring Brewery on Brainard Avenue, Schlather Brewery on York Avenue, and Cleveland-Sandusky Brewing Company on Carroll Avenue.

Other businesses thrived in this commercial ecosystem. Fries & Schuele, founded in 1868 as a small dry goods store, grew into a five-story department store rivaling downtown establishments. The neighborhood supported a remarkable range of enterprises, from Fred Herz's Merchant Tailor shop on Lorain Street to Herrman & Pfarr's Groceries on Pearl Street.

Through changing times, the West Side Market stood as an unwavering anchor of neighborhood commerce. The market's preservation of small-scale, personal commerce and the architectural legacy of the brewing industry would later prove crucial to Ohio City's revitalization, as new generations recognized the value of these historical commercial roots. The buildings, spaces, and community bonds forged during these foundational years created an enduring framework that would shape the neighborhood's future development.

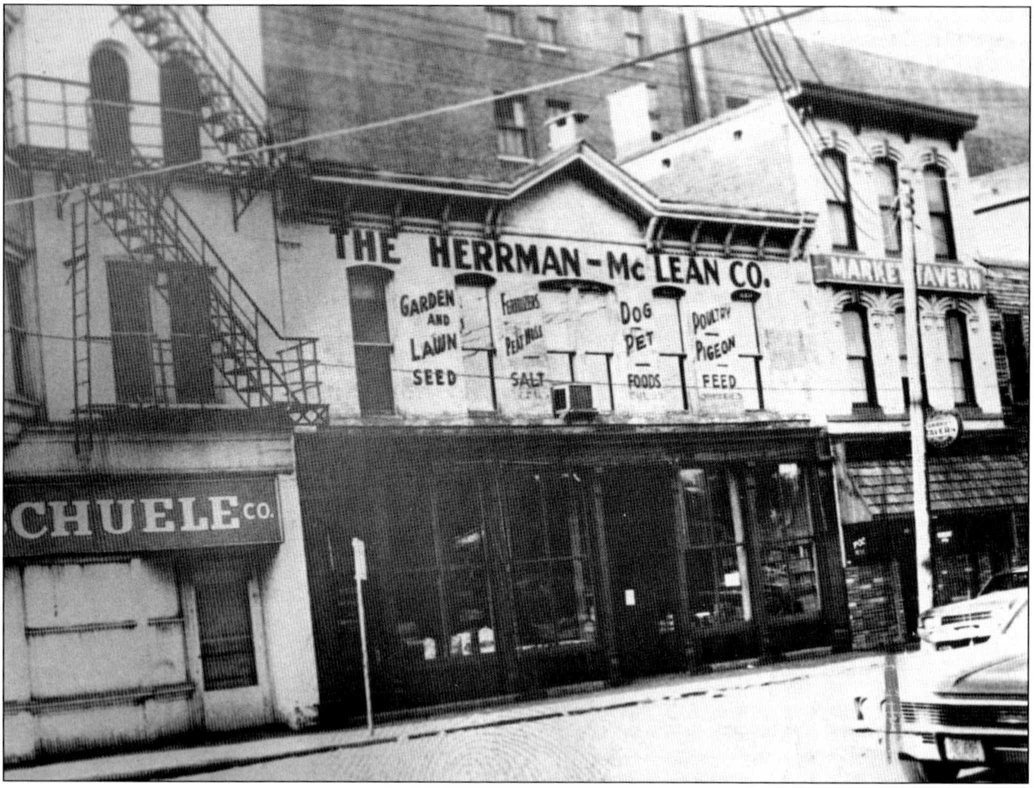

MARKET STREET COMMERCE. Market Street's commercial corridor exemplified Ohio City's diverse business district in the early 1900s. The Fries & Schuele Company (left), founded in 1868 as a dry goods store, grew into the West Side's premier department store. Next door, the Herrman-McLean building, built by wine merchant Jacob Bender in the 1870s, housed various businesses before becoming home to Great Lakes Brewing Company in 1988. (Michael Schwartz Library Special Collections, Cleveland State University.)

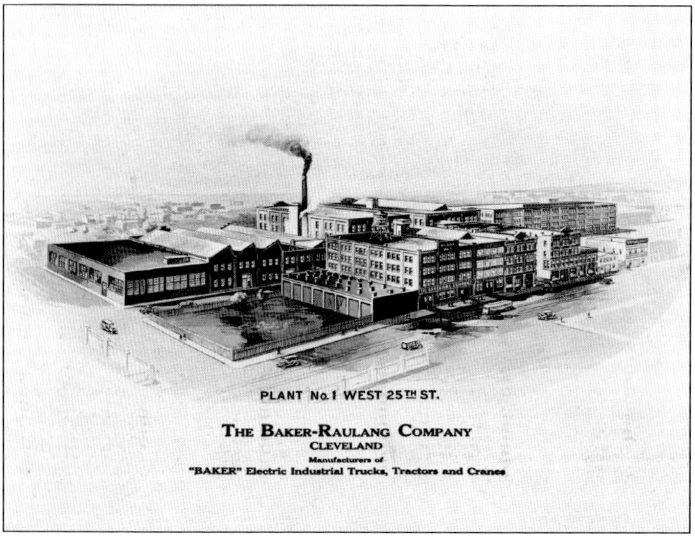

RAUCH & LANG CARRIAGE COMPANY. The Rauch & Lang plant at West Twenty-Fifth and Carroll Streets began as a premier carriage manufacturer in 1883 before transitioning to electric automobiles in 1905. After merging with Baker Motor Vehicle Company in 1915, they became the world's largest electric vehicle producer. As gasoline-powered cars dominated the 1920s market, the company shifted to manufacturing industrial lift trucks. (The Library of Congress.)

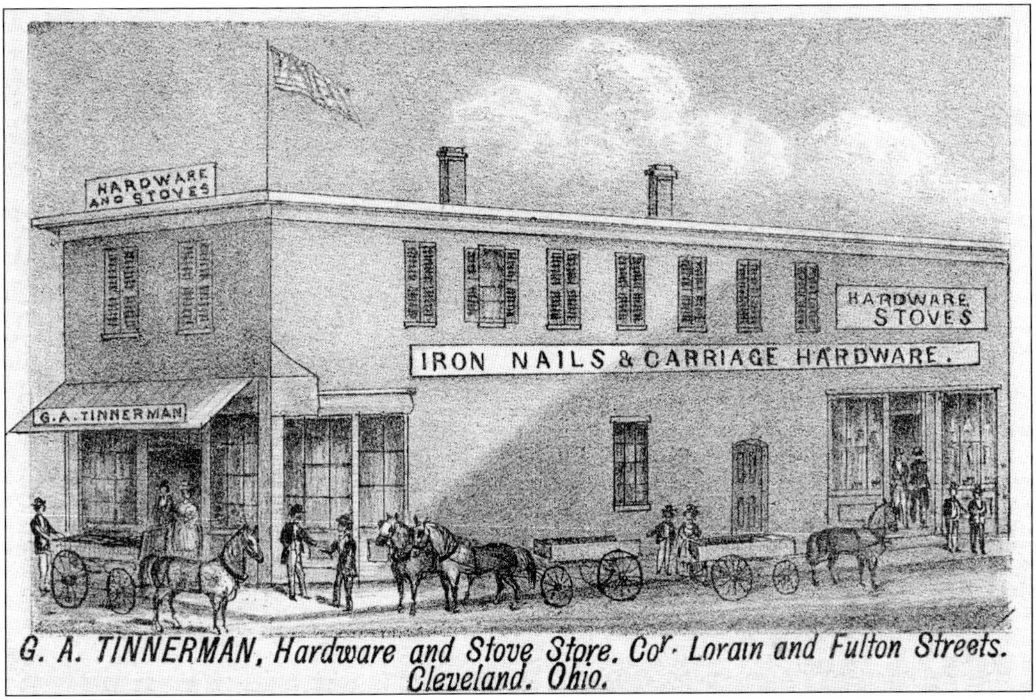

FROM HARDWARE TO HISTORY. This 1874 Cleveland Atlas sketch shows George A. Tinnerman's original hardware store at Lorain Street and Fulton Street. A Bavarian immigrant and skilled tinner, Tinnerman opened the store in 1870, selling cast iron stoves among other goods. His later dissatisfaction with these stoves led to innovations in steel range design that transformed his business into manufacturing. (Cleveland Public Library Photograph Collection.)

FROM STOVES TO HOMES. Built to accommodate the company's growth from its original hardware store location, the former Tinnerman Stove and Range Company headquarters at 2048 Fulton Road represents Ohio City's industrial evolution. This building served as the company's main facility until 1950. Today, it has been thoughtfully renovated into the Tinnerman Lofts residential complex. (Cleveland Public Library Photograph Collection.)

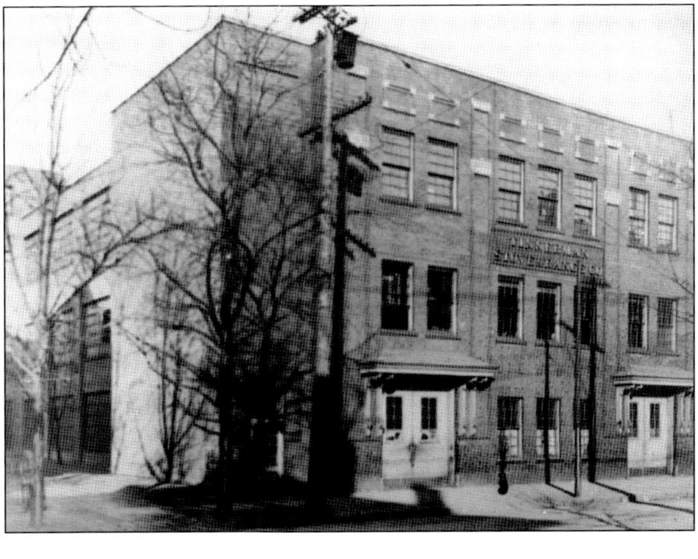

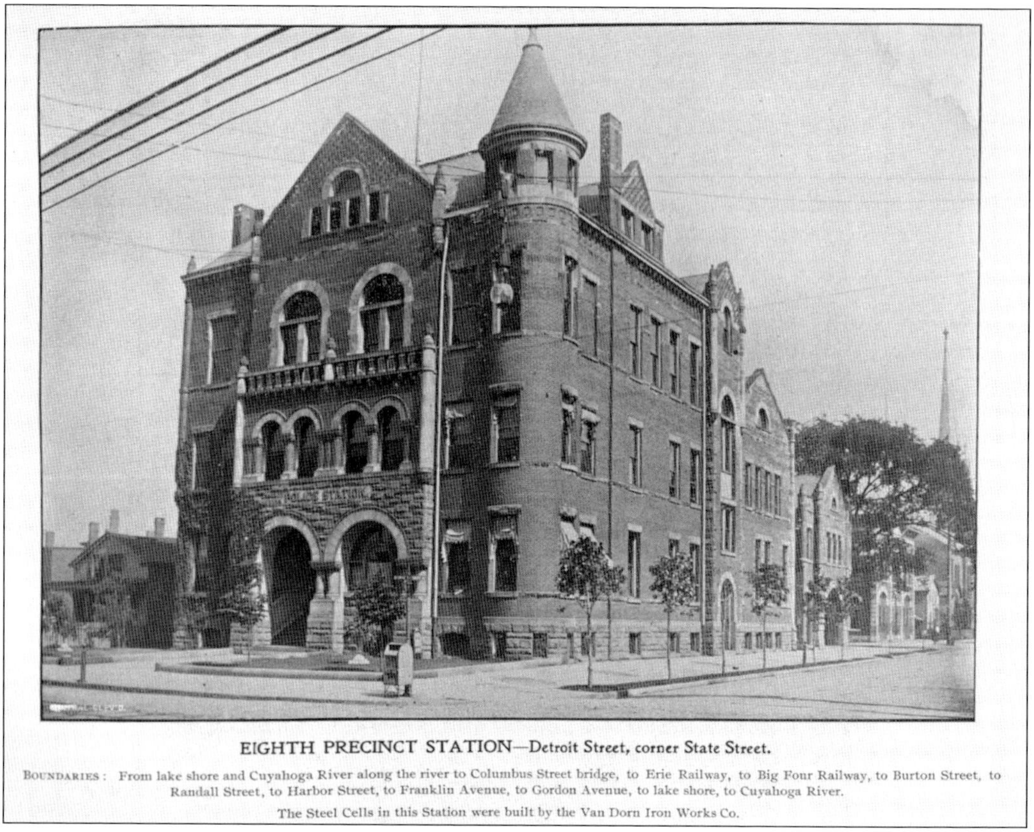

CIVIC CORNERSTONE. The Eighth Precinct police station at Detroit Avenue and State (West Twenty-Ninth) Street anchored Ohio City's growing municipal and business district. Built in 1892 on the former First Congregational Church property, it ranked second in importance only to Central Station. Originally the West Side Watch House in 1855, it served as Second District headquarters until 1954. (Michael Schwartz Library Special Collections, Cleveland State University.)

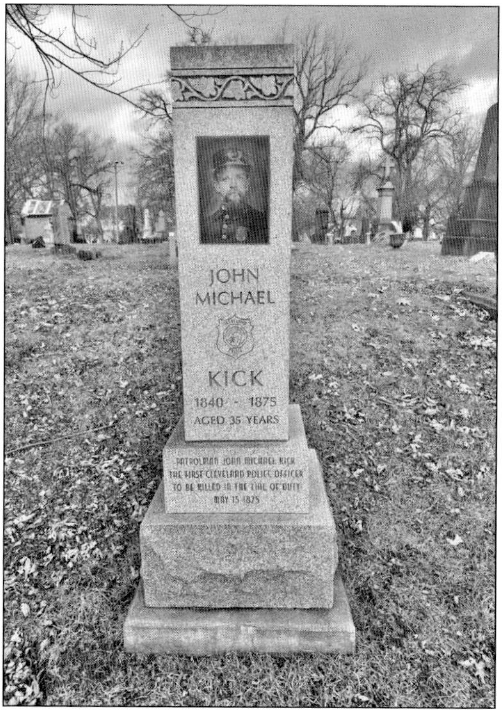

FIRST TO FALL. This memorial and the adjacent original gravestone in Monroe Street Cemetery honor Cleveland Patrolman Michael Kick, the city's first police officer killed in the line of duty. During a stakeout near Kentucky (West Thirty-Eighth Street) and Franklin Streets in 1875, Kick and fellow officers confronted suspected burglars, leading to a fatal shootout. His sacrifice is commemorated both here and on the National Law Enforcement Officers Memorial in Washington, DC. (Author's collection.)

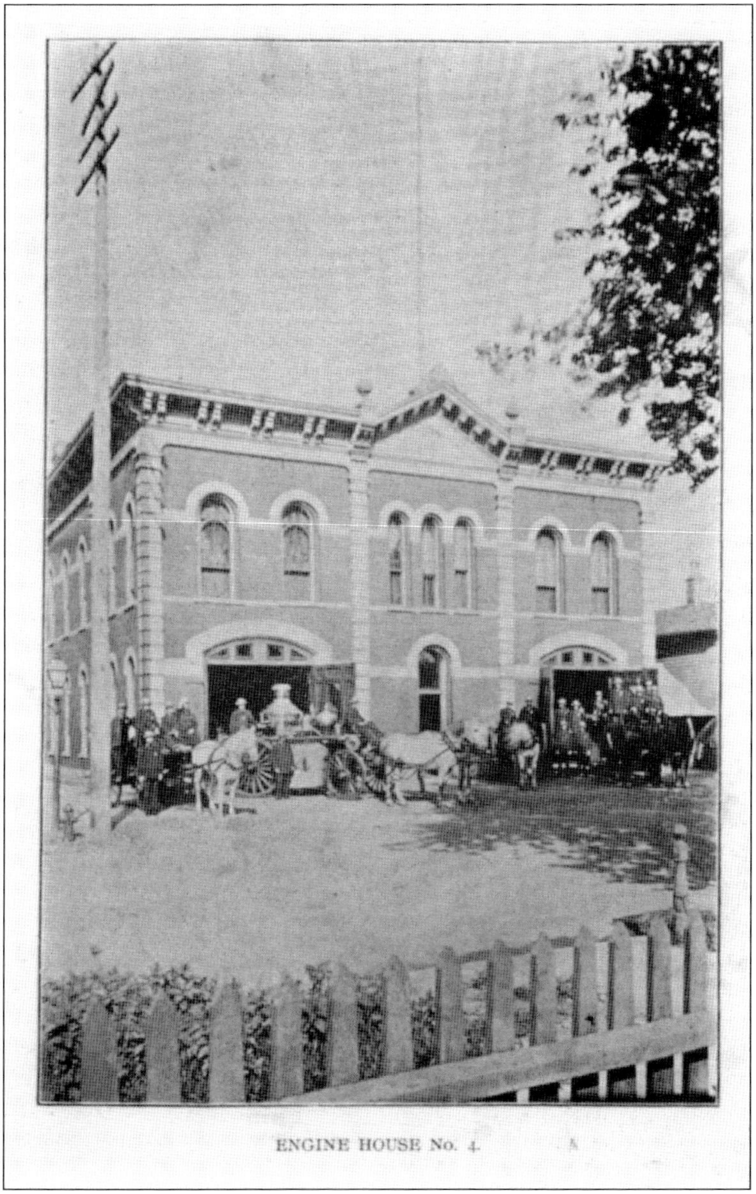

Guardians of a Growing City. Engine House No. 4, featured in this c.1890 Cleveland Fire Department yearbook, served a critical role in protecting Ohio City's expanding commercial district. Located on State Street (West Twenty-Ninth) at Church Avenue near the Eighth Precinct police station, the firehouse provided essential protection for a neighborhood dominated by wooden structures. The station's strategic placement reflected the era's growing concern for public safety as Ohio City's dense urban development increased fire risks. The two-story brick building, with its distinctive architectural features typical of late-19th-century firehouses, remains a neighborhood anchor today. Now home to Rising Star Coffee, Larder Delicatessen, and professional offices, the historic structure maintains its prominent place in community life. The building's successful adaptation from public safety to commercial use demonstrates Ohio City's ability to preserve its architectural heritage while meeting modern needs. (Michael Schwartz Library Special Collections, Cleveland State University.)

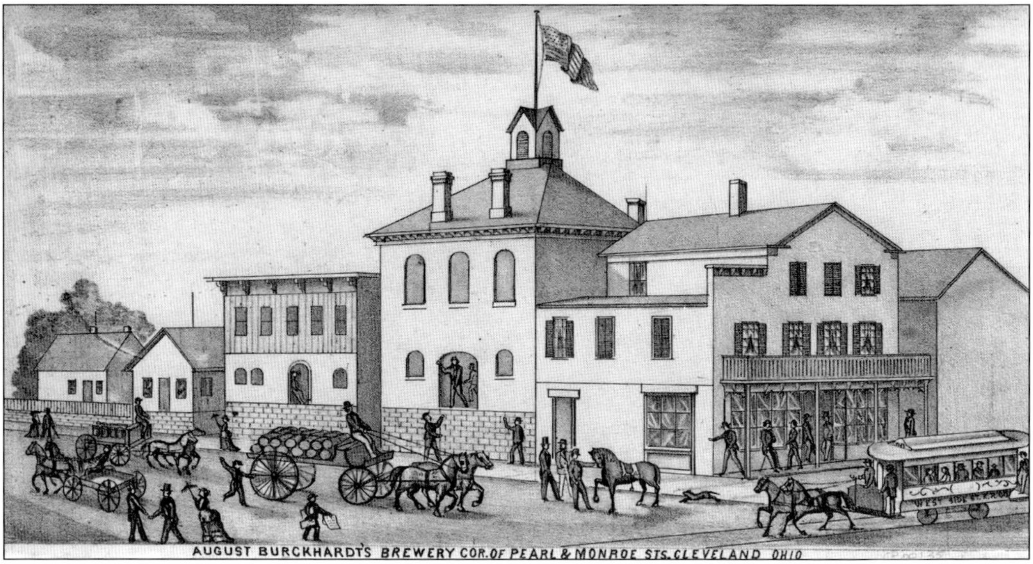

Burckhardt Brewery, c. 1870. August Burckhardt's Brewery, operating at Pearl (West Twenty-Fifth Street) and Monroe Streets from 1868 to 1876, represented the early wave of German brewers establishing themselves in Ohio City. Though short-lived, it exemplified the neighborhood's emerging brewing industry that would help define the area's commercial identity. (Cleveland Public Library Photograph Collection.)

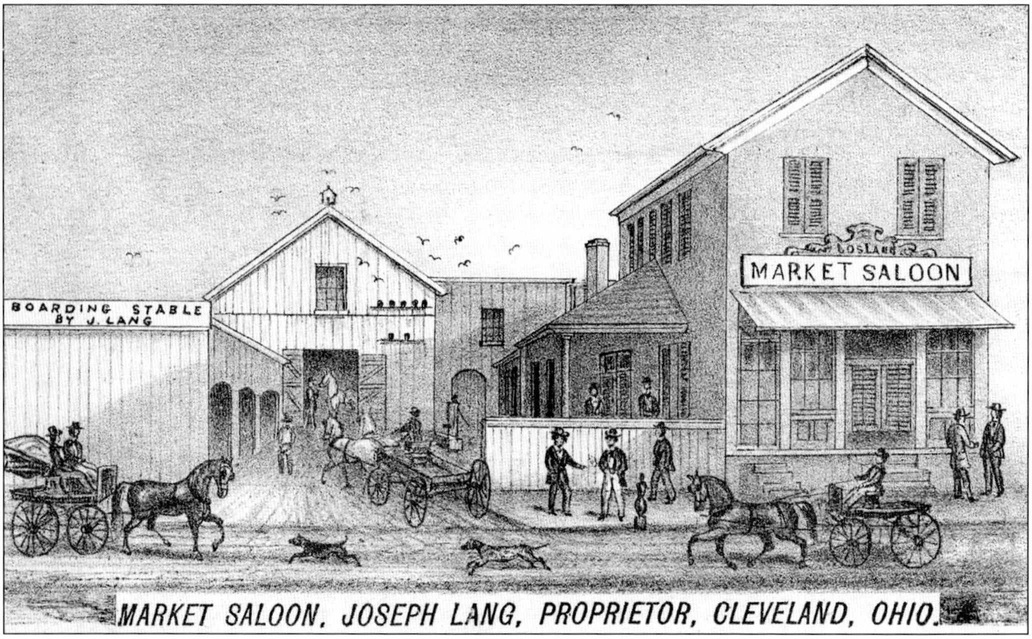

Market Saloon, c. 1870. The Market Saloon at 86 Lorain Street, operated by Joseph Lang in 1874, exemplified the tavern culture integral to Ohio City's commercial life. Beyond his role as proprietor, Lang contributed to the neighborhood's development as a civic leader and real estate developer. (Cleveland Public Library Photograph Collection.)

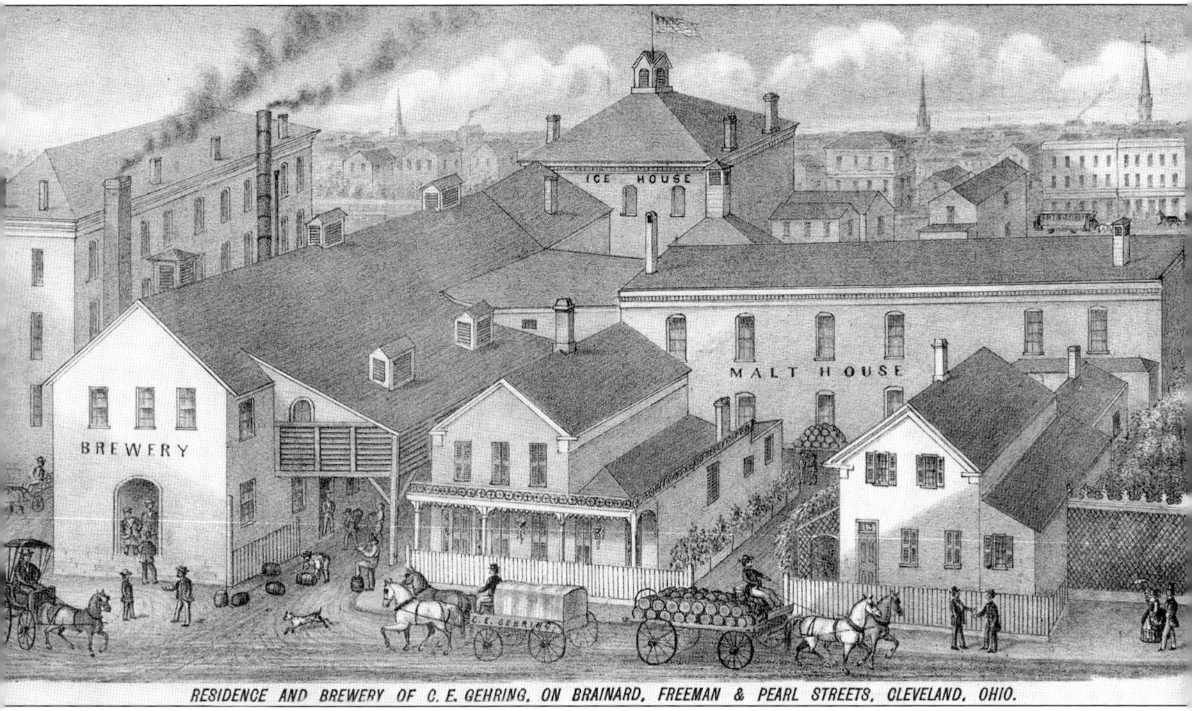

BREWING EMPIRE. This 1874 wood engraving from the *Atlas of Cuyahoga County* showcases the thriving C.E. Gehring Brewing Company complex at Freeman Avenue and Pearl (West Twenty-Fifth) Street. Carl Ernst Gehring, who learned brewing as an apprentice in Germany, immigrated to America in 1848 and established his brewery in 1857. From modest beginnings producing 1,800 barrels in his first year, Gehring built one of Cleveland's most successful brewing operations. The facility expanded to include a 155-barrel brew kettle, 36 fermenting tanks, a malthouse, two ice houses, and six lagering cellars. Gehring moved his family to a residence on the brewery property, where his four sons joined the business. Beyond brewing, Gehring served on Cleveland's city council, as police commissioner, and as president of Forest City Bank, while supporting numerous charitable causes, including homes for children and the elderly. His brewery's reputation for producing "Cleveland's best beer" helped establish Ohio City as the center of the city's brewing industry. (Michael Schwartz Library Special Collections, Cleveland State University.)

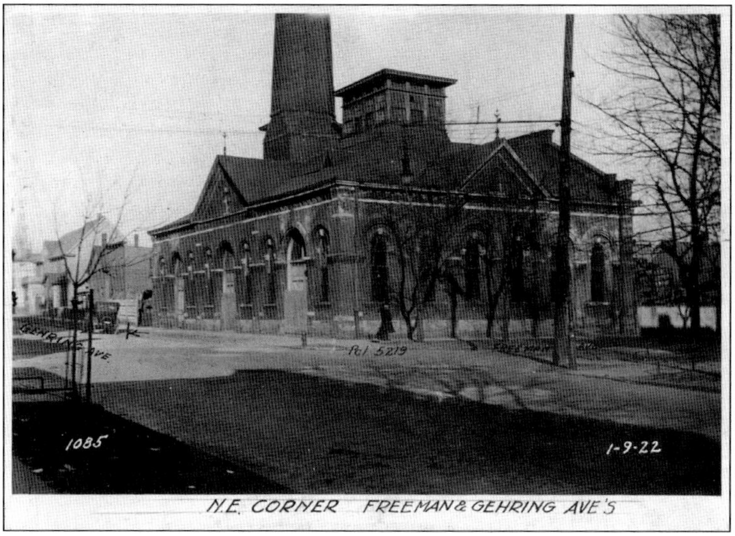

Prohibition's Toll. The Gehring Brewery at Freeman and Gehring Avenues, photographed in 1922, shows the facility after its 1898 absorption into the Cleveland & Sandusky Brewing Company. The once-prosperous brewery, which produced 68,000 barrels annually at its peak, closed in 1918 due to Prohibition. (Michael Schwartz Library Special Collections, Cleveland State University.)

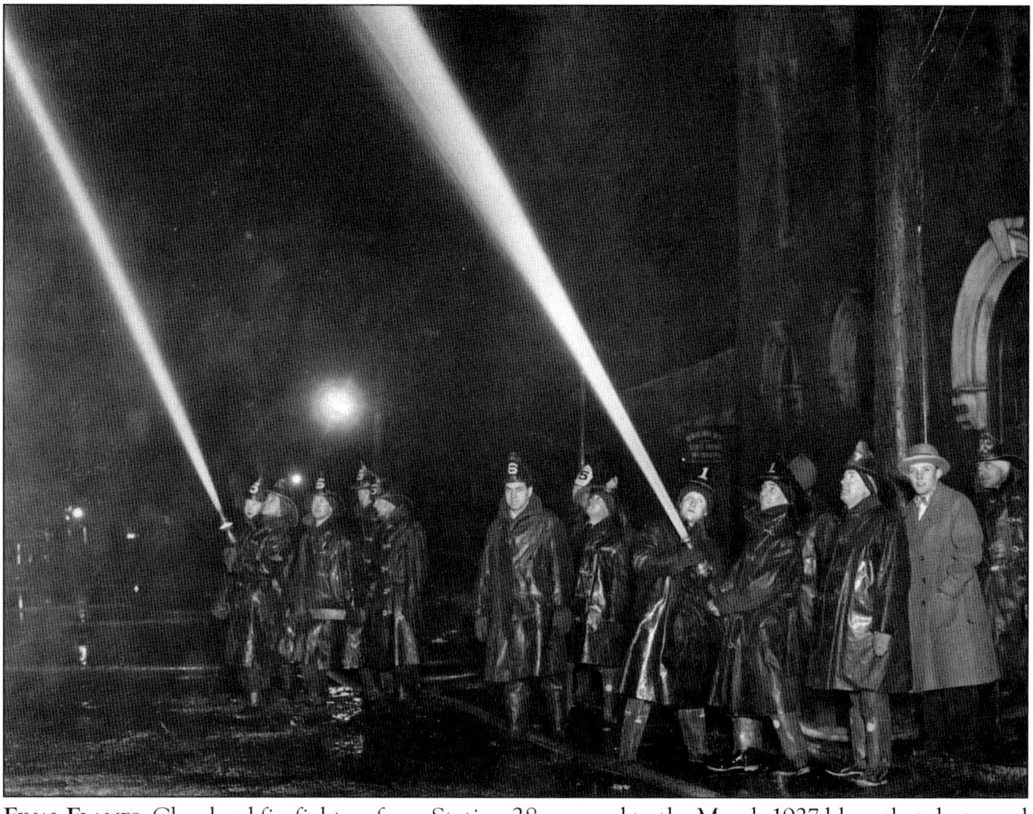

Final Flames. Cleveland firefighters from Station 28 respond to the March 1927 blaze that destroyed the remaining structures of the former Gehring Brewery complex. The fire, causing an estimated $40,000 in damage, marked the final chapter for this once-prominent Ohio City landmark. Only Gehring Avenue, named for the brewery's founder, remains as a testament to this important piece of brewing history. (Cleveland Public Library Photograph Collection.)

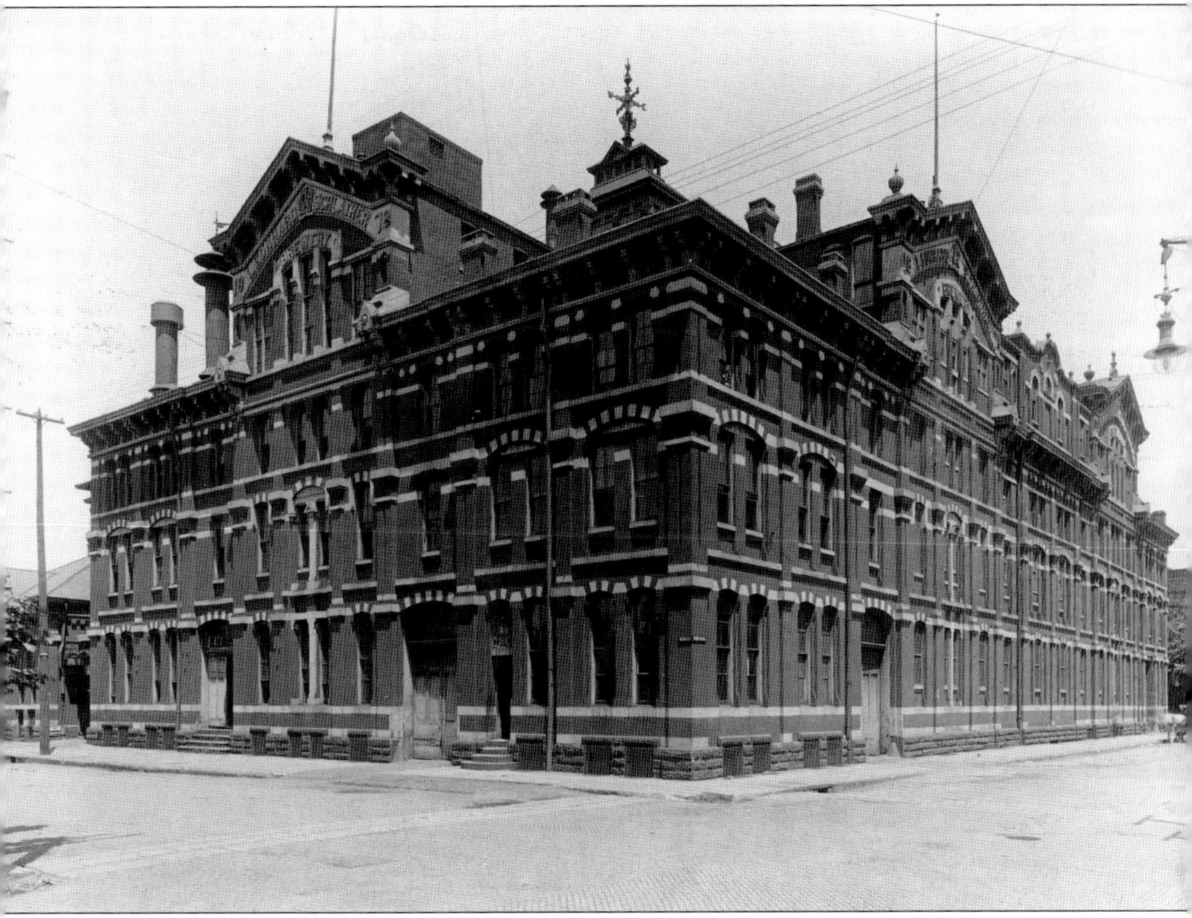

Schlather's Success Story. This 1885 photograph captures Leonard Schlather's brewery at York (now West Twenty-Eighth) Street and Carroll Avenue. The structure was designed in 1878 by architect Andrew Mitermiler. Schlather, a German immigrant from Ebenhausen, Württemberg, arrived in Cleveland in 1852 and founded his brewery in 1857. Starting as a small operation, Schlather steadily expanded, constructing a brick building at this location and adding to it as the business flourished across the area. By the late 19th century, Schlather Brewery had grown into one of Ohio City's largest breweries. In 1902, Schlather sold the business to Cleveland & Sandusky Brewing Company, which operated it until Prohibition in 1919. Leonard Schlather's success extended beyond brewing; he became a prominent philanthropist, cofounding St. Luke's Hospital and serving as a bank president and director. His legacy endures as a symbol of the industrious spirit that shaped Cleveland's history. (Cleveland Public Library Photograph Collection.)

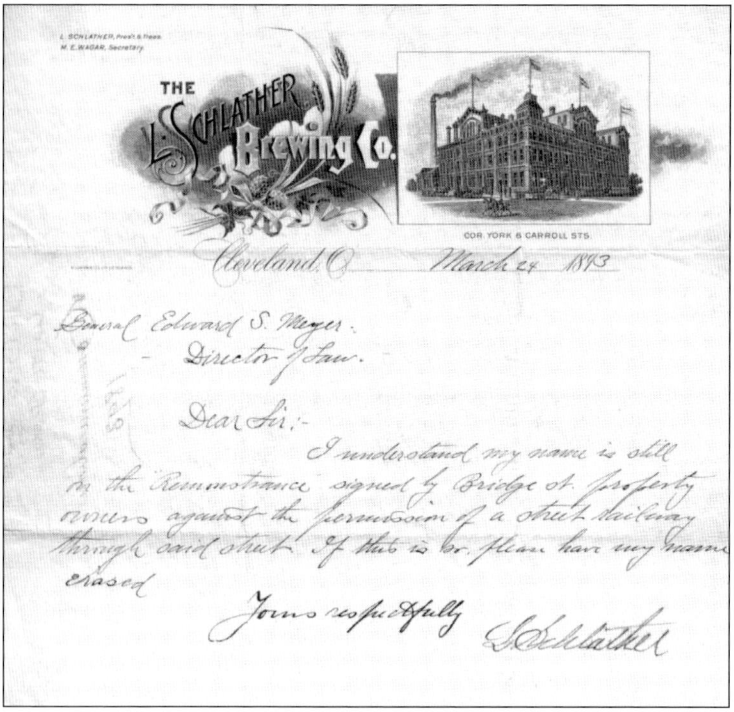

L. SCHLATHER, Pres't & Treas.
M. E. WAGAR, Secretary

THE L. SCHLATHER Brewing Co.

COR. YORK & CARROLL STS.

Cleveland, O. March 24 1893

General Edward S. Meyer.
Director of Law.

Dear Sir:-

I understand my name is still on the Remonstrance signed by Bridge st. property owners against the permission of a street railway through said street. If this is so, please have my name erased.

Yours respectfully
L. Schlather

A Brewer's Letterhead. This 1893 stationery from Leonard Schlather to Cleveland's law director reflects the prominence of Schlather's brewery in Ohio City. Featuring elegant design and official branding, the letterhead demonstrates Schlather's status as a leading businessman. By this time, his brewery had become one of Cleveland's largest, embodying the entrepreneurial spirit of the city's German immigrant community. (The City of Cleveland Archives.)

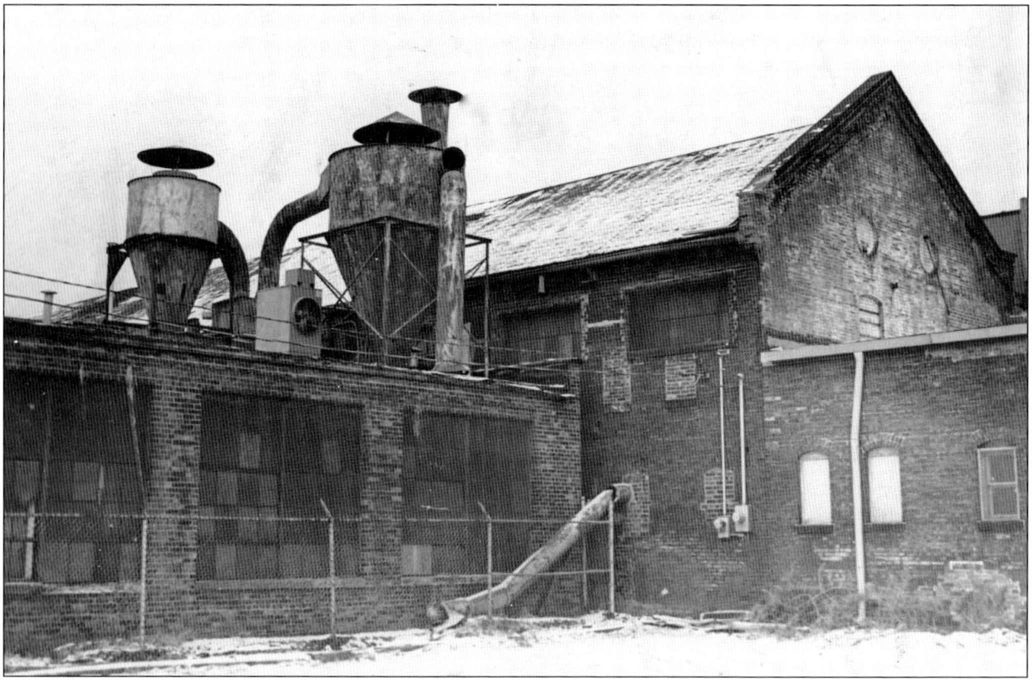

Brewing Heritage Preserved. This deteriorating structure at Carroll Avenue and West Twenty-Sixth Street, photographed in 1974, represents both decline and renewal in Ohio City's brewing heritage. Originally serving as Schlather Brewing Company's horse stables and bottling plant until 1933, the building found new life as part of Great Lakes Brewing Company's production facility. (Michael Schwartz Library Special Collections, Cleveland State University.)

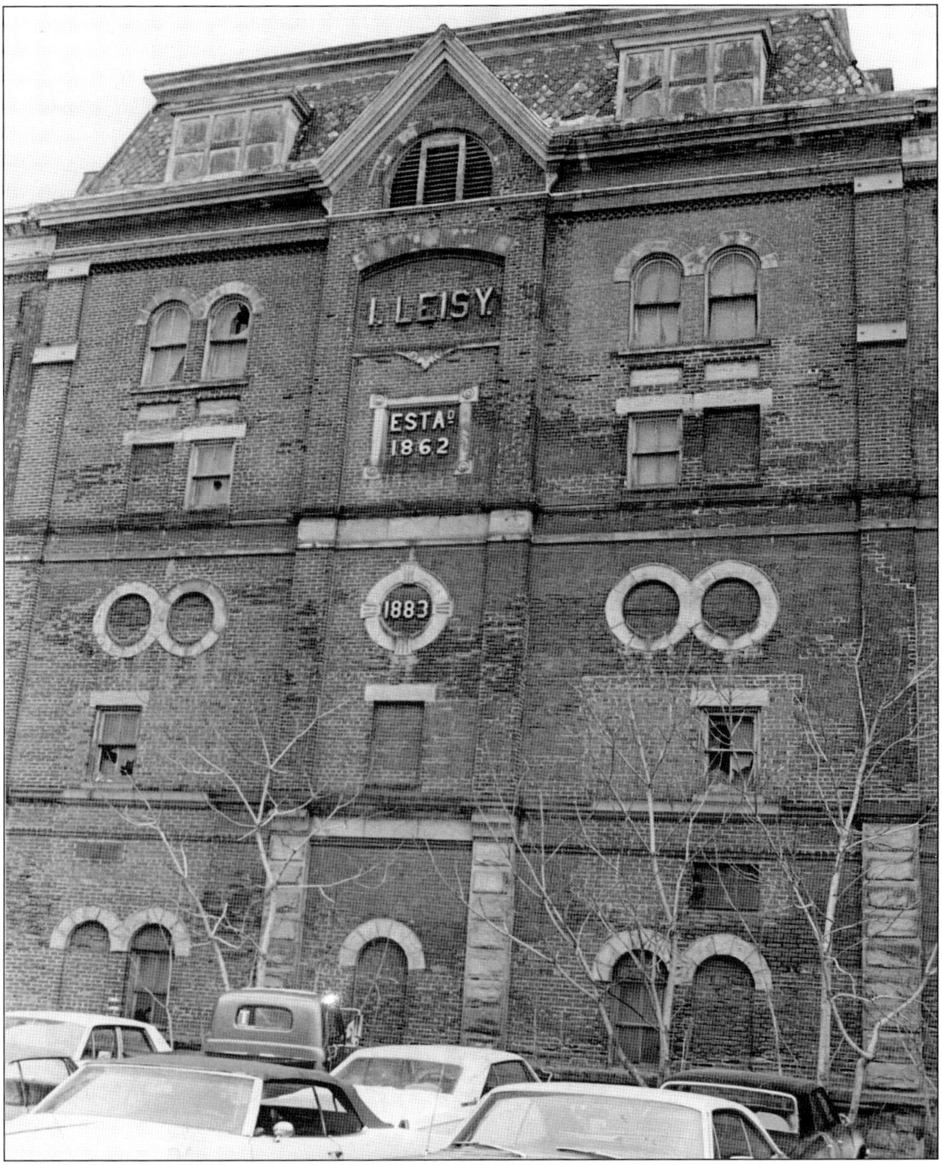

Leisy Brewery's Imposing Entrance. The entrance of Leisy Brewery at Fulton Road and Vega Avenue stood as a testament to one of Cleveland's most successful brewing enterprises. Founded by Bavarian immigrant Isaac Leisy in 1873 after purchasing Frederick Haltnorth's brewery for $120,000, the company quickly established itself as Cleveland's largest independent brewery. Under Isaac's leadership, production soared from 12,000 barrels in 1873 to over 90,000 by 1890. The brewery complex expanded to cover eight acres, employing 75 workers, mostly German-Americans. After Isaac's death in 1892, his son Otto maintained the brewery's independence despite industry consolidation trends. Though Prohibition forced its closure in 1923, the facility reopened in 1933. The brewery distributed its popular brands, including Black Dallas malt liquor, Dortmunder, and Mello-Gold beer, across six states. This 1974 photograph captures the entrance in its final days before demolition, years after the brewery's 1958 closure. The grand archway, once a symbol of Cleveland's vibrant brewing heritage, marked the end of one of America's longest-running family-operated breweries. (Michael Schwartz Library Special Collections, Cleveland State University.)

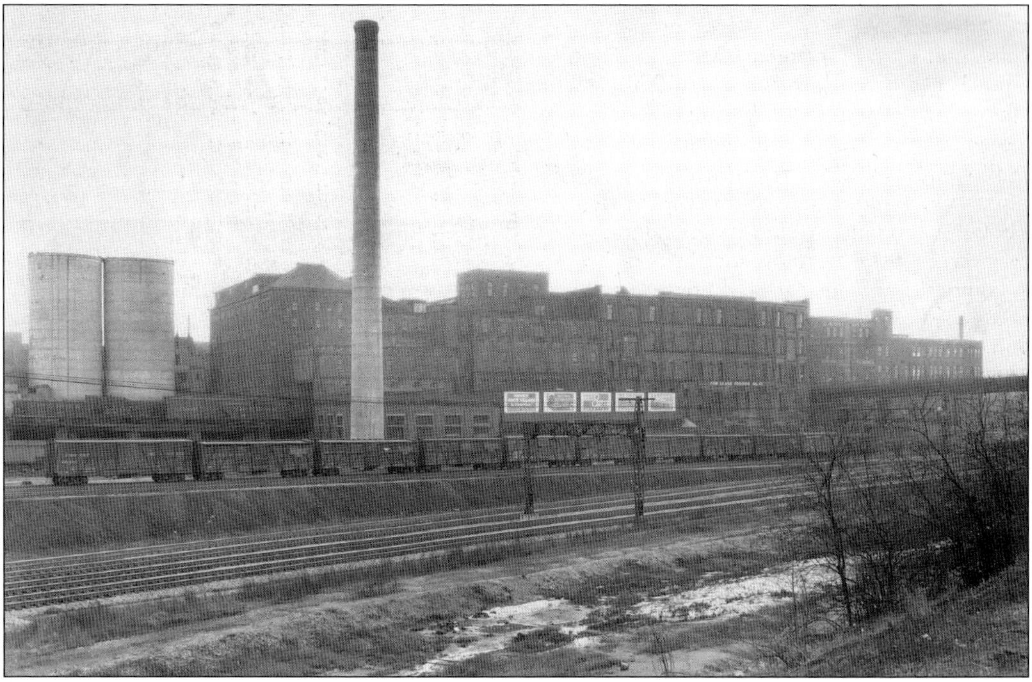

Rising from Prohibition. The Leisy Brewery complex, photographed in 1933 from the New York Central Railroad yard, captures a moment of rebirth as Herbert Leisy prepared to reopen the family business following Prohibition's repeal. Under his leadership, the facility was completely reequipped with modern machinery and expanded to achieve an ambitious annual production capacity of 750,000 barrels. (Michael Schwartz Library Special Collections, Cleveland State University.)

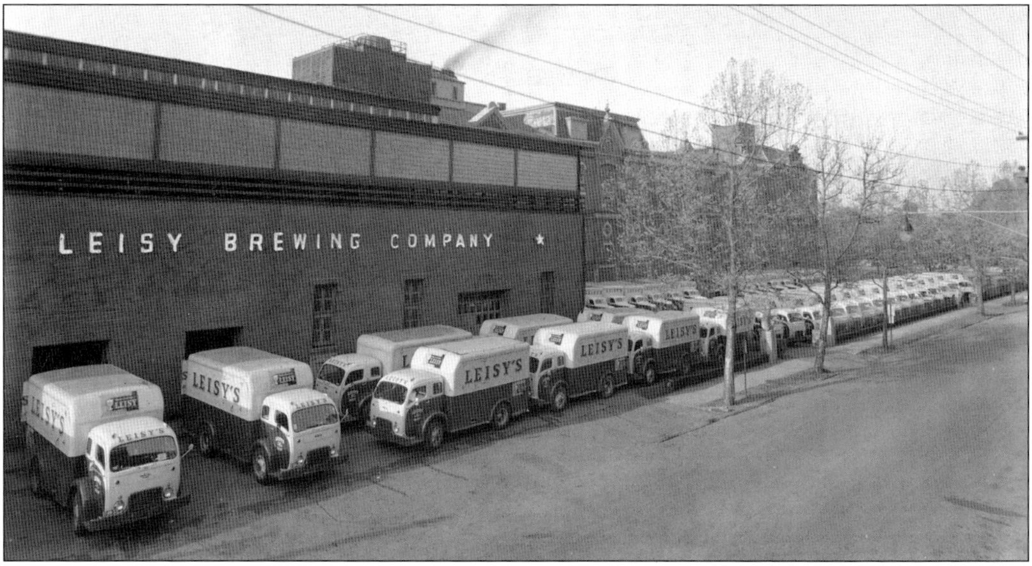

Delivering the Goods. Leisy Brewery's impressive fleet of delivery trucks in 1950 demonstrated the company's successful post-Prohibition revival. Under Herbert Leisy's leadership, the brewery modernized its operations and distributed its popular beers across six states. The trucks, replacing the horse-drawn wagons of earlier days, delivered up to 500,000 barrels annually to taverns and stores throughout the Midwest. (Cleveland Public Library Photograph Collection.)

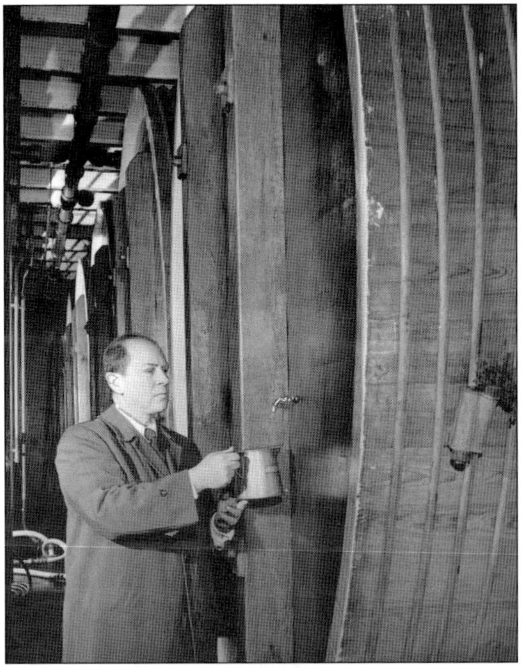

Testing Family Tradition. Herbert Leisy, grandson of founder Isaac, samples beer from aging casks in 1950. Under his leadership, the brewery reopened after Prohibition's repeal in 1933, maintaining the family's three-generation commitment to quality brewing. Though Cleveland's oldest independent brewery, Leisy's eventually succumbed to competition from national breweries, closing its doors in 1958. (Cleveland Public Library Photograph Collection.)

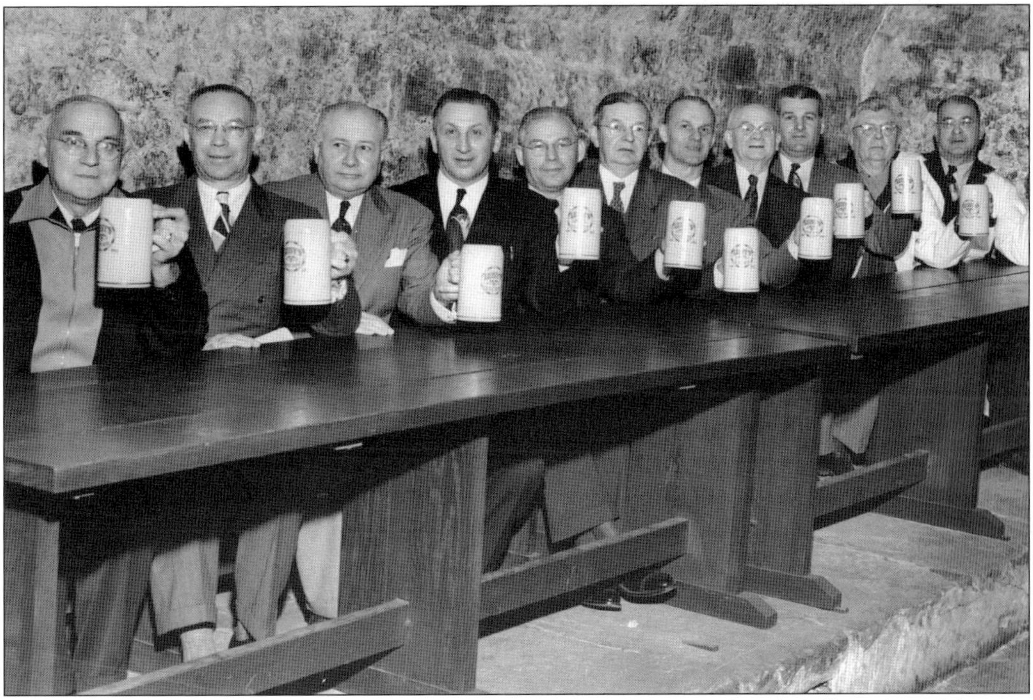

Toasting Traditions, 1952. Employees raise their mugs in the brewery's rathskeller. This celebratory image reflects the company's proud German heritage and brewing traditions. The rathskeller, a traditional German-style beer hall, was a central gathering place for workers and patrons alike. Under three generations of Leisy family leadership, the brewery maintained these cultural connections until its closure in 1958. (Photograph by Lou Moore, Cleveland Press Collection, Michael Schwartz Library Special Collections, Cleveland State University.)

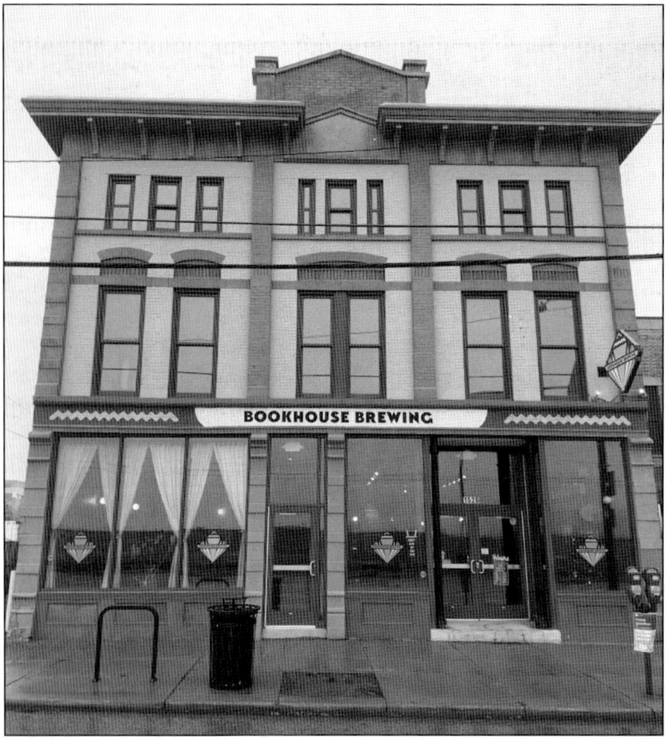

Historic Brewery Reopened. This historic structure at 1526 West Twenty-Fifth Street began as Jacob Baehr's brewery in the late 1800s before becoming part of the Cleveland & Sandusky Brewing Corporation. Much of the original architectural detail, including the distinctive ceiling, survives today as Bookhouse Brewing continues the building's long tradition of craft beer production in Ohio City. (Author's collection.)

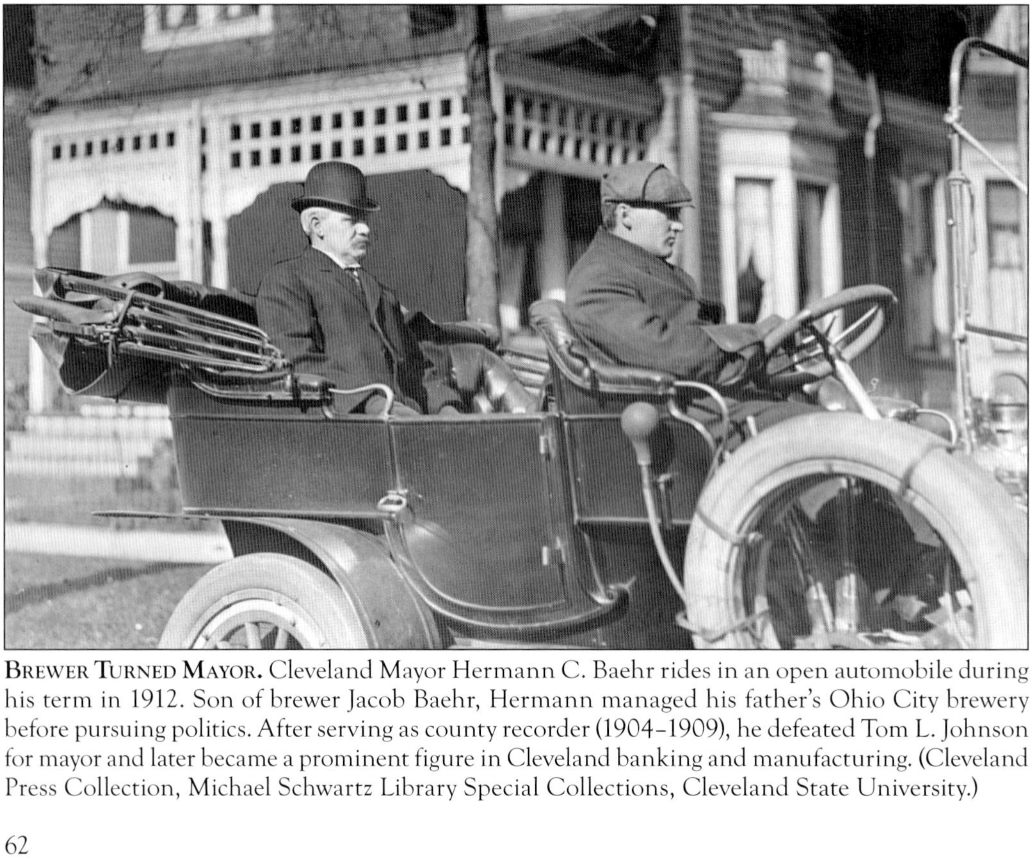

Brewer Turned Mayor. Cleveland Mayor Hermann C. Baehr rides in an open automobile during his term in 1912. Son of brewer Jacob Baehr, Hermann managed his father's Ohio City brewery before pursuing politics. After serving as county recorder (1904–1909), he defeated Tom L. Johnson for mayor and later became a prominent figure in Cleveland banking and manufacturing. (Cleveland Press Collection, Michael Schwartz Library Special Collections, Cleveland State University.)

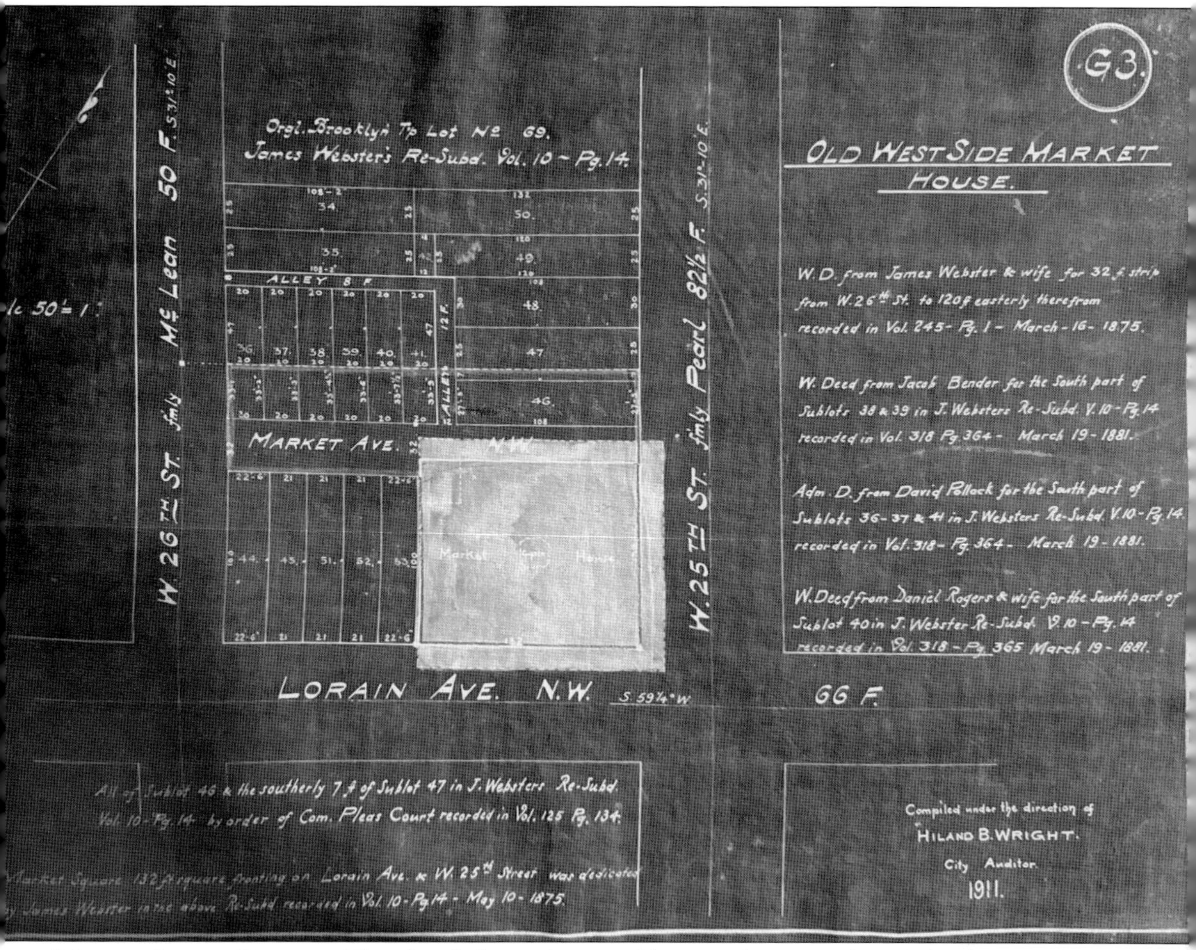

Market Square District. This detailed city planning blueprint by city auditor Hiland B. Wright captures Cleveland's historic Market Square district in 1911. With the construction of the new West Side Market already underway, this document offers a meticulous survey of the commercial district. Centered on the intersection of West Twenty-Fifth Street (then Pearl Road) and Lorain Avenue, the blueprint maps the network of parcels and properties surrounding the market site. The careful notations and measurements reflect both the ambitions of Cleveland's civic planners and their attention to the district's existing urban fabric. Market Street, shown in careful detail, would later become home to Great Lakes Brewing Company and other local institutions. This blueprint serves as both a technical document and a historical snapshot, preserving the precise dimensions of a neighborhood on the cusp of change that would define Ohio City's commercial heart for generations to come. (The Cleveland City Archives.)

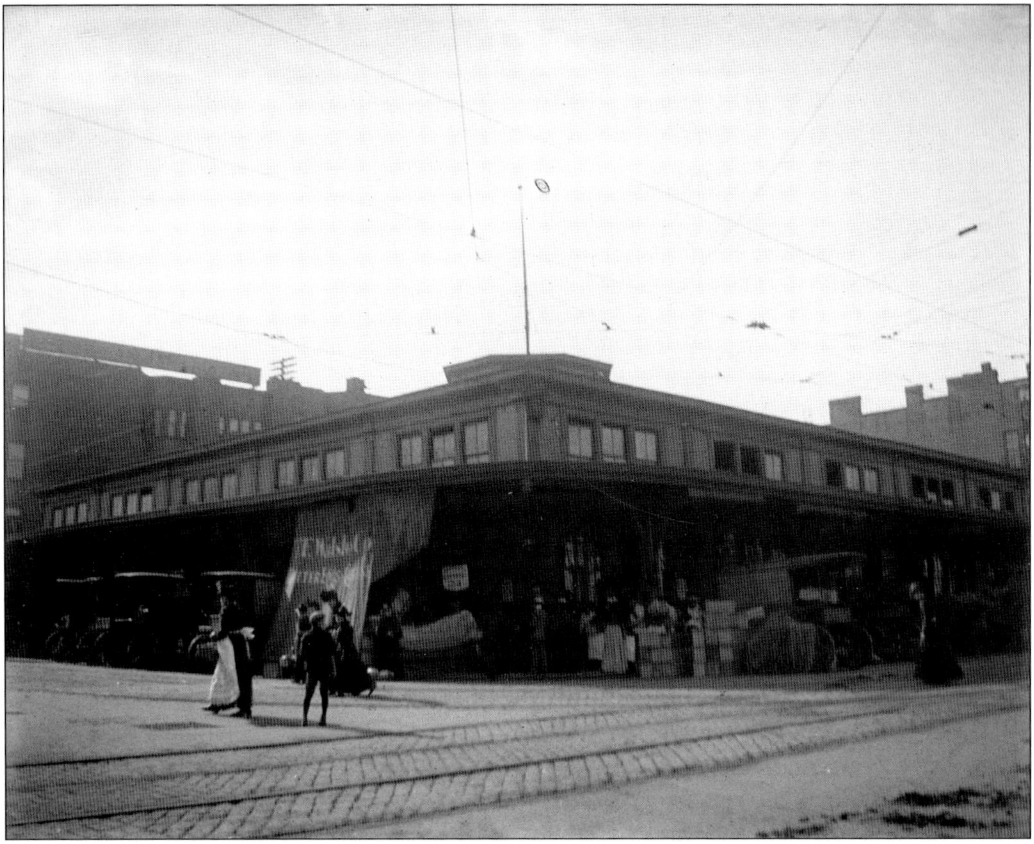

EARLY MARKET DAYS. This 1901 view of the wooden Pearl Street Market anchored the corner of Pearl and Lorain streets. The market's story began in 1840 when pioneers Josiah Barber and Richard Lord donated the land for an open-air marketplace. By 1868, this structure housed a bustling trade center serving the area's growing immigrant communities. Its overcrowded conditions would soon spark plans for a grander market house. (Cleveland Press Collection, Cleveland State University, Michael Schwartz Library Special Collections.)

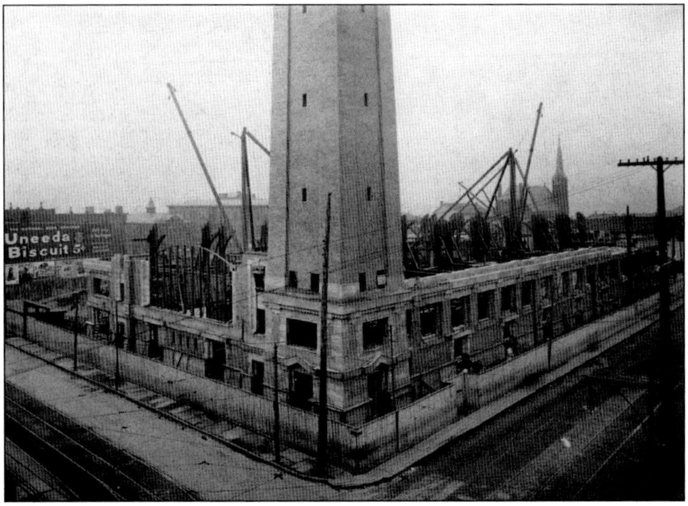

BUILDING A LEGACY. The construction of the new West Side Market in 1909 marked Cleveland's commitment to a permanent public marketplace. The ambitious project, championed by Mayor Tom L. Johnson, took nearly a decade from planning to completion. Architects Hubbell and Benes designed the imposing structure to serve generations of Cleveland shoppers. (Cleveland Public Library Photograph Collection.)

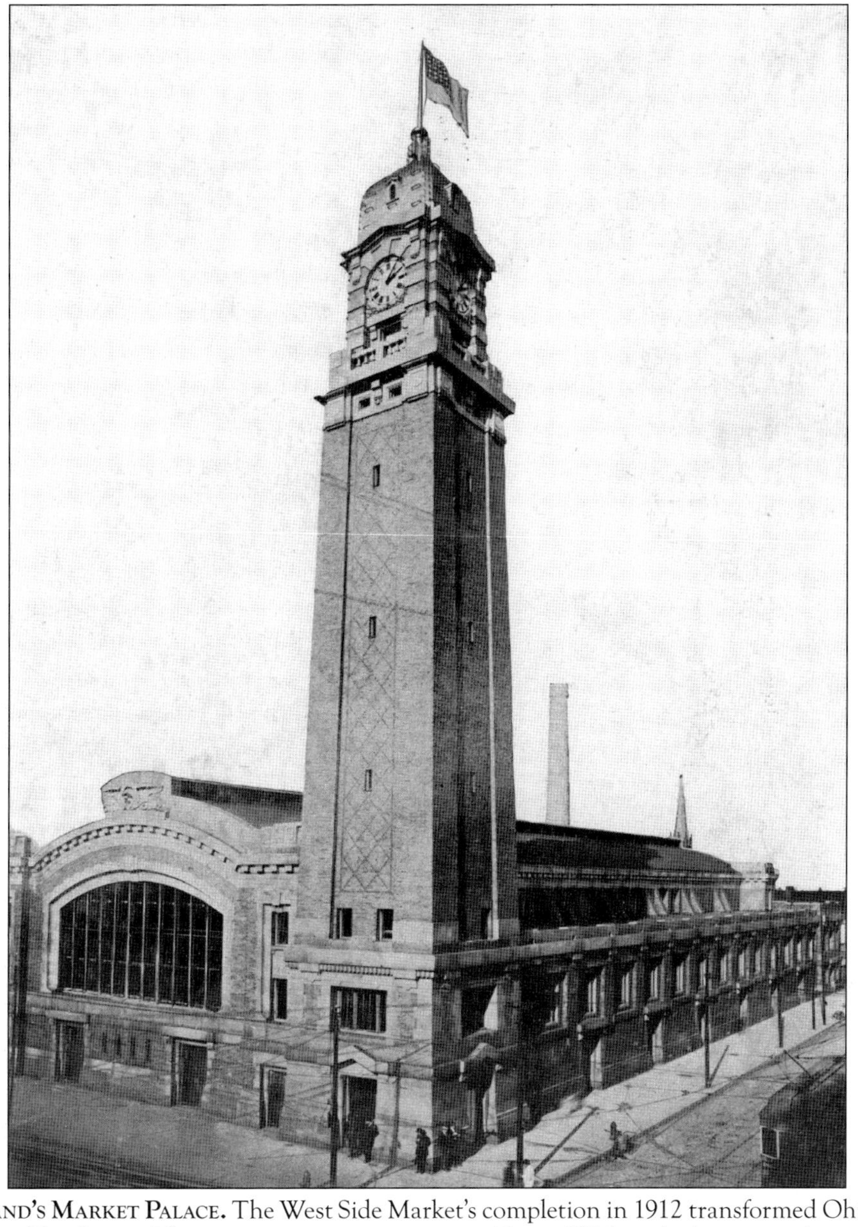

Cleveland's Market Palace. The West Side Market's completion in 1912 transformed Ohio City's commercial landscape. The imposing structure, crowned by its 137-foot clock tower and magnificent vaulted ceiling, opened on November 2. Inside, vendor stalls offered a diverse array of meats, dairy products, fresh bread, and specialty foods reflecting Cleveland's rich immigrant heritage. Outside, produce sellers initially worked from curbside stands until the construction of the covered arcade provided permanent shelter. The cost of over $730,000 represented Cleveland's bold investment in public commerce. Designed by architects Hubbell and Benes, the building's grand scale and artistic details elevate it beyond a marketplace to a civic monument. Over a century later, its significance was celebrated with designation as one of "10 Great Public Places in America" by the American Planning Association. Today, this National Historic Landmark ranks among Cleveland's most visited tourist destinations, drawing visitors from around the world to experience its historic charm and vibrant atmosphere. (Cleveland Public Library Photograph Collection.)

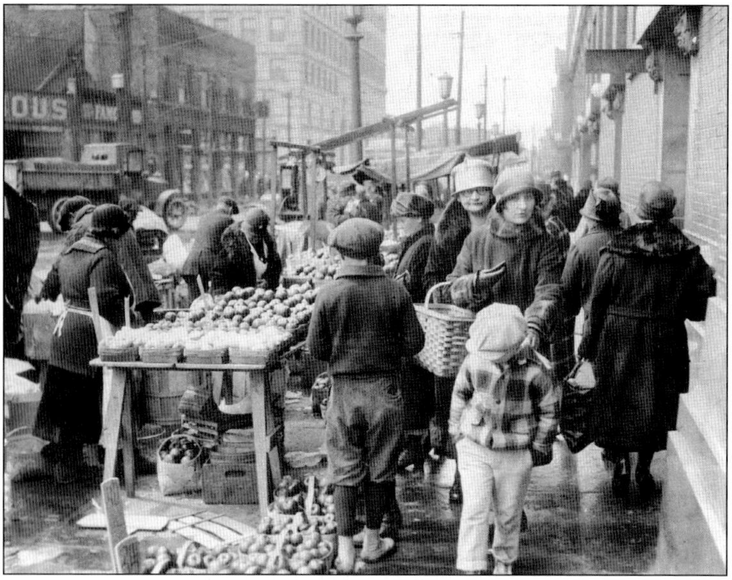

Market Day Bustle. Shoppers crowd the produce arcade in 1927, where vendors displayed fresh fruits and vegetables along the market's exterior. Originally operating from curbside stands, produce sellers gained permanent shelter when the city constructed covered walkways, expanding the market's capacity to 236 total vendor stalls. (Cleveland Public Library Photograph Collection.)

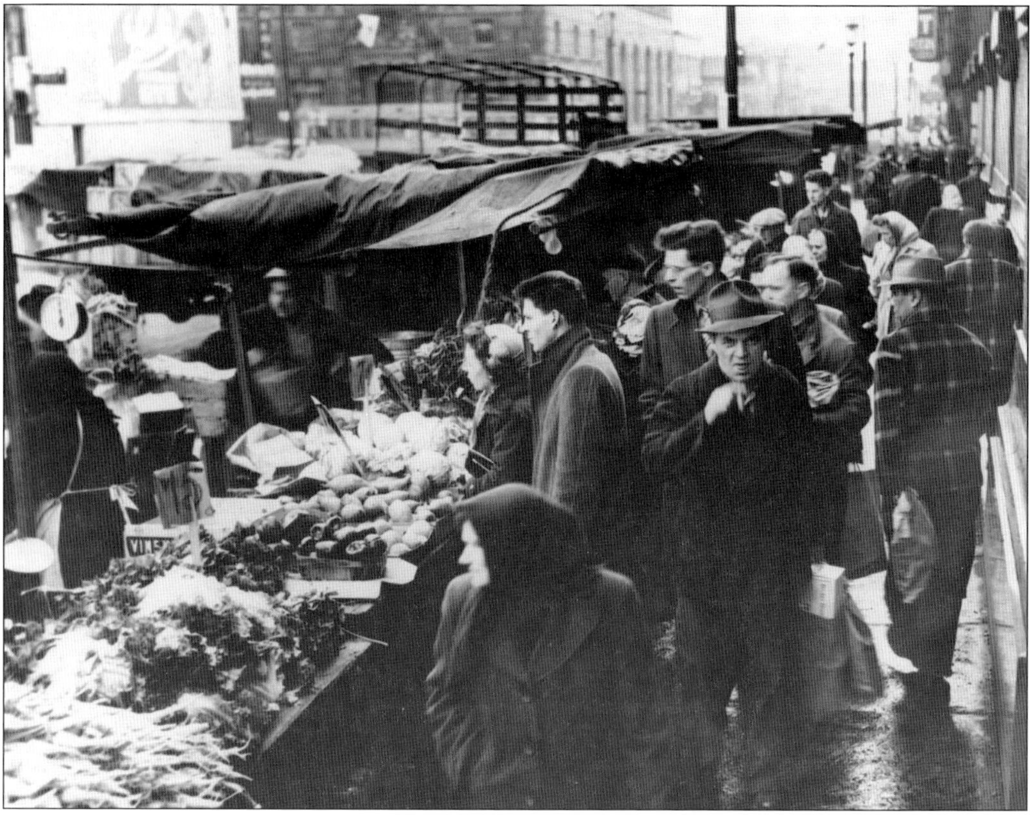

Market Life Along Lorain Avenue, 1950. The West Side Market's vibrant street life spills onto Lorain Avenue, where outdoor produce vendors maintain a tradition dating to the building's earliest days. Local shoppers browse the stalls that line the market's south facade, creating a lively scene that captures the everyday commerce connecting vendors and neighborhood customers. (Cleveland Public Library Photograph Collection.)

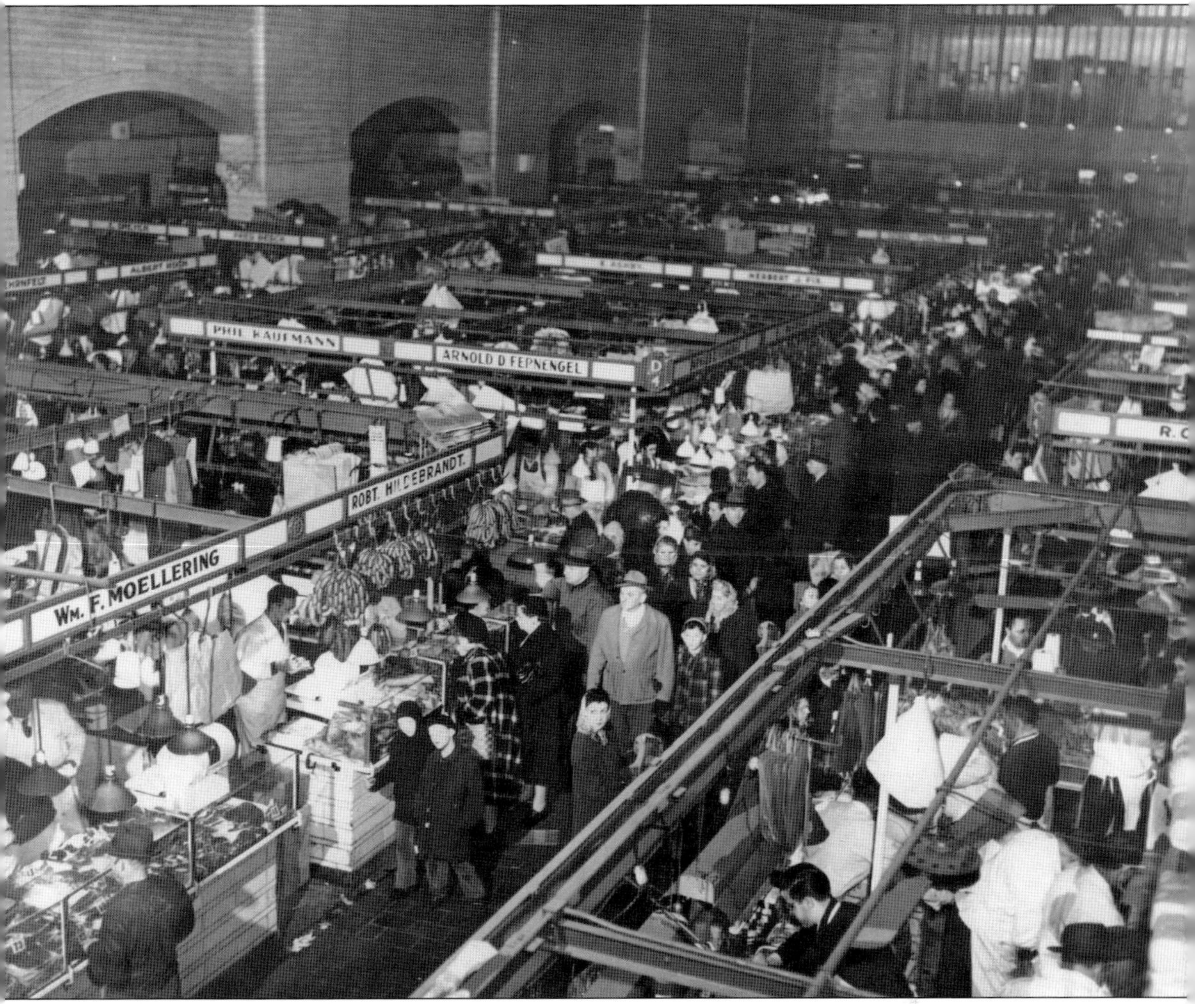

Commerce in Motion. The market's interior captures the essence of Cleveland's enduring public marketplace tradition. From this sweeping vantage point, the innovative design of architect W. Dominick Benes reveals the carefully planned clustering of vendor stalls in efficient quadrangles. Shoppers today continue to navigate the time-tested flow patterns, just as their predecessors have done for over a century. The elevated perspective from the balcony offers a view of the vendors arranging displays, customers examining produce, and neighbors exchanging greetings amid the stalls. While the interior's basic layout has remained remarkably unchanged since 1912, recent renovation projects aim to preserve this historic space while modernizing its aging infrastructure. This arrangement of space perfectly balances commerce with community, creating sightlines that showcase both the architectural grandeur and the human-scale interactions that have made the West Side Market Cleveland's culinary crossroads for generations. (Cleveland Public Library Photograph Collection.)

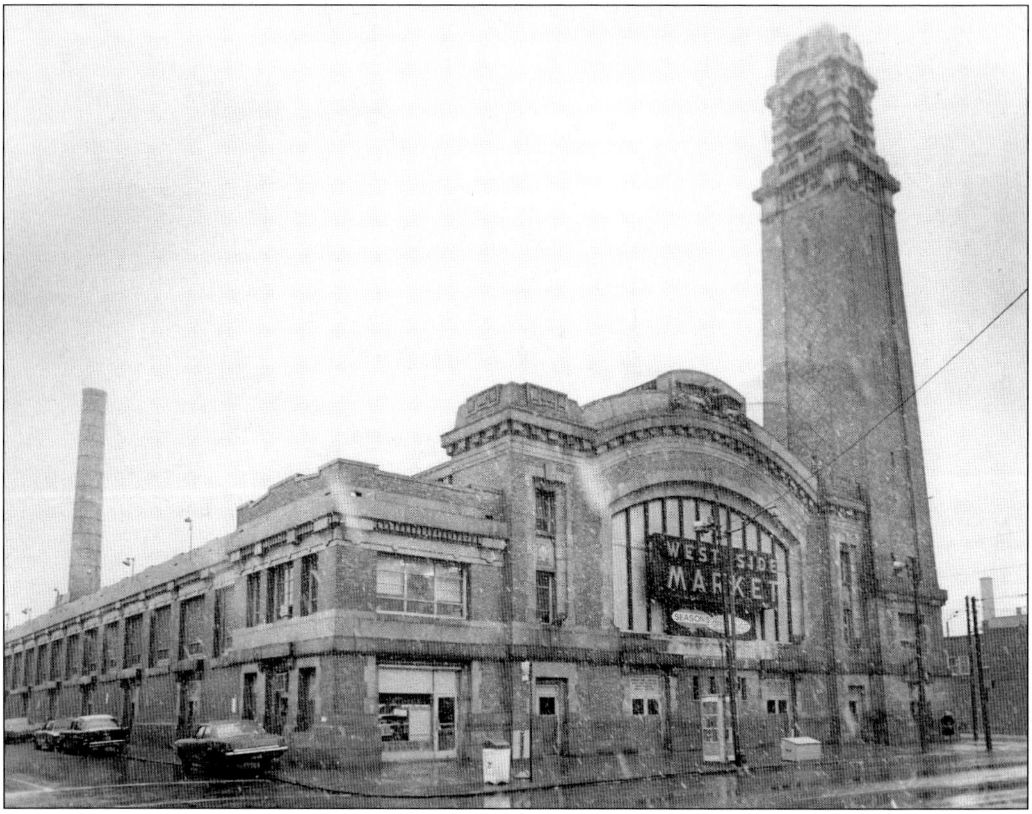

Market Through Time. These two views capture distinct perspectives of the West Side Market during a pivotal era. The 1972 frontal image showcases the building's iconic tower and the prominent "WEST SIDE MARKET" lettering, signage not present in the market's early days. The 1969 view from the parking lot reveals how the market adapted to changing times, as suburban shoppers drove from across Greater Cleveland to maintain connections with their heritage. Despite the era's urban challenges, when supermarket chains replaced corner grocers and many residents moved outward, the market maintained its vital role. Second- and third-generation families still returned for specialty foods and traditional favorites, while inside, many vendor stalls remained in the same families that had established them decades earlier. (Both, Cleveland Public Library Photograph Collection.)

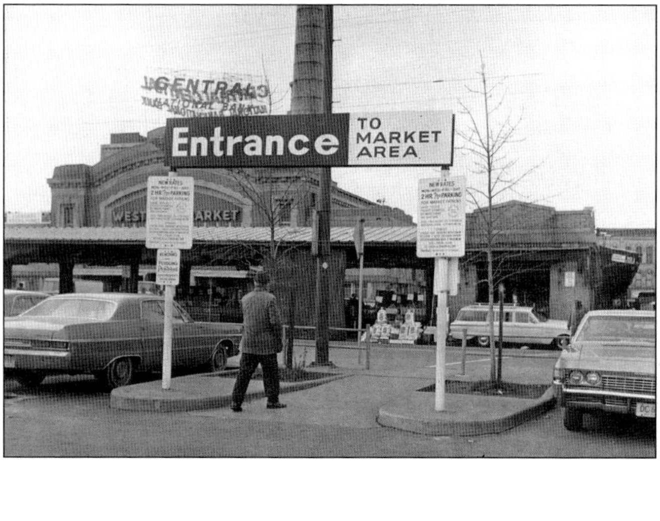

Five

Homes and Heritage

Residential Growth in Ohio City

Ohio City's residential architecture tells the story of a neighborhood where prosperity and working-class life existed in remarkable proximity. From the mansion-lined Franklin Avenue to the modest worker cottages on surrounding streets, the area's rapid development following its 1836 incorporation created a walkable community where wealth and labor lived within blocks of each other.

Franklin Avenue, once compared to Cleveland's grand Euclid Avenue, emerged as the neighborhood's premier residential street. Its wide, tree-lined thoroughfare showcased massive stone mansions and Italianate homes set back from decorative iron fences. Hannes Tiedemann's home, later known as the turreted Franklin Castle on Franklin Boulevard, became the neighborhood's most mysterious mansion, while the Carnegie West Library brought Beaux-Arts sophistication to Fulton Road. The childhood home of football pioneer John Heisman on Bridge Avenue represented the neighborhood's connection to national history.

Beyond Franklin's grandeur, the neighborhood displayed an architectural parade of Victorian-era styles. Middle-class homes featured Gothic Revival pointed arches, Second Empire mansard roofs, and elaborate Eastlake-style wooden ornamentation. Queen Anne homes showcased varied textures of brick, stone, and decorative shingles, while later Colonial Revival residences introduced classical elements like temple-front porches.

The most common dwellings were modest wooden frame houses that lined the neighborhood. These worker cottages, often built for immigrant families, featured simple gabled roofs facing the street and small stoops or porches. While plain in design, many incorporated elaborate decorative woodwork and varied textures of brick, stone, and shingle siding.

This architectural diversity reflected Ohio City's role as home to both industry owners and workers, merchants and craftsmen, bankers and laborers. The proximity of grand homes to modest cottages created a unique urban fabric that supported a vibrant community life, centered around nearby churches, schools, and the West Side Market.

This architectural diversity, preserved through decades of change, continues to define Ohio City's character. Iron picket fences, brick alleys, and small yards with mature trees enhance the intimate urban scale. From grand boulevard homes to simple worker cottages, these buildings tell the story of a neighborhood where people of different backgrounds and means created a vibrant community together.

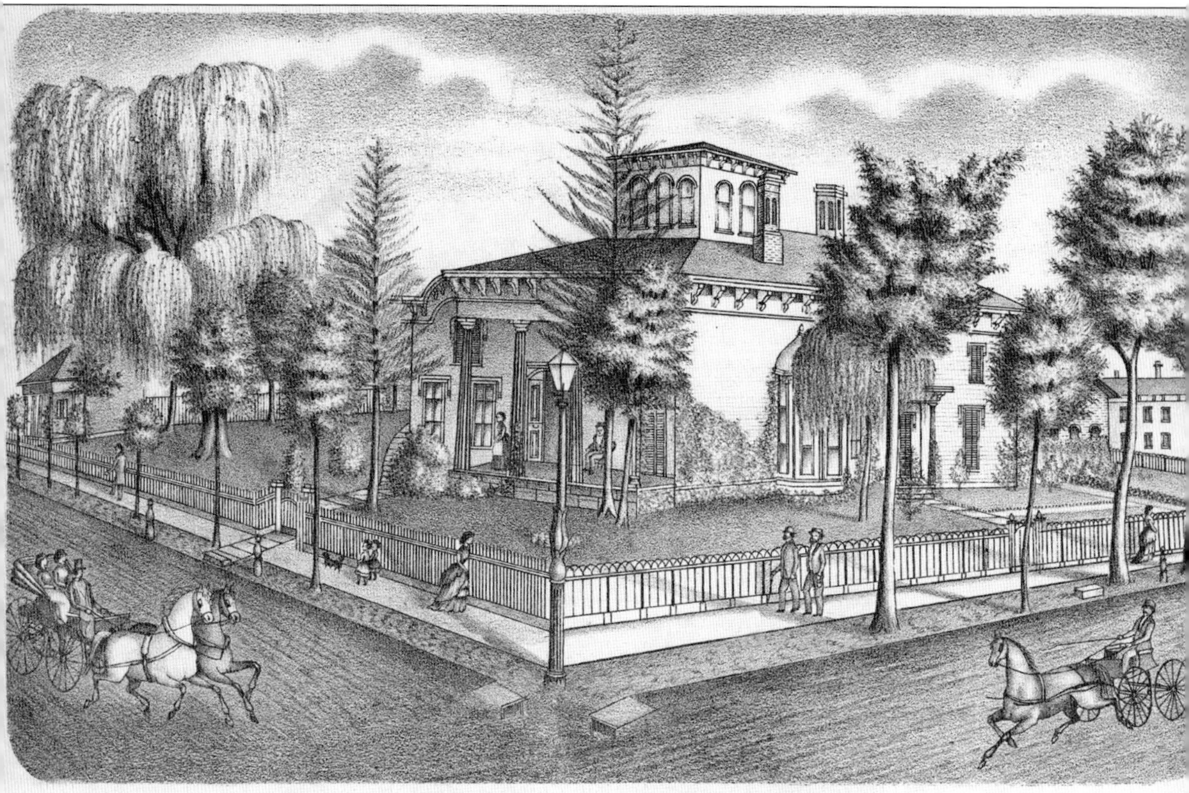

RES. OF C. L. RUSSELL
Nº 94 Washington St Cleveland, Ohio.

EARLY OHIO CITY GRANDEUR. This 1874 *Atlas of Cuyahoga County* engraving depicts one of Ohio City's most impressive early residences. Built in 1836 on Washington Street (renamed Washington Avenue in 1906), this mansion belonged to Charles Winslow, a prominent investor in the Buffalo Company, which sought to transform the west bank of the Cuyahoga into a thriving commercial center rivaling Cleveland. The Buffalo Company played a pivotal role in Ohio City's early development, investing heavily in land speculation and infrastructure. Winslow's mansion reflected this optimistic era of growth as the settlement transitioned from West Village to the incorporated City of Ohio. The property later became home to C.L. Russell, a leading figure in Ohio City's resistance during the infamous Bridge War. This grand residence stood for over seven decades on ground now traversed by the Memorial Shoreway, its 1912 demolition marking one of many transformations that would reshape Ohio City's historic landscape. (Cleveland State University, Michael Schwartz Library Special Collections.)

FROM HEIGHTS TO HARBOR. Irish Bend in the Flats, 1885. This view captures the working-class Irish settlement known as "Irish Bend" along the Cuyahoga River's edge. The stark contrast between Ohio City's heights and the industrial riverside is evident in the modest wooden dwellings. Irish immigrants created a transitional zone between the prosperous Market Square district and the industrial Flats. This area led to "The Angle," another Irish enclave that defined Ohio City's industrial frontier. (Cleveland Public Library Photograph Collection.)

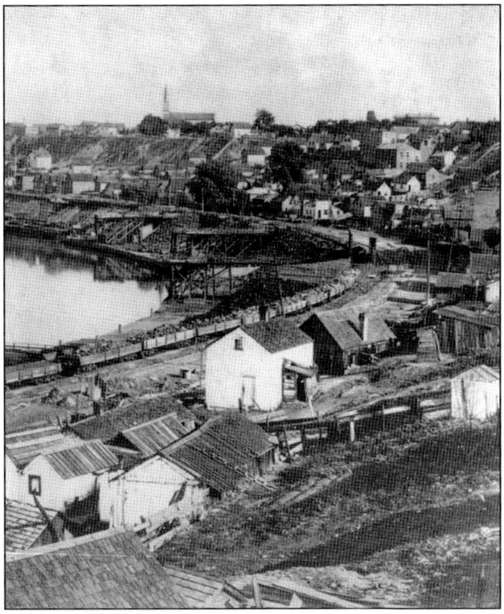

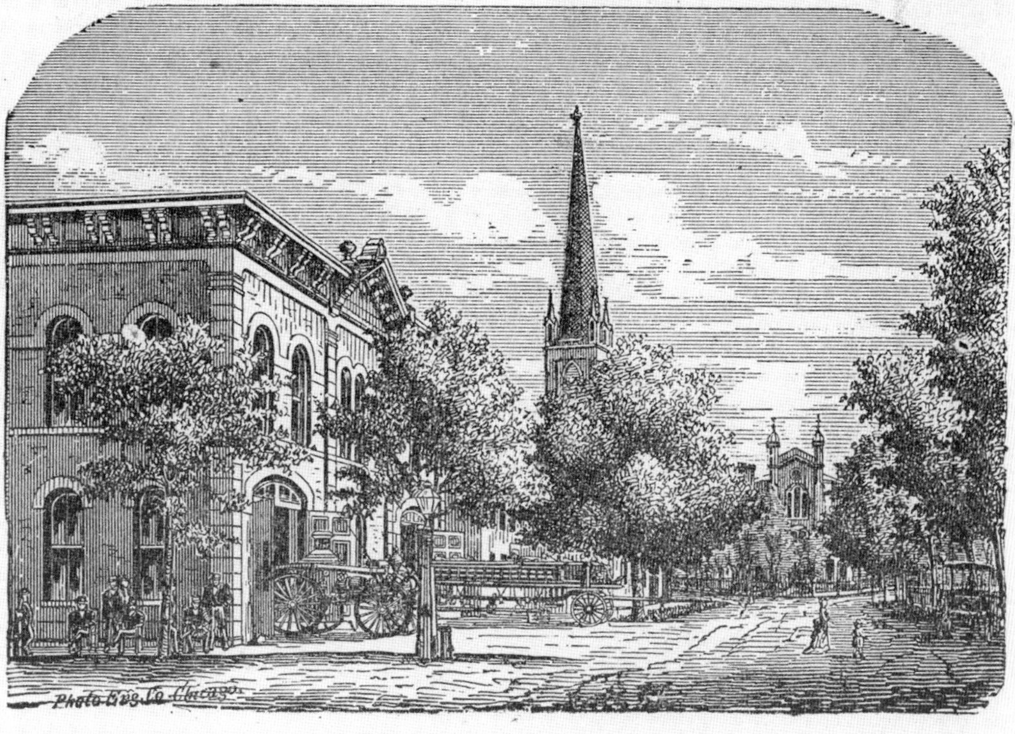

CHURCH STREET—WEST SIDE.

CHURCH STREET'S CONTRASTS. This 1876 engraving of Church Street captures a neighborhood where wealthy merchants and working-class families lived in remarkable proximity. The fire department stands prominently in the foreground, while church steeples pierce the sky—shared institutions serving a community where elegant mansions and modest workers' cottages coexisted just blocks apart. (Cleveland State University, Michael Schwartz Library Special Collections.)

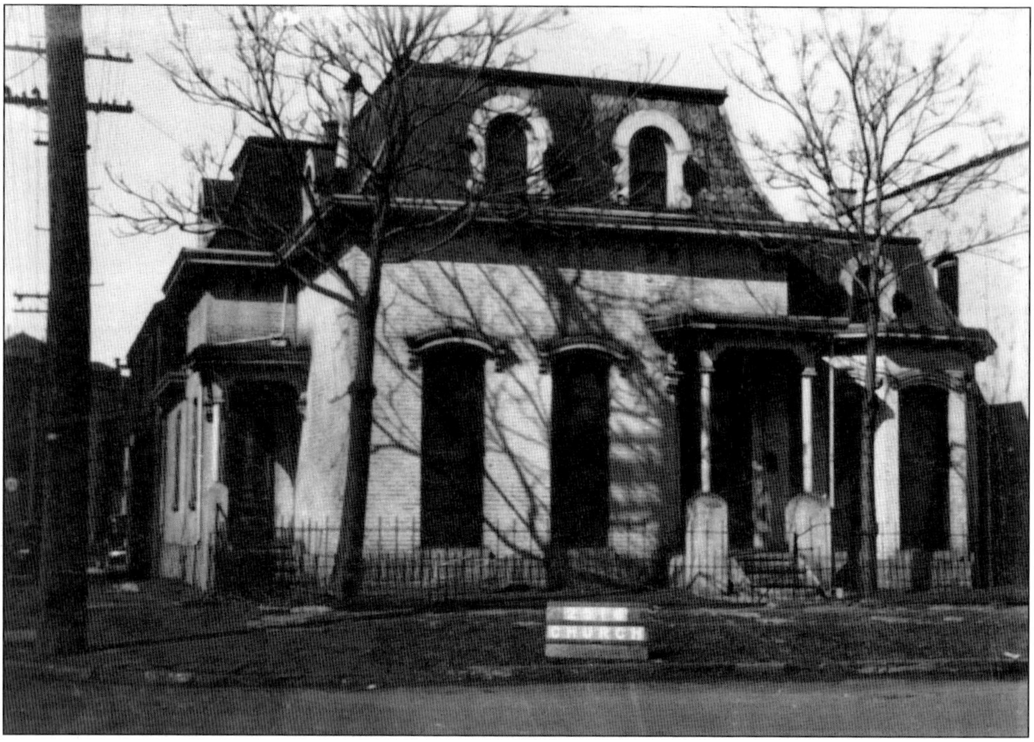

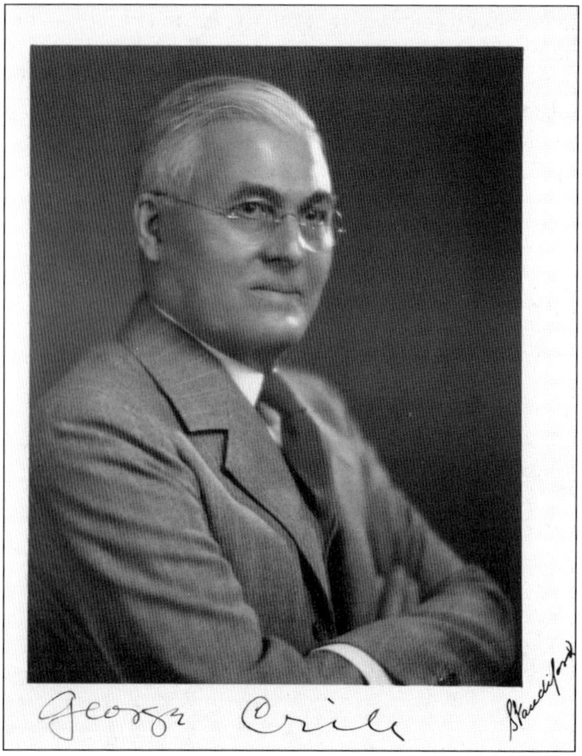

House Calls on Church Avenue. This residence at 2516 Church Avenue, built in 1870 in Barber and Lord's original Ohio City subdivision, served as both home and office to Dr. George Crile, one of Cleveland's most distinguished medical pioneers. The design, featuring an octagonal bay window and distinctive mansard roof, reflects the era's architectural fashion while providing a professional setting suited to a physician's practice. Dr. Crile, photographed here in 1931, achieved international recognition for performing the first successful direct blood transfusion and developing innovative anesthesia techniques. His surgical advances, particularly during World War I, preceded his role as cofounder of the Cleveland Clinic. Today, this designated Cleveland landmark stands isolated among warehouses, a reminder of the professional class that once called Ohio City home. (Both, Cleveland Public Library Photograph Collection.)

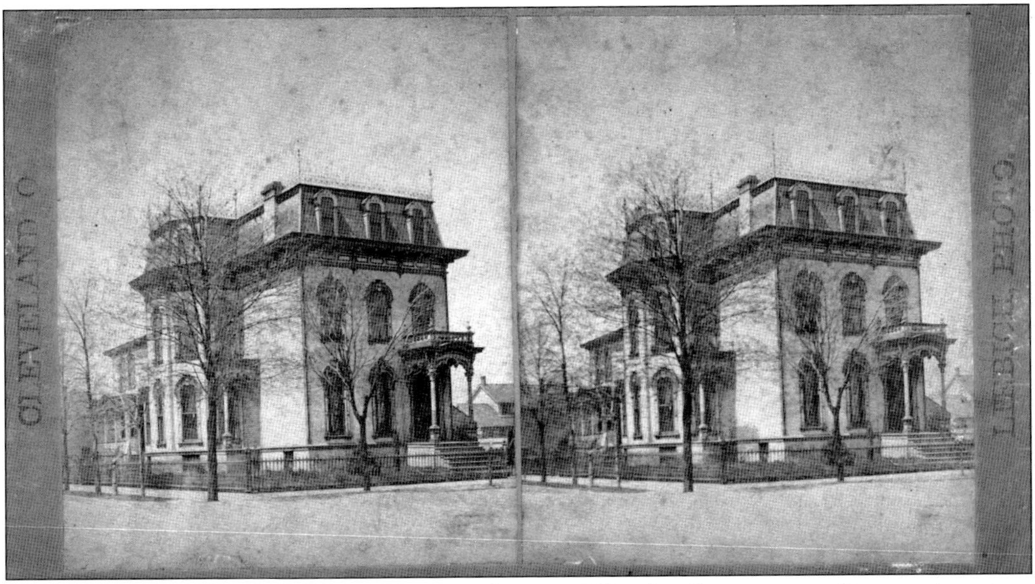

The Schlather and Leisy Estates. These residences of Cleveland's prominent German-American brewers reflect both their commercial success and deep neighborhood ties. The stereograph (above) of Leonard Schlather's York Street (now West Twenty-Eighth) residence, captured between 1876 and 1898 by photographers Moritz and Arthur K.A. Liebich, showcases another interpretation of Victorian grandeur. Isaac Leisy's mansion (below) on Vega Avenue, photographed in 1939 but built in the 1880s, stood adjacent to his brewery complex, allowing him to oversee operations while maintaining a dignified family home. These homes represented more than personal wealth— they demonstrated the brewers' commitment to living near their businesses and workers, a practice that helped maintain the neighborhood's unique social fabric where industrial success and community life intersected. (Above, Michael Schwartz Library Special Collections, Cleveland State University; below, Cleveland Public Library Photograph Collection.)

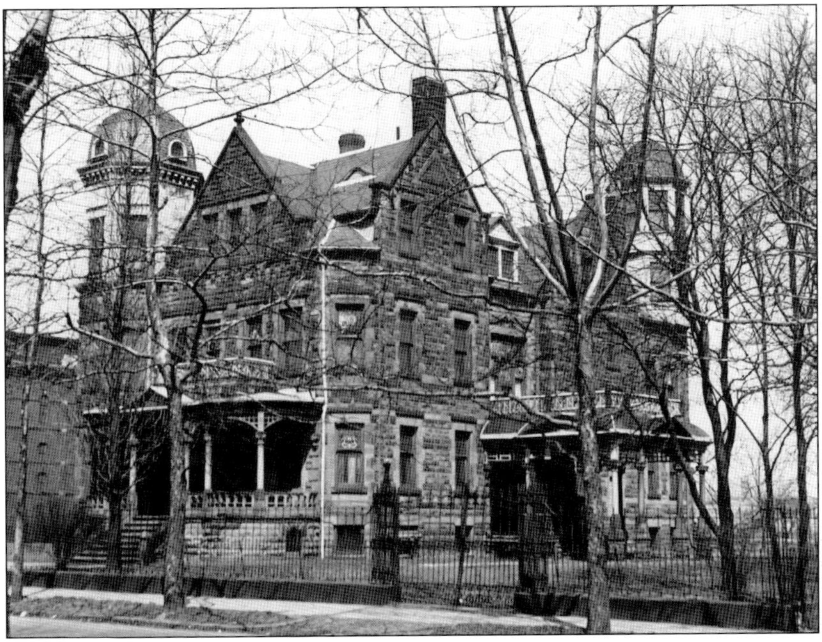

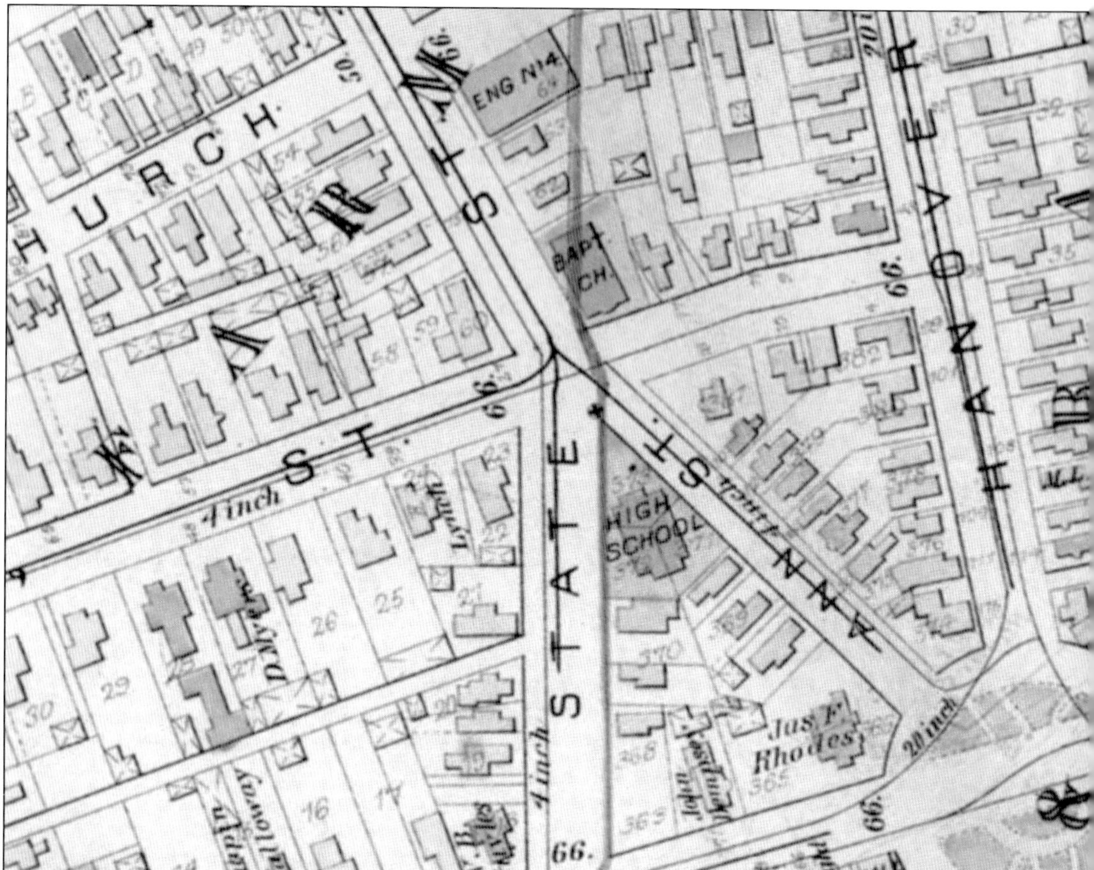

Franklin Circle's Golden Age. This late-19th-century plat map reveals Franklin Circle as the centerpiece of Ohio City's most prestigious address. The detailed parcels show how the area, particularly Franklin Avenue (now Boulevard), attracted the city's industrial and political elite. Prominent residents included Mayor William Castle and Nelson Sanford, a lumber merchant. The Rhodes family dominated this landscape; Daniel Pomeroy Rhodes, who married into Ohio City

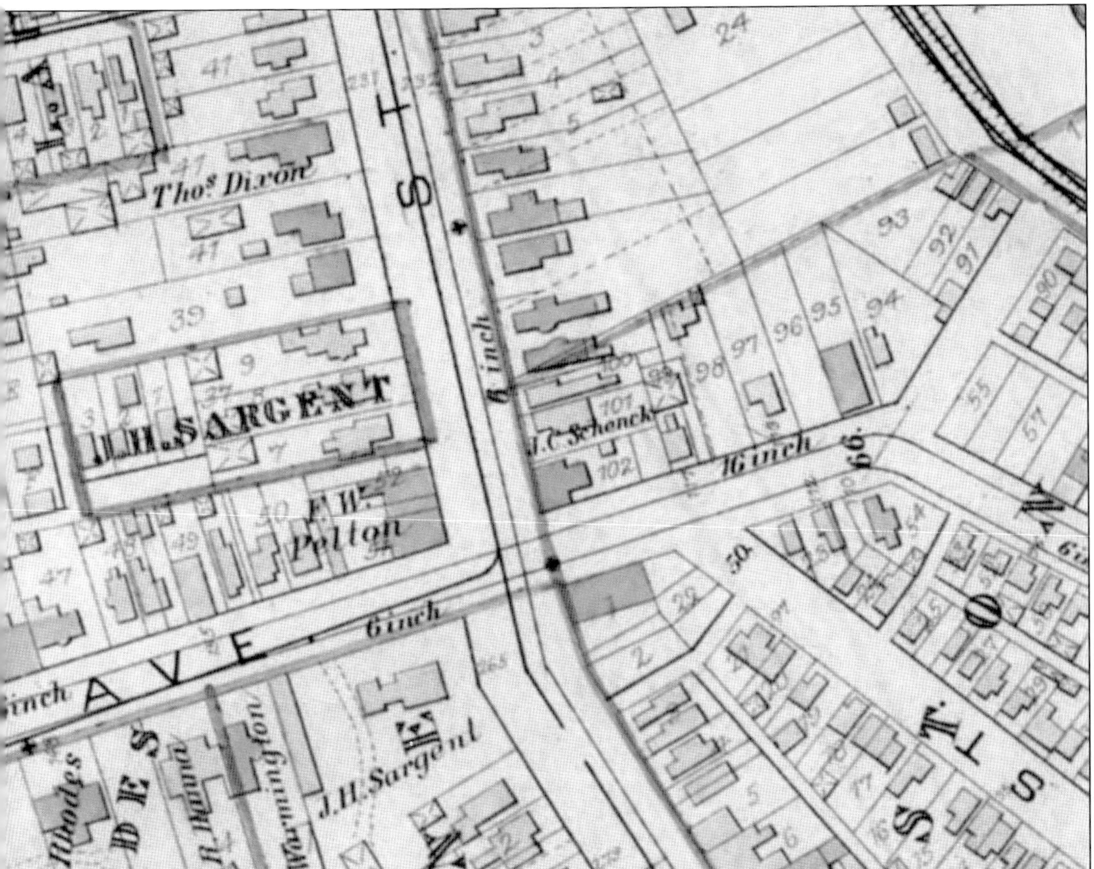

pioneer Josiah Barber's family, his sons Robert Russell and James Ford Rhodes, and his son-in-law Marcus Hanna all owned mansions around the Circle. Franklin Circle Christian Church and several of the renovated historic residences survive today as reminders of the west side's version of Millionaire's Row. (This image is from a G.M. Hopkins Company Map, published in 1881.)

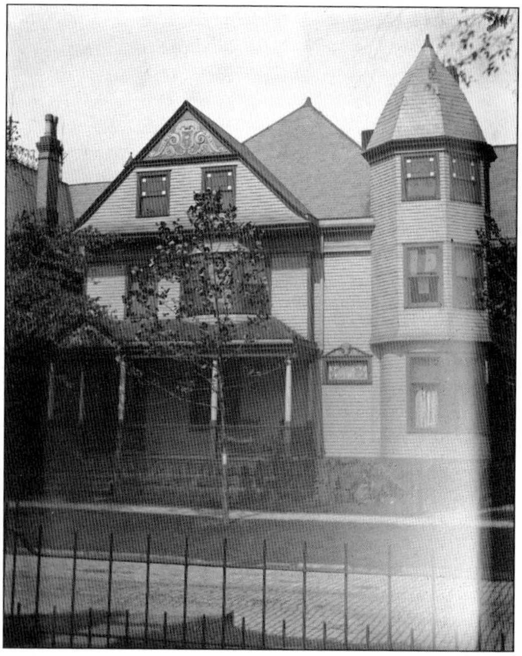

A Physician's Home. Built around 1890 by William Ketteringham, this well-preserved residence at 2826 Franklin Boulevard later became home to Dr. Charles Gentsch, a Georgetown Medical School graduate who served as a reserve officer in World War I. The house stands as an example of the professional class who made Franklin Boulevard their home in the late 19th century. (Kettering Collection, Cleveland Public Library Photograph Collection.)

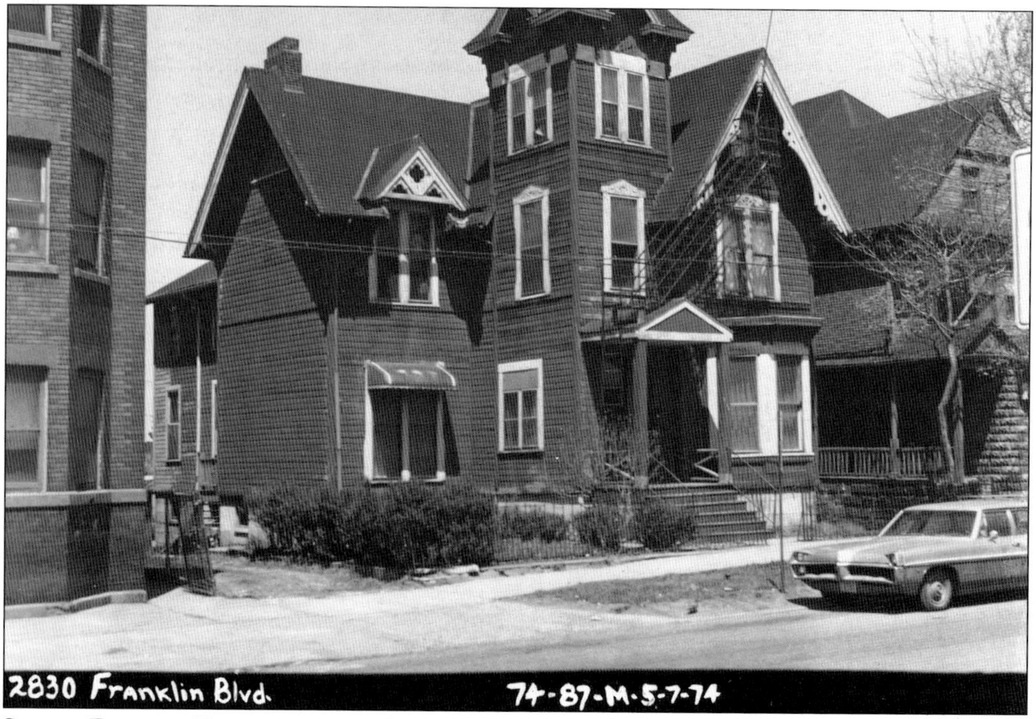

Spitzer-Dempsey House, 1974. Built in 1879 for banker C.M. Spitzer at 2830 Franklin, this architecturally unique home later became the residence of Civil War veteran Col. John Dempsey, whose son James helped establish the law firm Squire, Sanders & Dempsey. Following decades as a boarding house, the vacant mansion became associated with tragedy in 1981 when the body of missing paper carrier Tammy Seals was discovered inside. The house has been renovated. (Cleveland City Hall Collection, Cleveland Public Library)

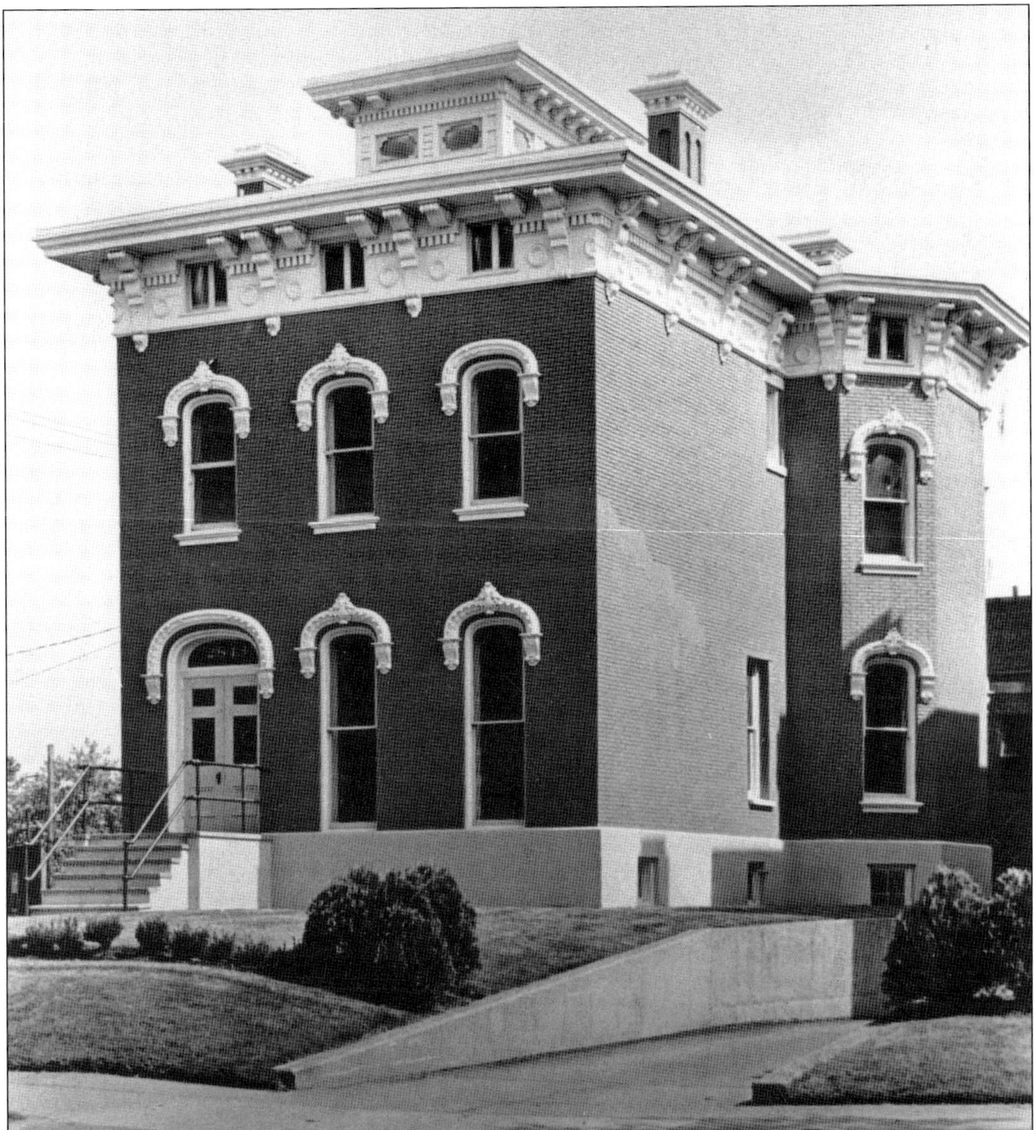

The Nelson Sanford House. Built in 1861 for lumber merchant and community leader Nelson Sanford, this distinguished Italianate residence at 2843 Franklin Boulevard represents the pinnacle of mid-19th-century architectural craftsmanship. The Cleveland Leader praised its completion in 1863, highlighting the sophisticated design that remains evident today. The exterior features exceptional sculpted brackets, roundels, and a cornice adorned with dentils and modillions. Inside, the main entrance hall showcases a masterfully crafted curving wooden staircase with turned balusters, ornamental stringers, and a fluted newel post, complemented by elaborate molded cornices. While the brick stoop was added later, the house maintains its original character despite its evolution from private residence to county ownership and now serves as apartments. This preservation success story illustrates how architectural heritage can be adapted for modern use while maintaining its historical significance. (Michael Schwartz Library Special Collections. Cleveland State University.)

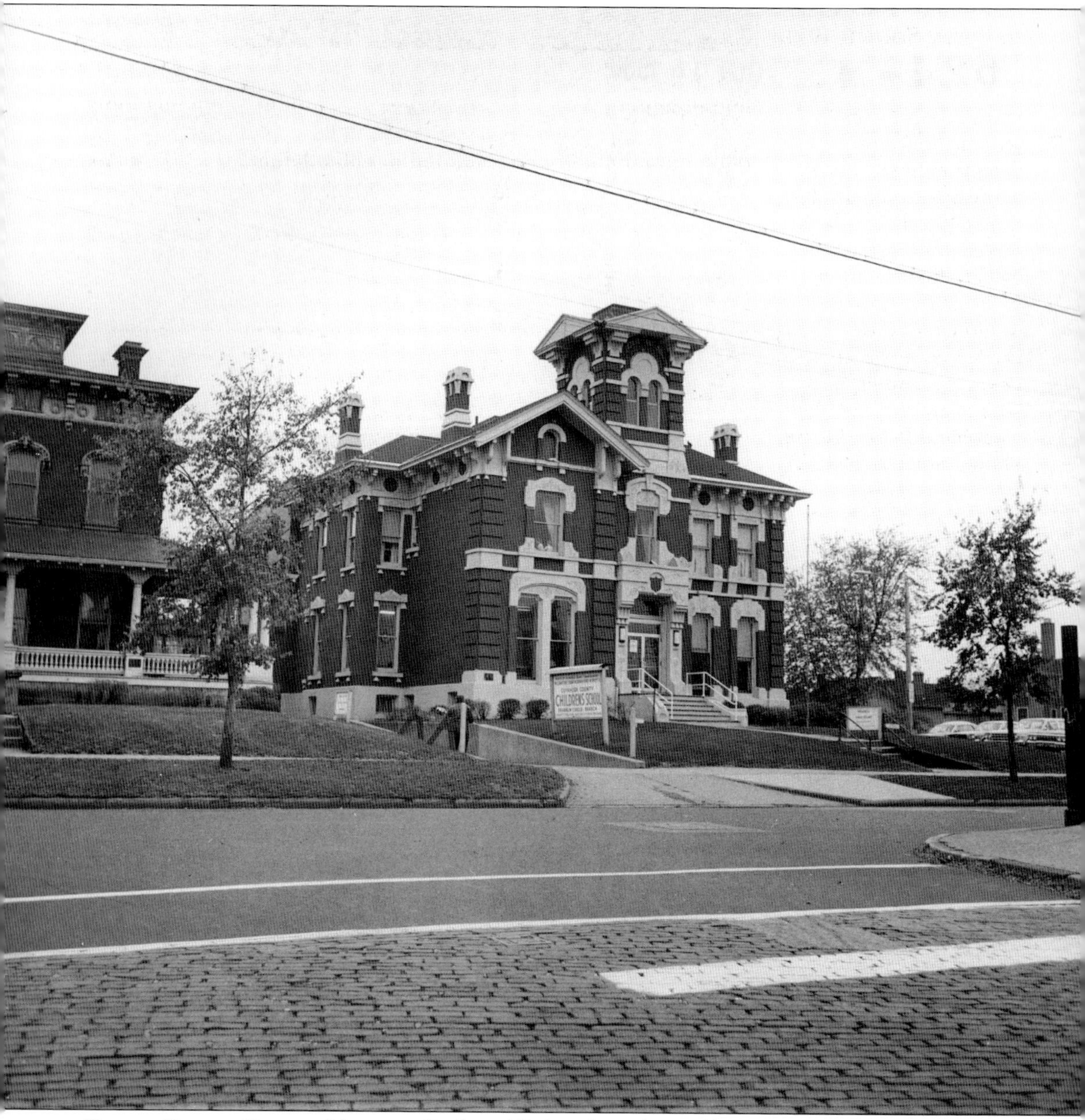

Robert Russell Rhodes Mansion. Built in 1874 in the Italian villa style, this impressive mansion reflects both Ohio City's pioneer heritage and its continued adaptability. Robert Russell Rhodes, a prominent banker and businessman, commissioned the home. His great-grandfather Josiah Barber was among Ohio City's earliest settlers, while his own generation represented the area's industrial wealth. After Rhodes sold the property in 1888, it began a remarkable century of institutional service under county ownership, serving variously as a juvenile detention home, nursing facility, welfare department, school, and county archives. The mansion demonstrates extraordinary versatility, recently transforming into modern apartments while preserving its architectural character. Today's residents enjoy the same soaring 12-foot ceilings and architectural details that once graced the Rhodes family home, now complemented by contemporary amenities—a testament to how historic preservation can meet modern needs. (Cleveland Public Library Photograph Collection.)

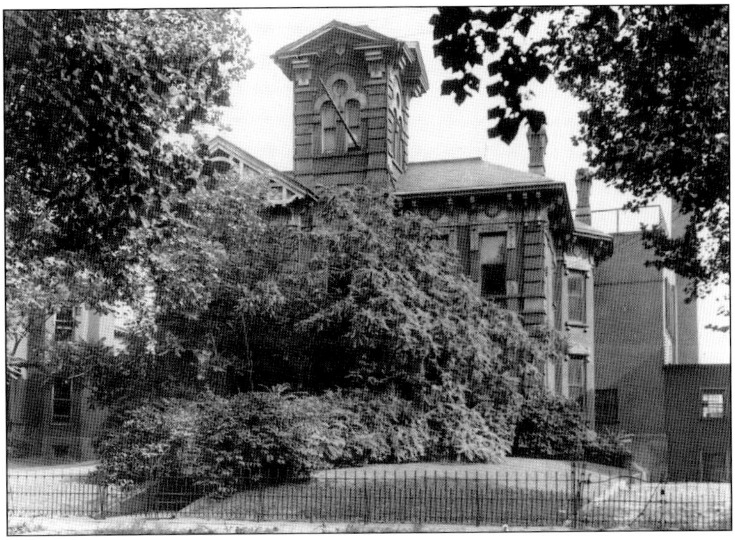

FROM PRIVATE MANSION TO PUBLIC SERVICE, 1934. This view captures the Robert Russell Rhodes mansion during its years as the county detention home, one of many institutional roles the 1874 Italian villa served after its purchase by Cuyahoga County in 1914. The building would later house various county agencies before becoming the county archives in 1978. (Cleveland Public Library Photograph Collection.)

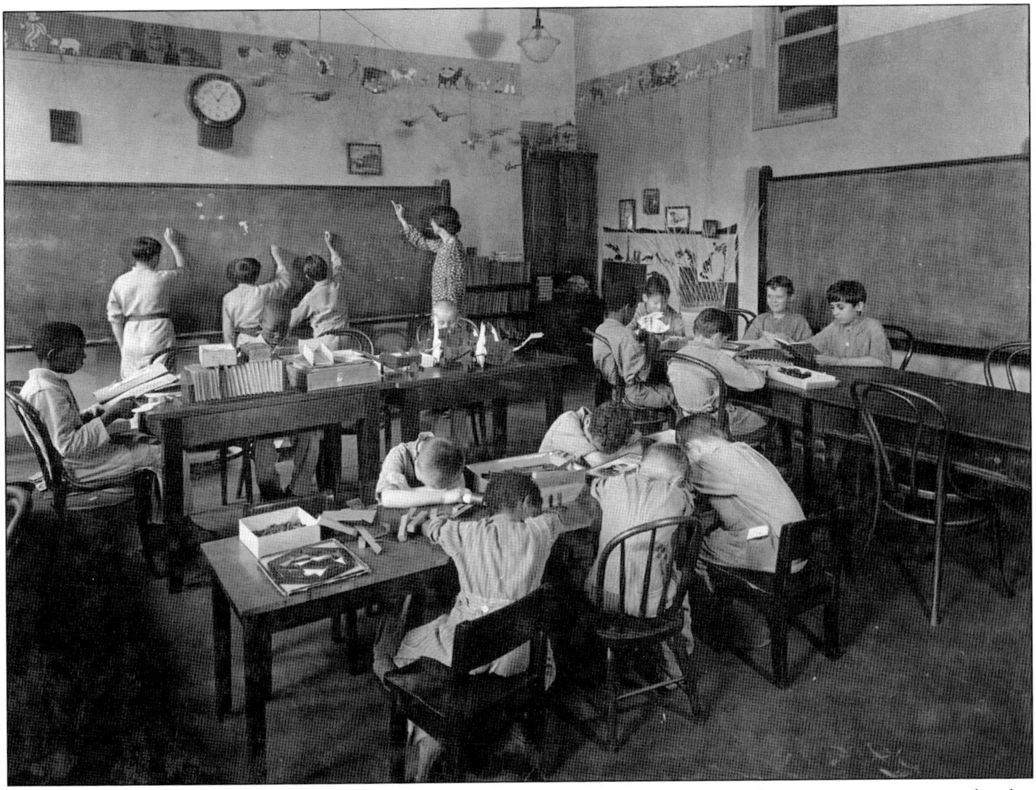

LEARNING AND LIFE IN THE DETENTION HOME, 1925. This poignant classroom scene inside the former Rhodes mansion shows young residents at the County Detention Home—some at the blackboard, others resting their heads on a shared table. The space, once dedicated to education in challenging circumstances, has since been transformed into a modern apartment. (Cleveland Public Library Photograph Collection.)

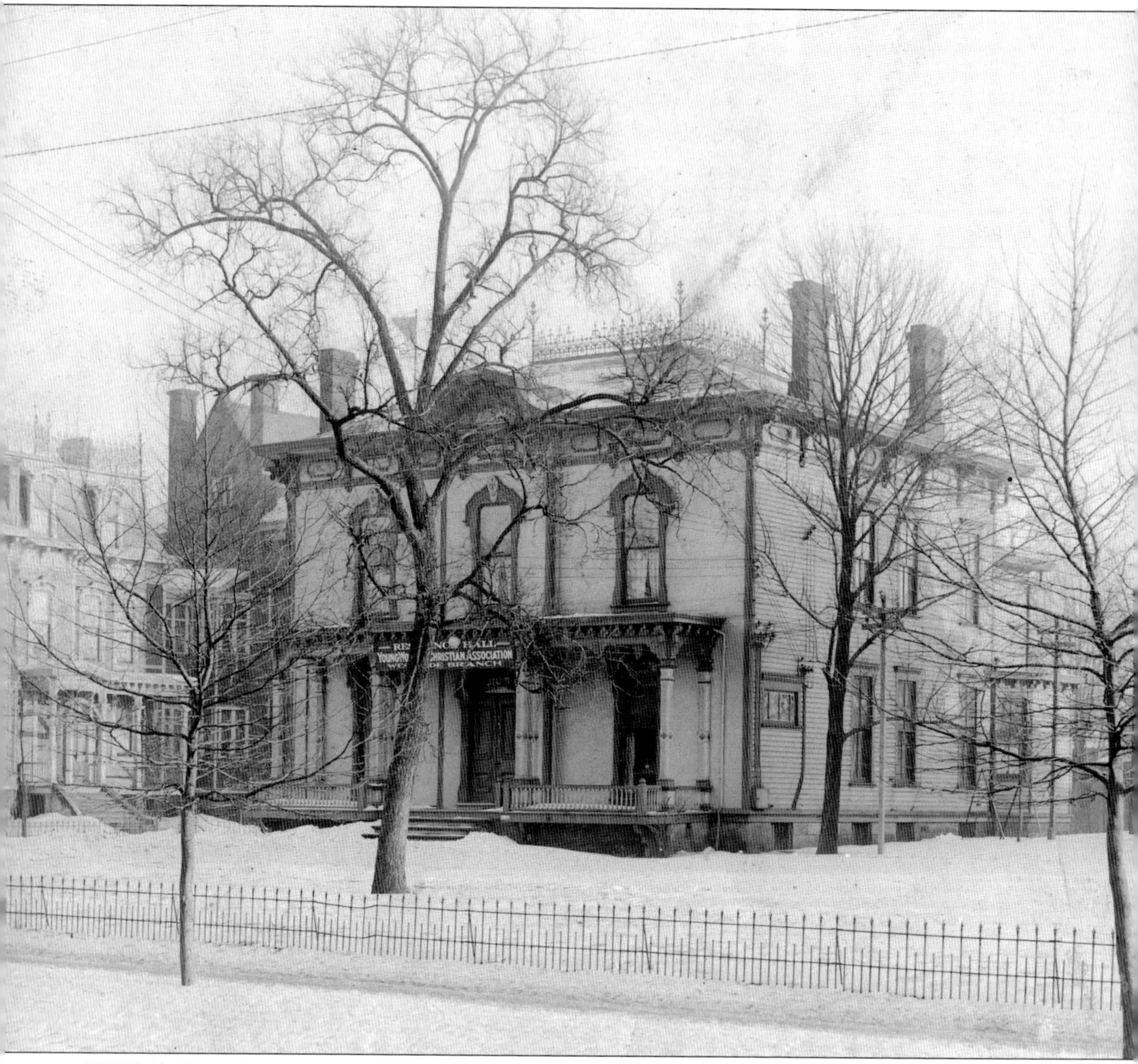

YWCA's West Side Branch, 1920. This photograph captures the former Coffinberry mansion at 3105 Franklin Boulevard during its service as the YWCA's junior girls' department. Built in 1875 for Judge James Coffinberry, whose family accident prompted Cleveland's first railroad crossing gates, the Italianate residence found new purpose in 1913 when the YWCA established its west side branch. Located diagonally across from the West Side YMCA, this mansion and the neighboring Cook-Bousfield house provided vital services for the west side girls. The banner proudly announcing its role as a YWCA residence hall symbolizes the transformation of Franklin Boulevard's grand homes to meet community needs. In 1928, this historic house was razed to make way for a modern YWCA residence hall. In January 2025, plans were reported to create "Franklin Yard," a mixed-use development incorporating the surviving Cook-Bousfield mansion. (Cleveland Public Library, Photograph Collection.)

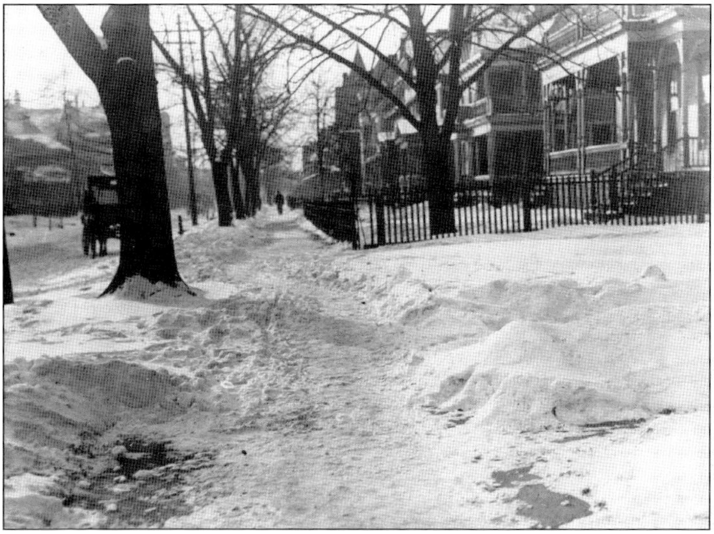

Winter on Franklin Boulevard, 1912. This snowy vista looking west along Franklin Boulevard's north side captures the grandeur of Ohio City's premier residential street. The stately mansions, including several that still stand today, showcase the neighborhood's peak era when wealthy industrialists and merchants made their homes along this tree-lined avenue. (Cleveland Public Library Photograph Collection.)

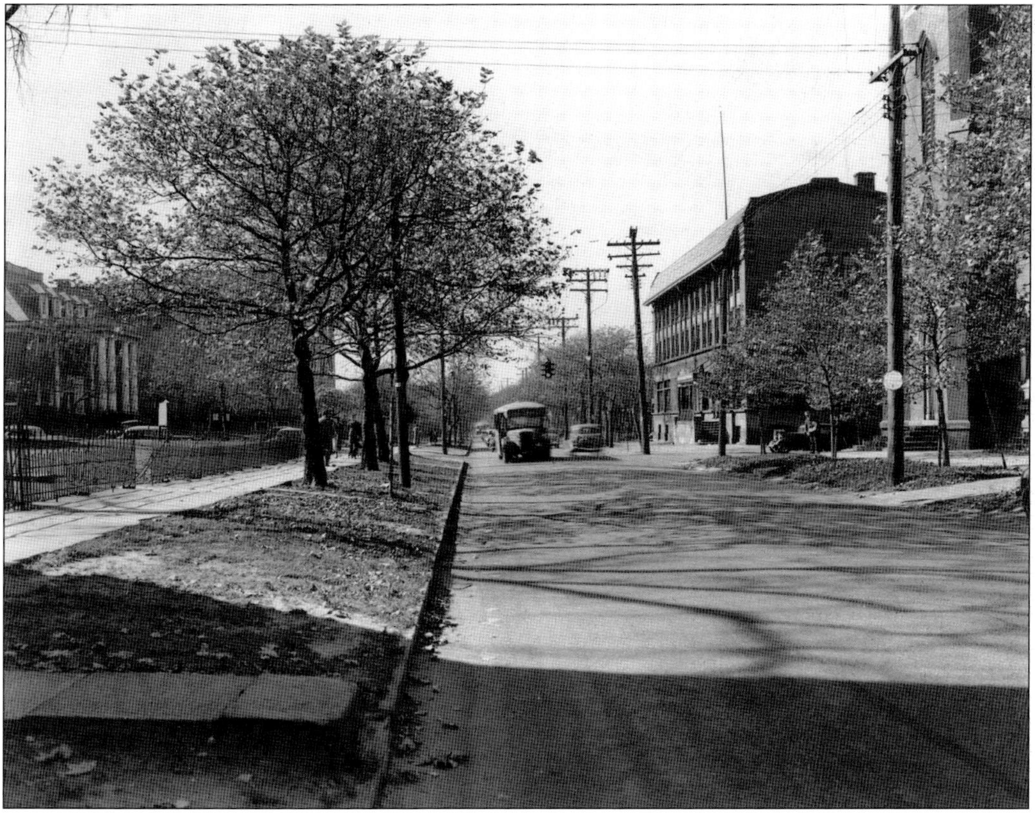

Franklin Boulevard's Changing Character, 1935. Two decades after the winter scene of prosperous Franklin Boulevard, this 1935 Depression-era view near West Thirty-Second Street shows the thoroughfare's evolution. While the Franklin Boulevard Methodist Church and YWCA remain prominent landmarks, the street scene reflects the neighborhood's transition as many grand homes began accommodating multiple families. (Cleveland Public Library Photograph Collection.)

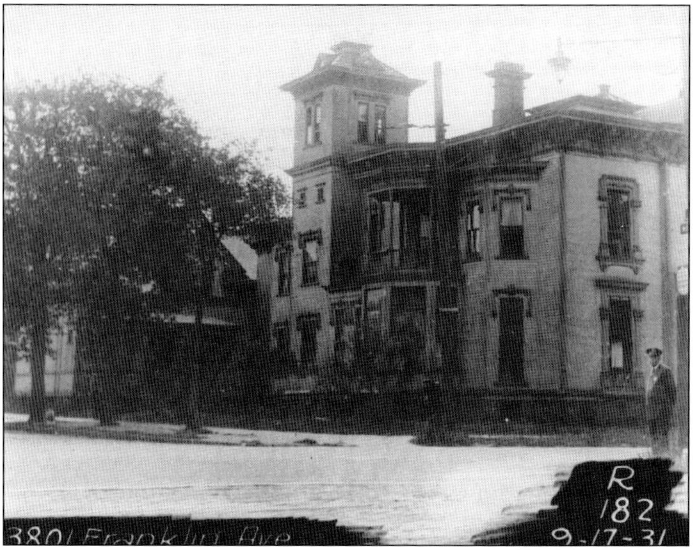

The Seymour Mansion Restored. Built in 1874 for Vermont-born real estate investor Belden Seymour, this Italianate mansion at 3805 Franklin Boulevard reflects both grandeur and resilience. After serving as a crowded tenement house during the Depression years and surviving multiple fires in later decades, the 7,500-square-foot home has been meticulously restored and is now serving as The Eleanor luxury apartments. (Cleveland Public Library, Photograph Collection.)

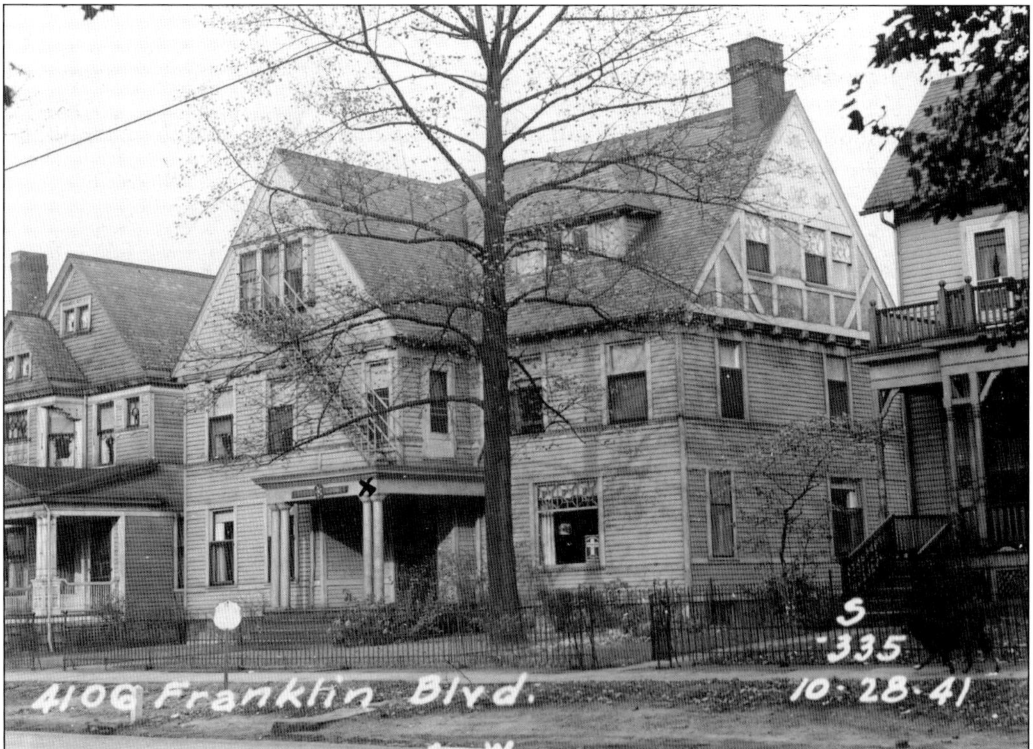

The Andrew Squire House, 1941. Built around 1891 for prominent corporate attorney Andrew Squire, cofounder of Squire, Sanders & Dempsey (now Squire Patton Boggs), this home illustrates the evolution of Ohio City's grand homes. By 1941, when this photograph was taken, the property had become the Lutheran Center, beginning a tradition of faith-based community outreach that continues today at this site through Lutheran Family Services. (Cleveland Public Library, Photograph Collection.)

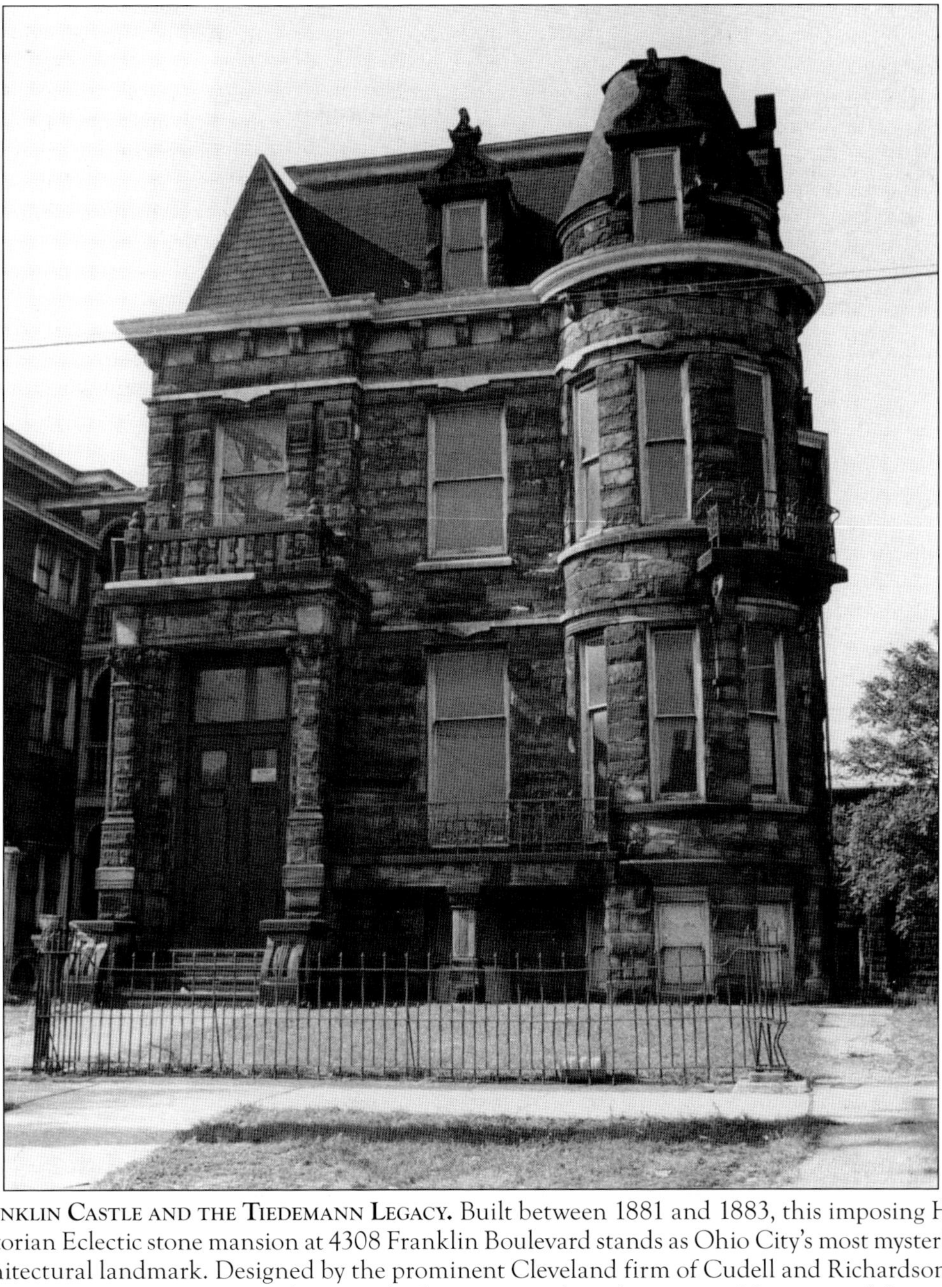

FRANKLIN CASTLE AND THE TIEDEMANN LEGACY. Built between 1881 and 1883, this imposing High Victorian Eclectic stone mansion at 4308 Franklin Boulevard stands as Ohio City's most mysterious architectural landmark. Designed by the prominent Cleveland firm of Cudell and Richardson for German immigrant Hannes Tiedemann, the four-story residence boasts over 20 rooms and distinctive features, including a round corner tower and rock-faced sandstone construction. Tiedemann, who made his fortune in wholesale groceries and banking, built the house not only as a family home but as temporary lodging for newly arrived German immigrants. After the Tiedemanns' departure in 1896, the house served various purposes, most notably as Eintracht Hall, home to the German-American League for Culture from 1921 to 1968. Local lore speaks of ghostly footsteps echoing through its halls and unexplained phenomena. While tales of Hannes's wife Luise Tiedemann's spirit and other supernatural occurrences have drawn paranormal investigators for decades, the house has undergone extensive restoration efforts. (Cleveland Public Library Photograph Collection.)

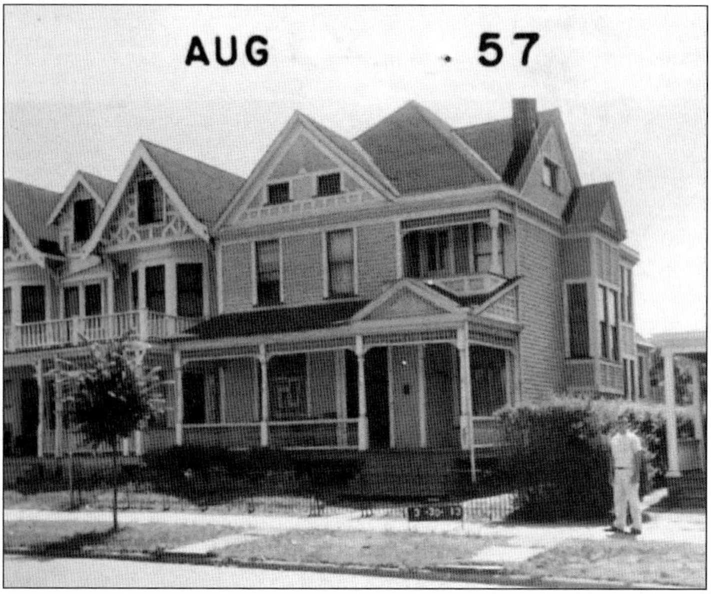

The William Ford House, 1957. Built in 1891 for William and Ella Ford on land owned by Ella's family, this Queen Anne masterpiece at 4201 Franklin Boulevard stands as one of the street's most intact Victorian homes. Photographed by the county appraiser here in 1957, the house would later undergo an award-winning restoration (2014–2017), preserving its original features, from Lincrusta wallpaper to ornate woodwork. (Cuyahoga County Archives.)

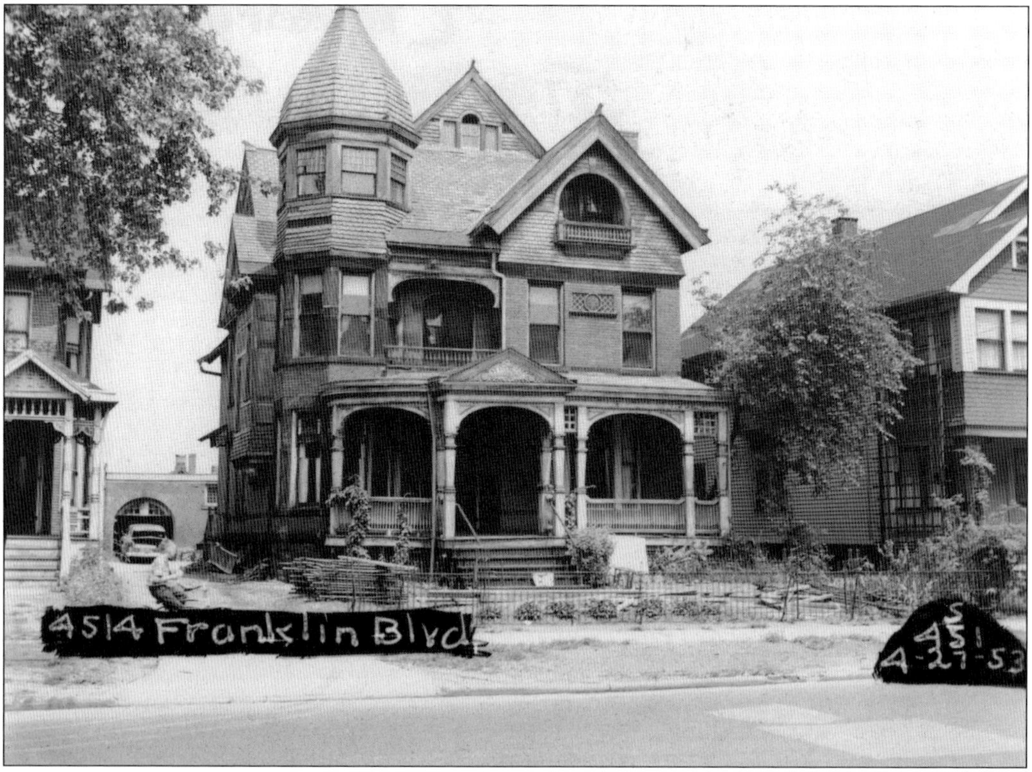

A Lumber Baron's Legacy, 1953. Built in 1887 for lumber magnate Abraham Teachout, this Queen Anne–style residence at 4514 Franklin Boulevard reflects its original owner's trade through millwork and varied wood detailing. The home's interior features a unique dining room floor crafted from six different wood species. Restored by Charles and Alice Gould Butts, the house stands as a testament to both Victorian craftsmanship and dedicated preservation efforts, despite the loss of its original wraparound porch. (Cleveland Public Library Photograph Collection.)

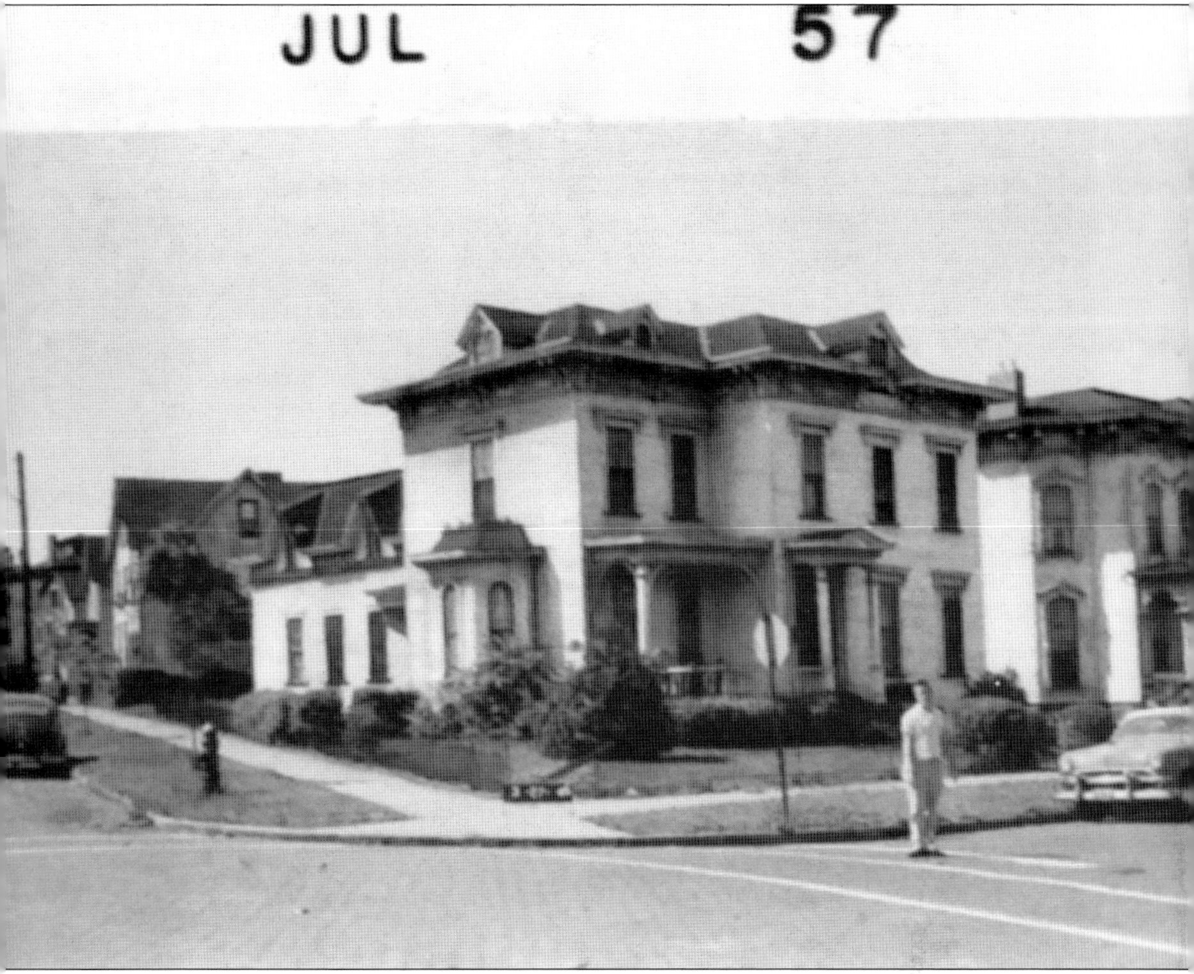

The Beverlin House. This 1957 county appraiser photograph shows the stately Italianate residence at 2901 Clinton Avenue, built in 1855 for early Ohio City mayor John Beverlin and his wife, Gracia. The home stands as one of three Cleveland Landmarks on this historic block. The imposing home reflects both its original architectural grandeur and later Victorian modifications, including the Second Empire–style windows added above the cornice around 1891. The Beverlins, who raised five children here, later built another Italianate house next door at 2913 Clinton, possibly for their son Clarence, a house carpenter. Today, this corner property continues its legacy of careful stewardship through ongoing restoration efforts that honor Clinton Avenue's historic single-family character. (Cuyahoga County Archives.)

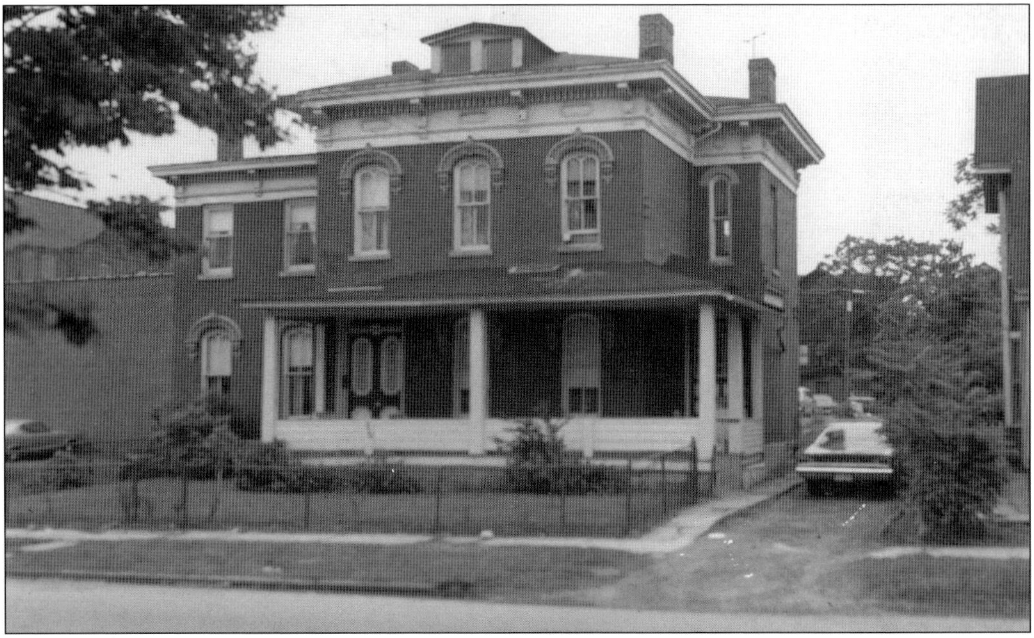

The Sanderson Legacy, 1971. This 1971 view of 3101 Clinton Avenue captures the Italianate mansion, built in 1868 for Globe Ironworks stakeholder Robert Sanderson, during its years as a Catholic Diocese youth facility. Though missing its front porch in this photograph, the house has since undergone an award-winning restoration that enhanced its original architectural splendor, including ornate marble fireplaces and 12-foot ceilings. (Cleveland Public Library Photograph Collection.)

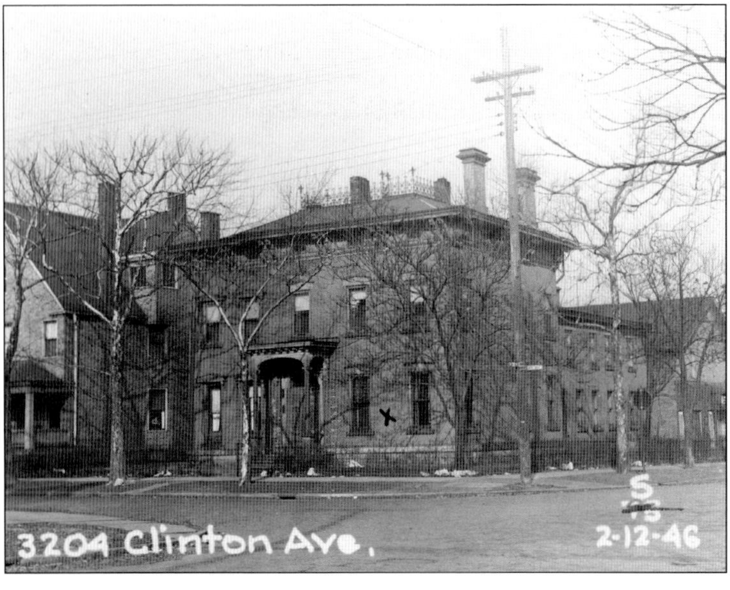

A Clinton Avenue Home Through Time, 1946. Built around 1890, this house at 3204 Clinton Avenue was home to Dr. Frederick C. Taylor and his sisters in the early 1900s, with his funeral held here in 1911. The rear property later housed the Clinton Bar from the 1950s to the 1980s and the Christian Fellowship Church in the 1990s before its recent restoration as a multi-family residence. (Cleveland Public Library Photograph Collection.)

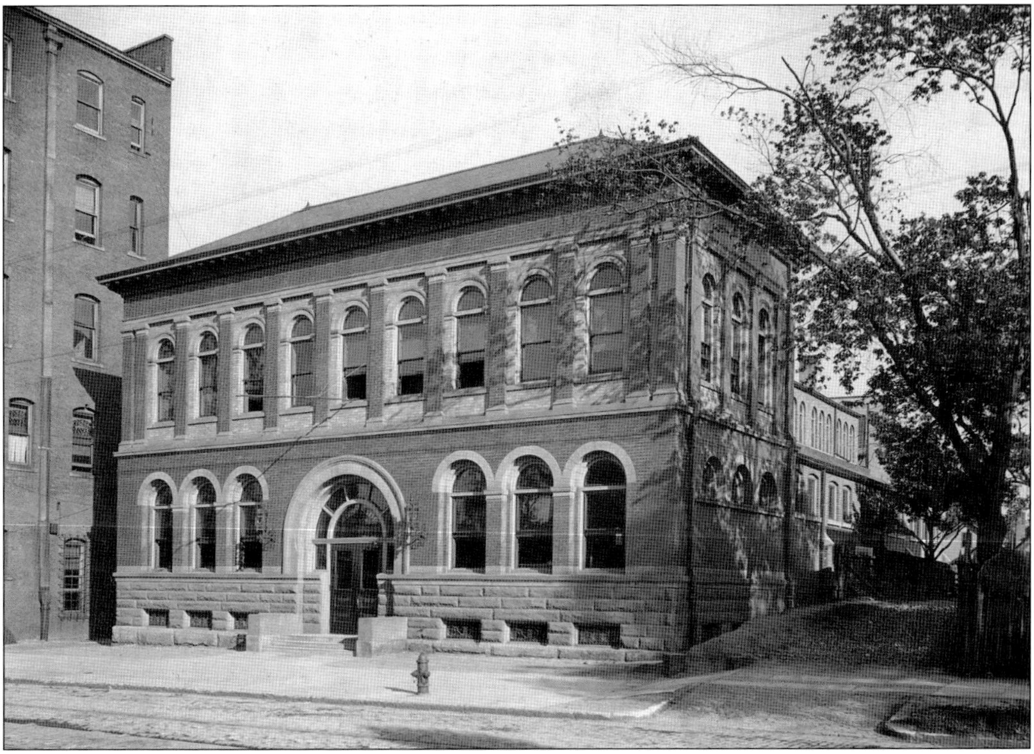

The West Side Library. These images capture the West Side Library's second location at 2515 Franklin Boulevard, which served the neighborhood from 1897 to 1910. Operating in space leased from People's Savings and Loan, the library occupied the building's entire first floor. At 60 by 110 feet, this facility represented a significant expansion from the library's original quarters, reflecting Ohio City's growing population and demand for public services. The second image showcases the library's interior, where the expansive main room occupies the entire first floor. A newspaper reading gallery overlooked the stairway, providing additional space for patrons. The building was designed to accommodate the growing demand for reading materials and public gathering spaces. The building's transformation continues today as part of Cinecraft Productions, a testament to the adaptability of Ohio City's historic structures. (Both, Cleveland Public Library Archives Collection.)

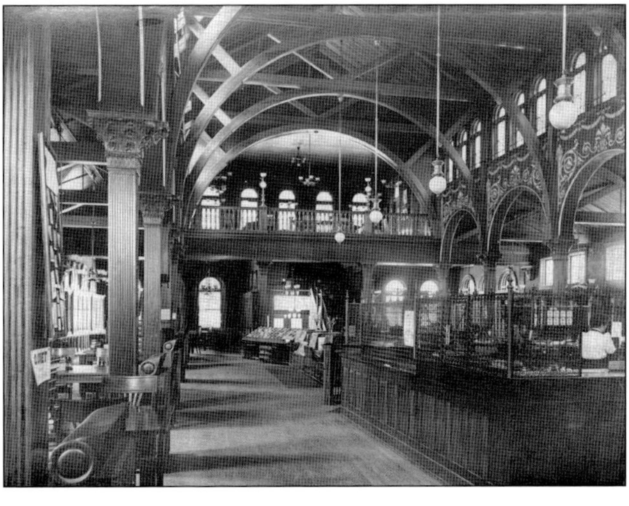

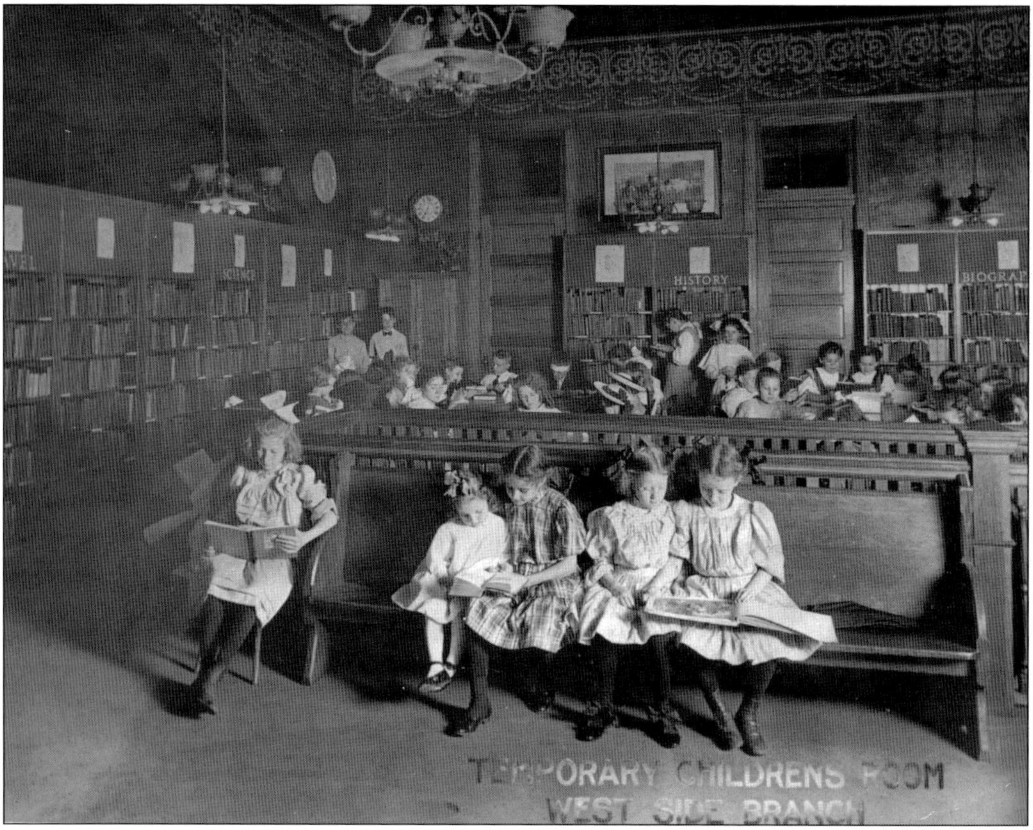

Learning Across Generations. This 1897 photograph of the Children's Reading Room at the West Side Library's Franklin Boulevard location captures an essential community service in action. The ornate space features high ceilings and labeled bookshelves organizing the collection by subject, reflecting the era's approach to public education. (Cleveland Public Library Photograph Collection.)

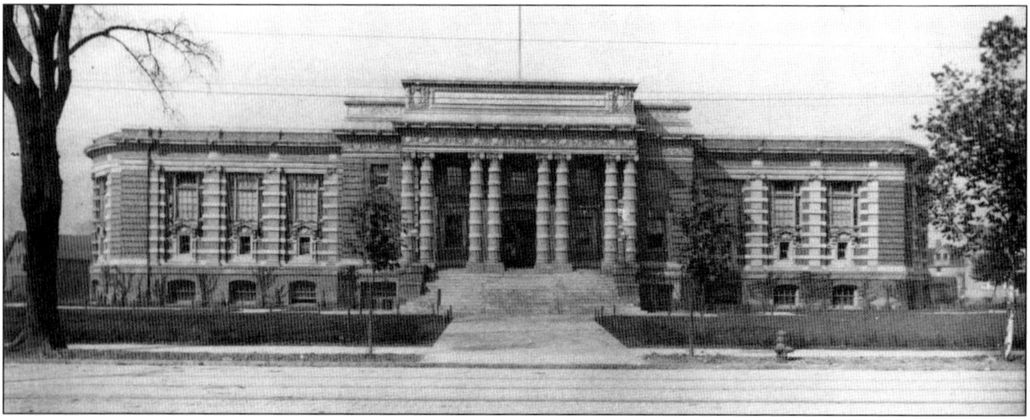

Carnegie West, a Literary Landmark, 1910. Designed by Ellis Island architect Edward Tilton in modified Renaissance style, Carnegie West Library stands as the oldest operating branch in Cleveland's library system. The brick, limestone, and terracotta building features classical elements and intricate architectural details. Andrew Carnegie's philanthropic vision helped create this enduring Ohio City cultural anchor in Frank Novak Park. (Cleveland Public Library Archive Collection.)

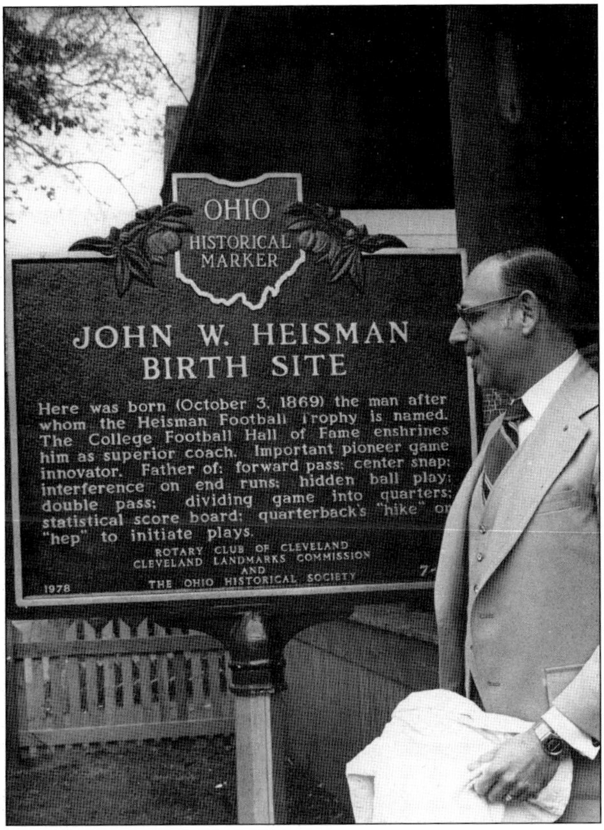

UNRAVELING HEISMAN'S TRUE BIRTHPLACE. These images tell a story of historical detective work in Ohio City. The 1978 photograph to the left shows the Ohio Historical Marker at 2825 Bridge Avenue, where Edward J. Wagner of West Side Savings and Loan had championed efforts to create a Heisman museum based on then-accepted local history. However, subsequent research revealed that the legendary football pioneer was actually born at 3928 Bridge Avenue, shown here in a 1957 county appraiser photograph. Born on October 23, 1869, John Heisman would go on to revolutionize college football through innovative coaching and rule changes. While the original marker location represented well-intentioned preservation efforts, the discovery of his true birthplace demonstrates the importance of thorough historical research. (Left, Cleveland Press Collection, Michael Schwartz Library Special Collections, Cleveland State University; below, Cuyahoga County Archives.)

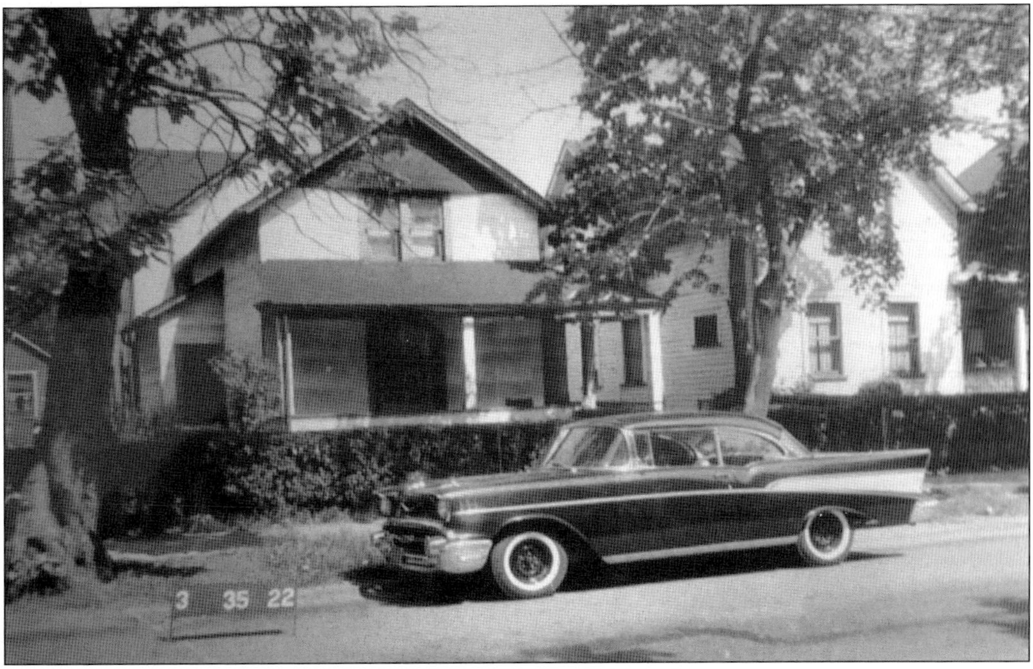

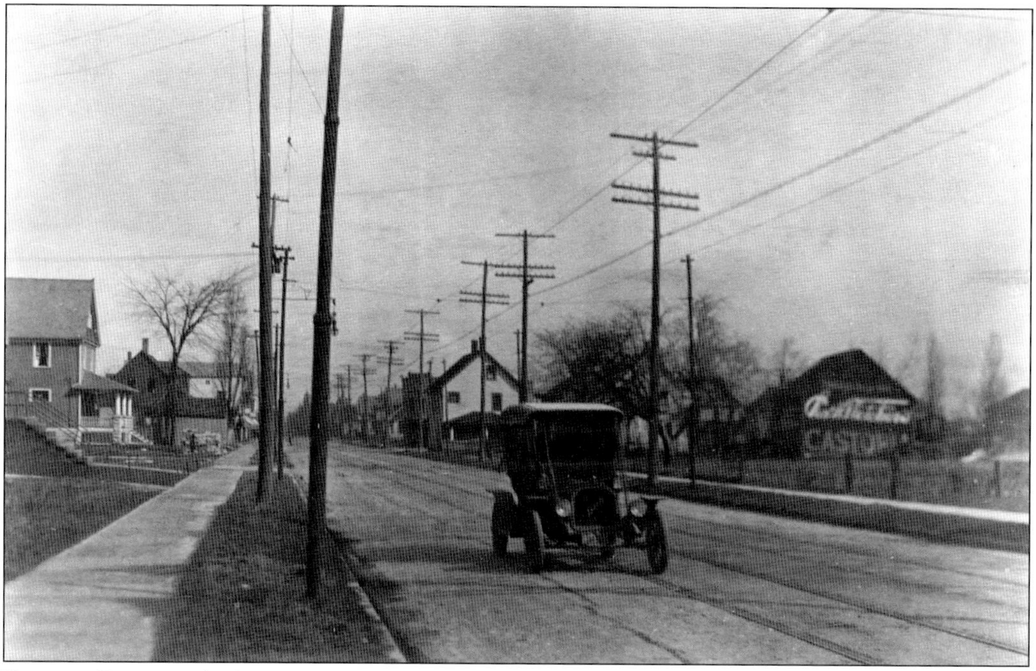

BEYOND FRANKLIN'S GRANDEUR, C. 1910. This view along West Forty-First Street reveals the more modest character of Ohio City's outer streets. While Franklin Boulevard showcased the neighborhood's wealthy elite, this well-developed streetscape, with its paved road, sidewalks, and telephone poles, demonstrates how urban infrastructure extended throughout the area, serving both grand mansions and working-class homes alike. (Cleveland Public Library Photograph Collection.)

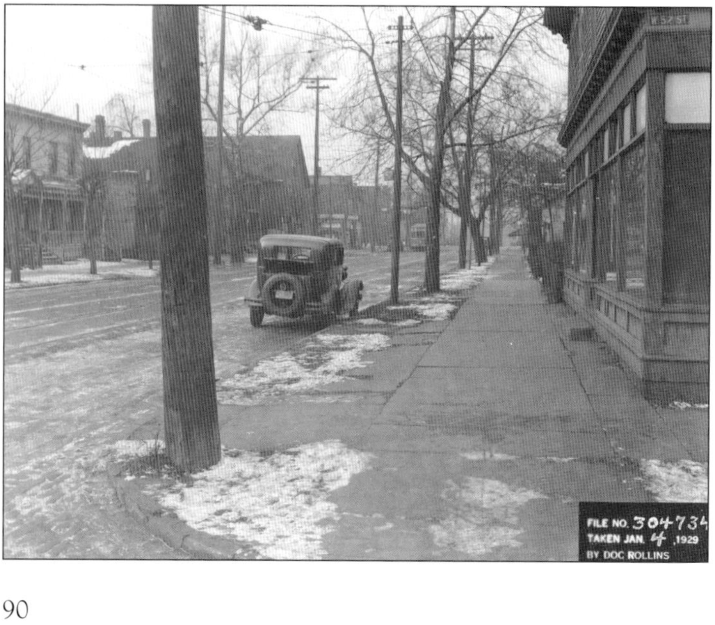

NEIGHBORHOOD COMMERCE, 1929. Looking west at West Fifty-Second Street, this view captures the mix of small storefronts and homes just beyond Ohio City's unofficial border. The snow-covered street reflects a community where local businesses and residential life flourished. This area served as a vital link to the expanding neighborhoods further west. (Cleveland Public Library Photograph Collection.)

Six

Daily Life and Commerce 1930s–1950s

Despite the economic strain of the Great Depression and the rationing during World War II, Ohio City residents adapted, demonstrating resourcefulness in their businesses and social spaces. The postwar boom brought modern storefronts and new businesses, while streetcar lines continued delivering shoppers to West Twenty-Fifth Street's department stores and specialty shops.

The mid-20th century was a defining era for Ohio City, which was increasingly referred to as "the Near West Side." The neighborhood was marked by bustling streets, thriving businesses, and a strong sense of community. West Twenty-Fifth Street and Lorain Avenue remained the commercial heart of the area, lined with department stores, grocers, bakeries, and specialty shops catering to its diverse residents. Business owners knew their customers by name, and local merchants were deeply woven into the fabric of daily life.

Entertainment venues added another dimension to neighborhood life. Movie theaters like the Rialto, Lorain-Fulton, and Marvel offered escape and entertainment, their marquees illuminating evening streets. These theaters became gathering spots where generations of families shared weekend outings and first dates.

Neighborhood bars were more than places to grab a drink—they were social hubs where workers gathered after shifts, exchanged news, and formed lifelong friendships. Taverns, corner cafés, and meeting halls played a key role in maintaining cultural traditions, hosting celebrations, political discussions, and even job networking. These establishments helped preserve the ethnic identity of Ohio City's early immigrant groups while also integrating new arrivals, including Appalachian, Puerto Rican, and Eastern European families seeking opportunities in Cleveland's manufacturing sector.

Small businesses were the backbone of the neighborhood, with family-run butcher shops, tailor stores, hardware suppliers, and independent grocers supporting daily life. Market culture flourished, with the West Side Market remaining a vital source of fresh produce, meats, and baked goods for households across the city. Many vendors had operated their stalls for generations, building lasting relationships with families who shopped there for decades. Just as businesses were passed down, so too were customer loyalties, with children and grandchildren continuing to frequent the same stalls their parents had trusted.

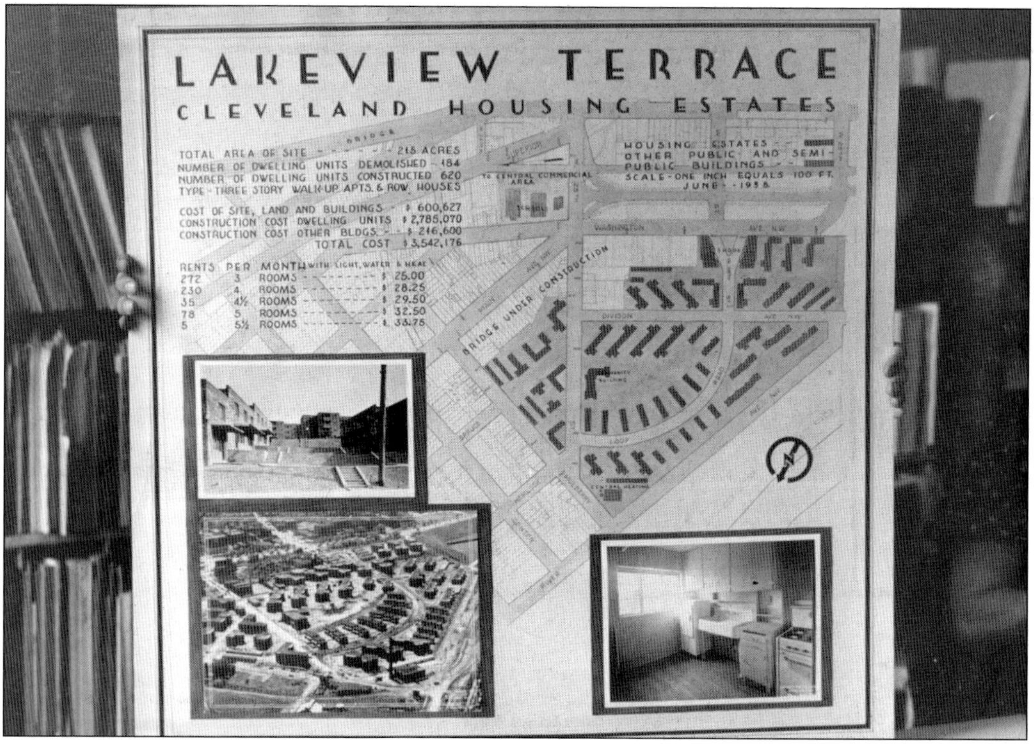

Lakeview Terrace. These two images capture Cleveland's first public housing project during its early years. The 1938 promotional poster showcases the innovative design of Lakeview Terrace—built into a hillside overlooking Lake Erie and the Cuyahoga River, featuring abundant green spaces, playgrounds, and a community center. The 1941 street view reveals the completed development's integration into the neighborhood landscape. Designed as transitional housing for working families, Lakeview Terrace represented a progressive approach to urban housing, offering an alternative to overcrowded tenements. The development's amenities, including WPA murals, reflected the era's optimistic vision of public housing as a stepping stone to better lives. Today, Lakeview Terrace remains Cleveland's oldest public housing complex. (Both, Michael Schwartz Library Special Collections, Cleveland State University.)

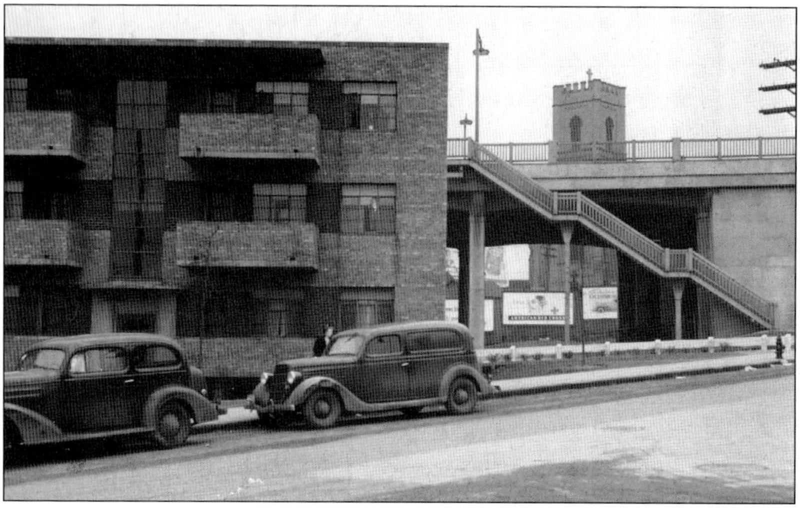

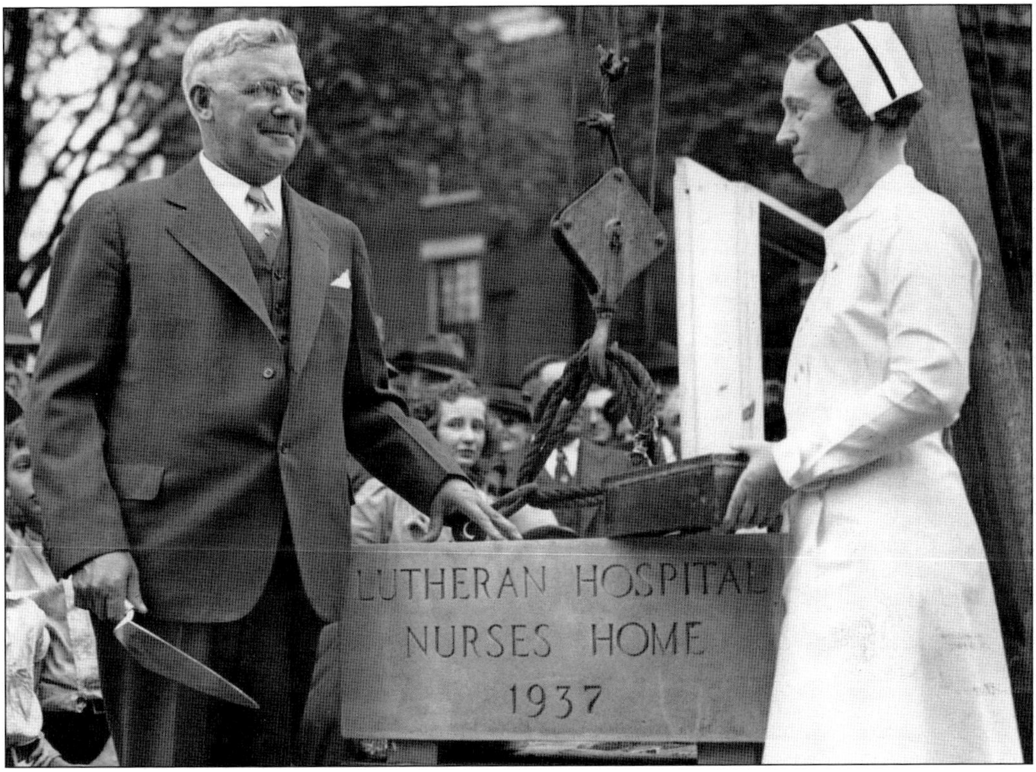

Lutheran Hospital's Evolution. These two images trace Lutheran Hospital's growth along Franklin Boulevard. The 1937 photograph shows the newly constructed Nurses Home, marking an era when the hospital expanded beyond its original Franklin Circle location. By 1963, as seen in the second image, the modernized façade reflected the hospital's continued development as a major medical center. From its humble beginnings in 1896, Lutheran Hospital grew into a vital healthcare institution, adding specialized departments and expanding its facilities through multiple renovations. Today, it continues its mission of serving Ohio City and the greater Cleveland community from its historic Franklin Boulevard campus. (Above, Michael Schwartz Library Special Collections, Cleveland State University; below, Cleveland Public Library Photograph Collection.)

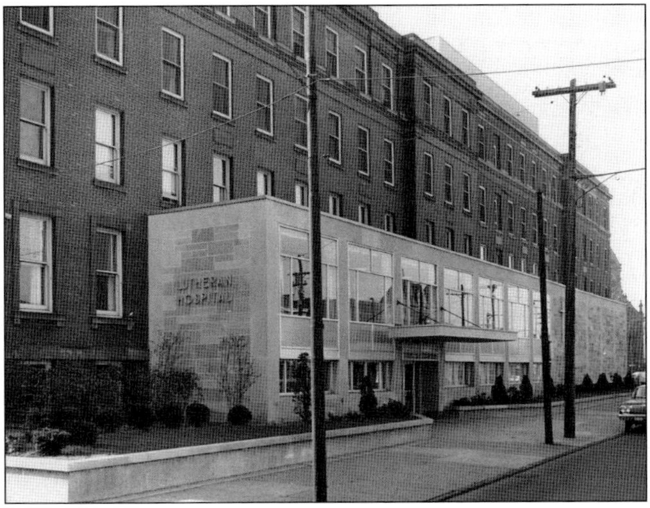

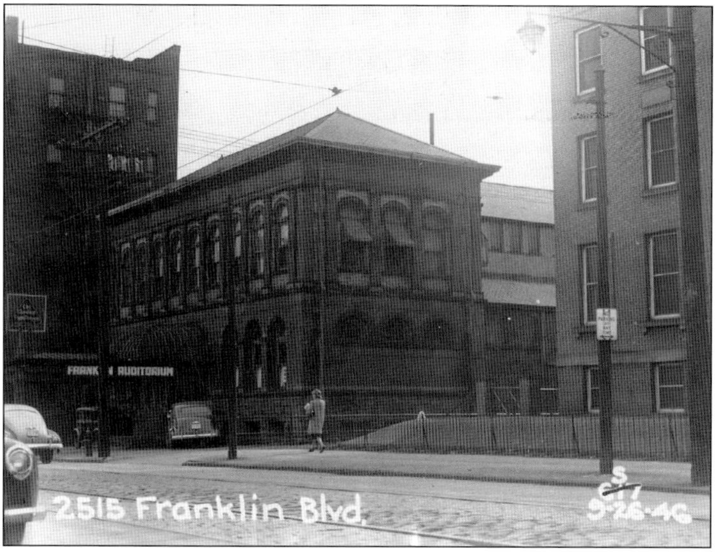

FROM PUBLIC HALL TO FILM STUDIO, 1946. Located at the corner of West Twenty-Fifth and Franklin Boulevard, this building served as Franklin Auditorium under owner Marie Adams, hosting community events from 1940 to 1946. The following year, Cinecraft Productions purchased the property, transforming it into a film studio that continues to operate today. (Cleveland Public Library Photograph Collection.)

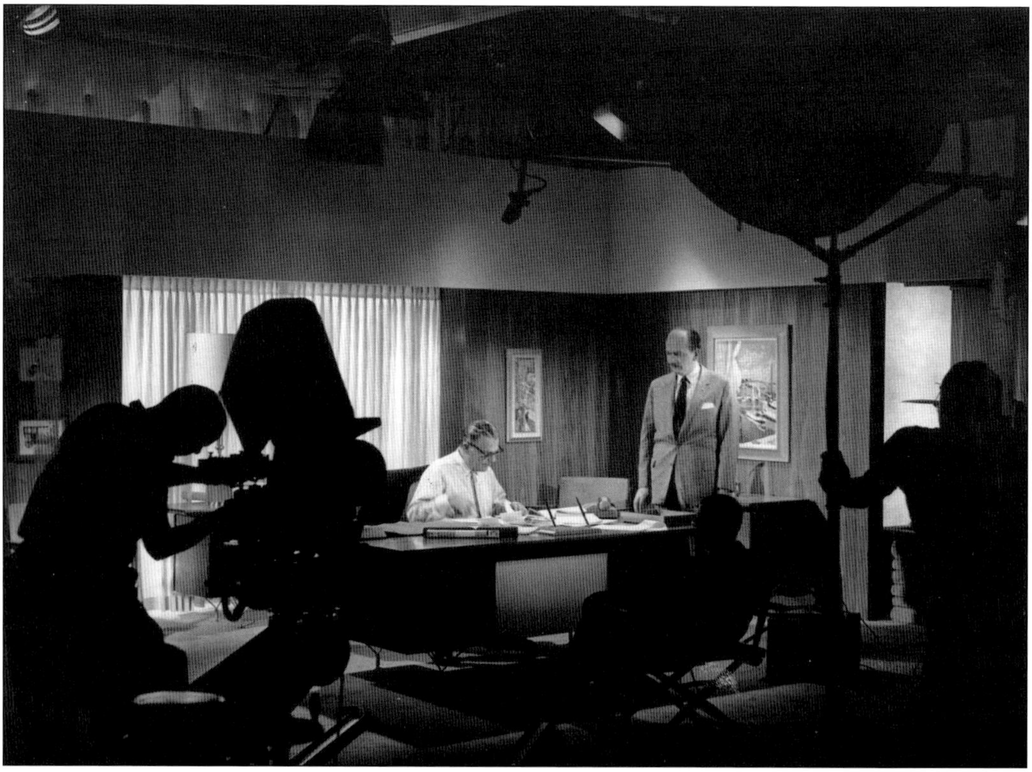

PIONEER FILMMAKERS AT WORK, 1959. Brian Donlevy and Bill Patterson during a filming session at Cinecraft Productions' Franklin Boulevard studio. As early innovators in commercial filmmaking, Cinecraft made history here by producing the nation's first infomercial—a 1950 demonstration film for Vitamix blenders, created in collaboration with WEWS television. (Michael Schwartz Library Special Collections, Cleveland State University.)

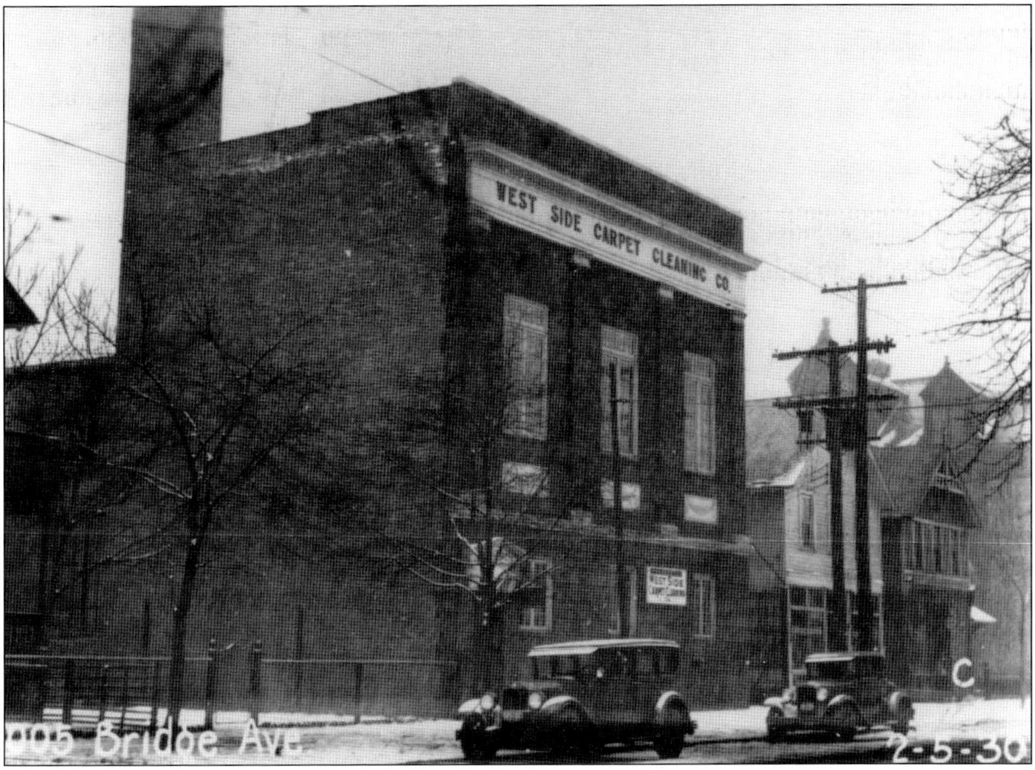

West Side Carpet Cleaning. This 1930 view shows the West Side Carpet Cleaning Company with 1920s automobiles parked outside. The business appeared in Cleveland Plain Dealer advertisements from at least 1913 through 1995, serving Ohio City families across generations. While the building's distinctive exterior remains unchanged, it now houses apartments, reflecting the neighborhood's modern transformation. (Cleveland Public Library Photograph Collection.)

Service Milk Company. This 1946 photograph at 2615 Hancock Avenue captures workers loading milk crates into a delivery van at Service Milk Company. The business later played an unexpected humanitarian role when its trucks were used to transport Hungarian refugees arriving in Cleveland during the 1956 revolution. (Cleveland Public Library Photograph Collection.)

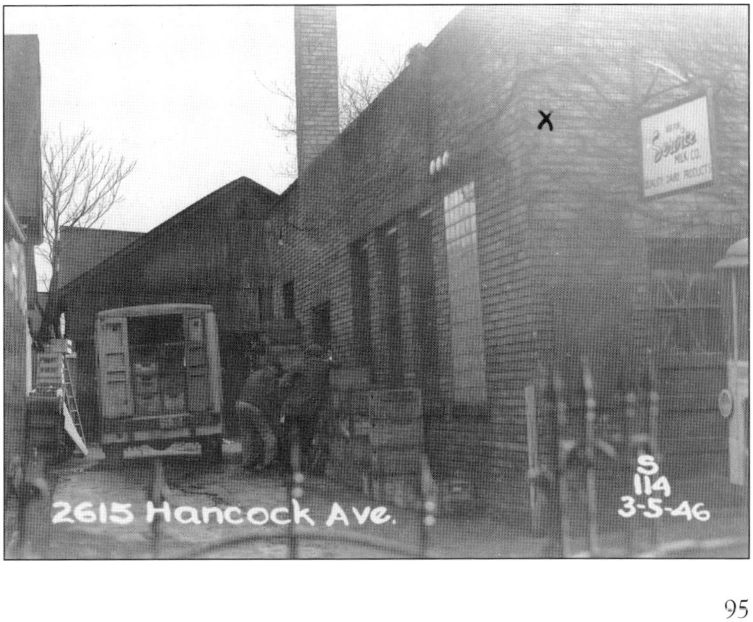

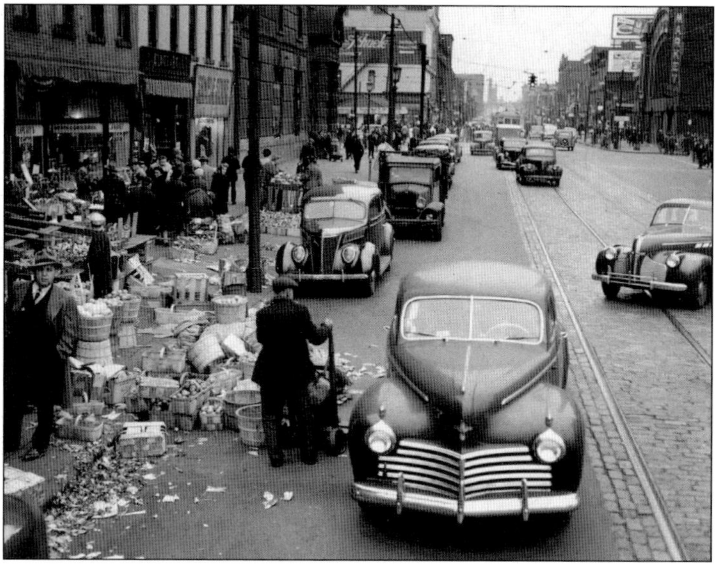

Market Day Cleanup, West Twenty-Fifth Street. This 1944 view looking north toward the West Side Market captures the aftermath of a busy market day, with discarded produce crates littering the sidewalk where vendors had earlier displayed their goods. The bustling street scene reflects the vibrant commerce that centers around the market's southern approach. (Cleveland State University, Michael Schwartz Library Special Collections.)

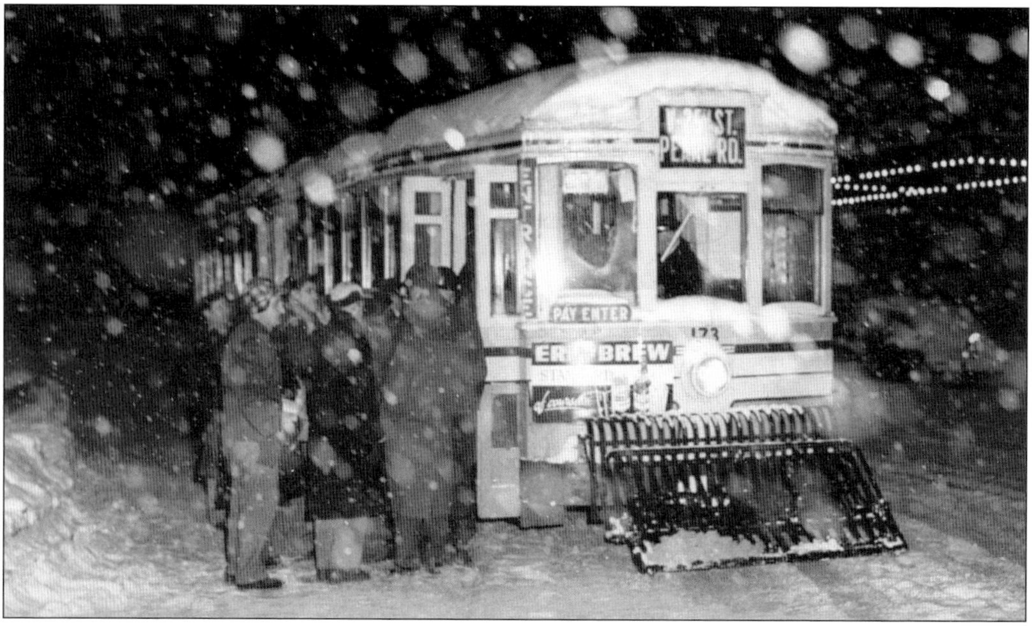

West Twenty-Fifth Street Streetcar Line, November 1950. This snowy scene captures the bustling West Twenty-Fifth Street streetcar line, a vital transit route for Ohio City residents. The streetcar features an Erin Brew advertisement prominently displayed on its front, highlighting the neighborhood's ties to local breweries. The line was an essential link for commuters and shoppers throughout the west side. (Cleveland Public Library Photograph Collection.)

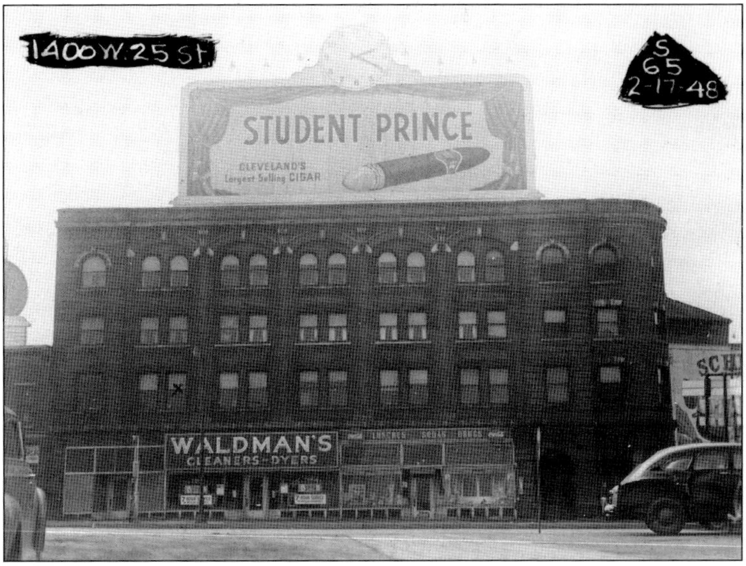

WALDMAN'S AND WEST TWENTY-FIFTH. This 1948 view captures the bustling corner of West Twenty-Fifth Street where Waldman's Cleaners, established in the 1920s, shared space with a neighborhood drugstore. Now home to Forest City Apartments, the building represents the evolution from daily commerce to residential use in modern Ohio City. (Cleveland Public Library Photograph Collection.)

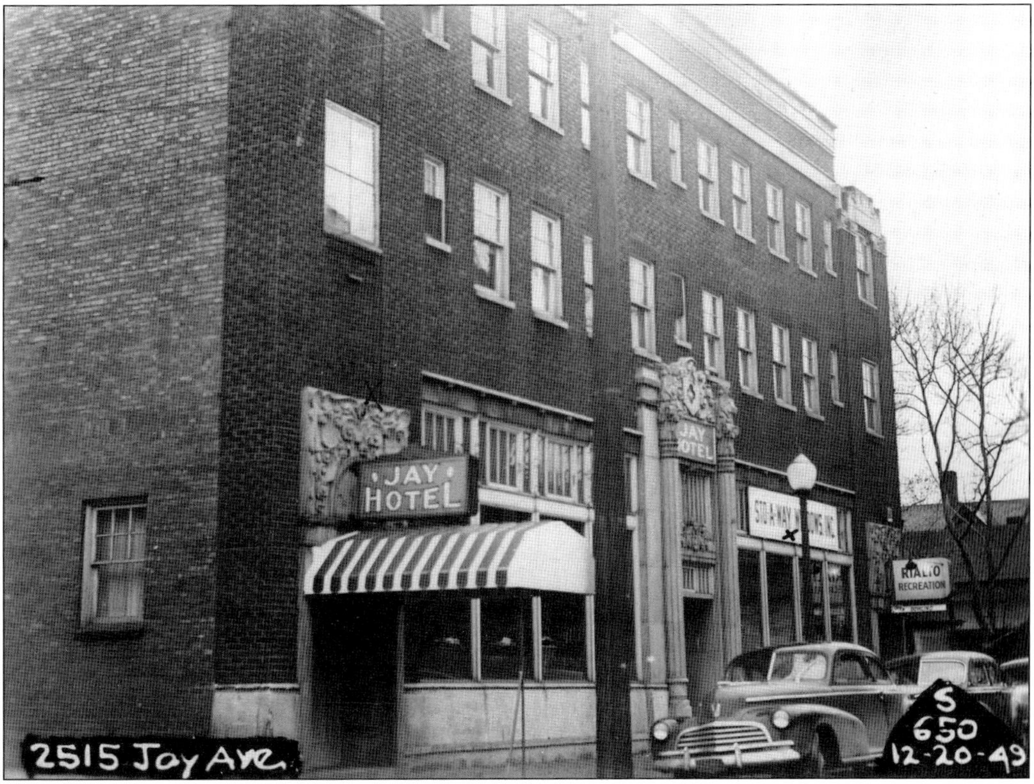

THE JAY HOTEL, 1949. This view captures the Jay Hotel at 2515 Jay Avenue, with Rialto Recreation visible in the background. Built in 1924, the building served multiple purposes over the decades—from post office to bowling alley—before its long tenure as a residential hotel. Today, the renovated structure houses apartments and commercial spaces. (Cleveland Public Library Photograph Collection.)

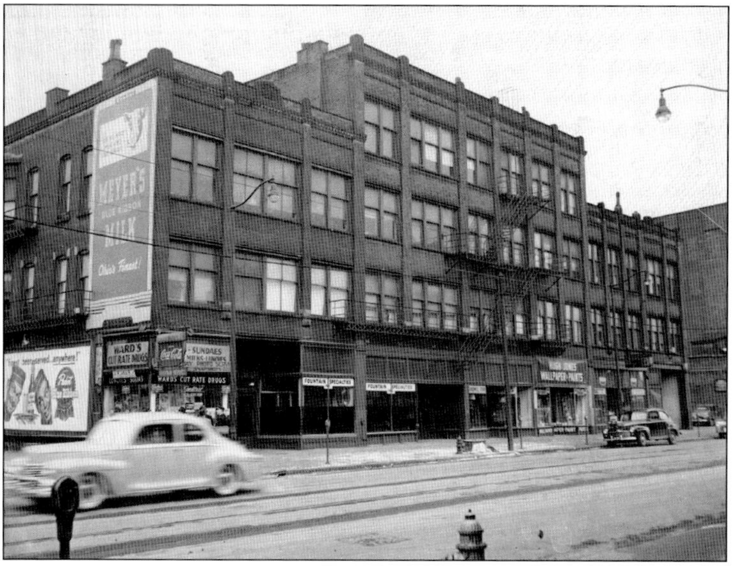

West Twenty-Fifth Street Storefronts, 1950. This 1950 view of 1714-1720 West Twenty-Fifth Street shows typical mixed-use buildings where retail shops operated at street level with rooming houses above. The site gained notoriety years earlier as the location of a tragic 1931 police shooting that claimed officer John Cleary's life in 1938. (Michael Schwartz Library Special Collections, Cleveland State University.)

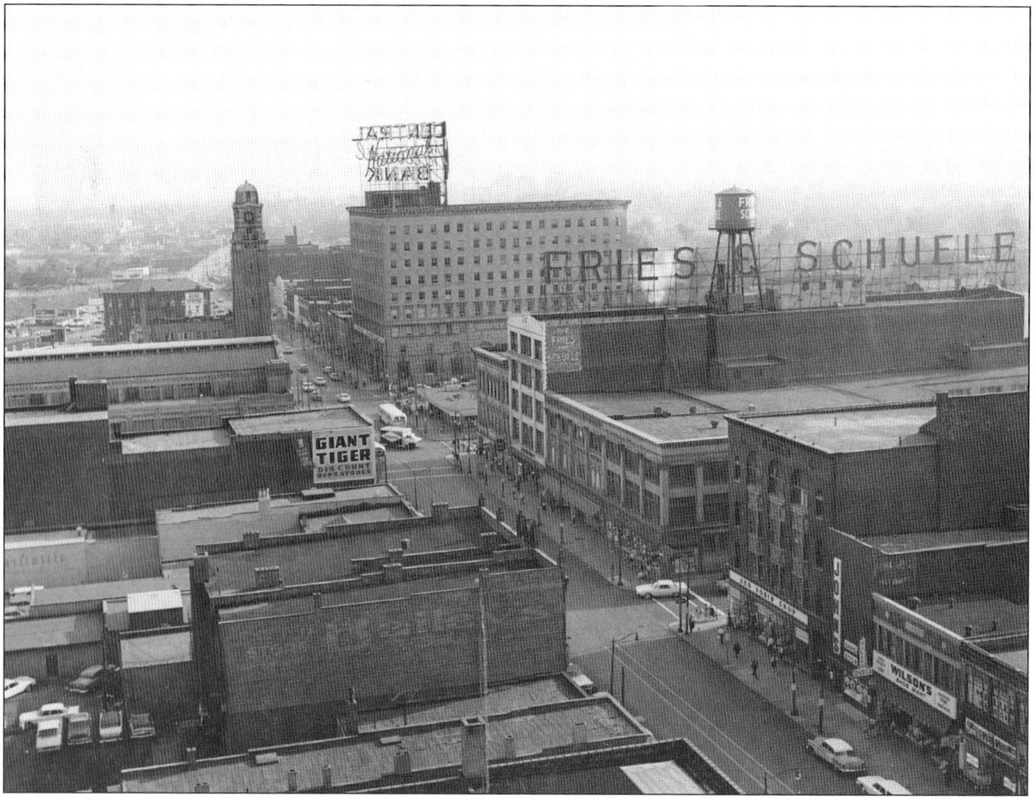

West Twenty-Fifth Street's Commercial Core, 1963. This elevated view south along West Twenty-Fifth Street captures the bustling retail corridor that defined Ohio City's commercial heart. Department stores and specialty shops line both sides of the street toward Lorain Avenue, with the West Side Market's clock tower visible in the distance. The scene shows both national chains and family businesses serving local and destination shoppers alike. (Cleveland Public Library Photograph Collection.)

Hidden Enterprise on Lorain, 1933. This seemingly ordinary storefront at 3702 Lorain Avenue concealed a secret gambling club behind an unmarked door. The photograph, with its telling arrow marking the entrance, documents the neighborhood's less visible enterprises during the Depression era. (Michael Schwartz Library Special Collections, Cleveland State University.)

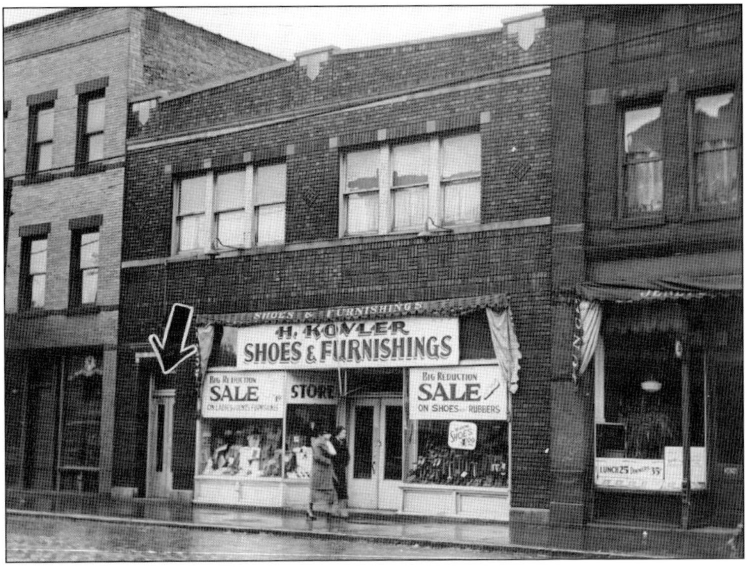

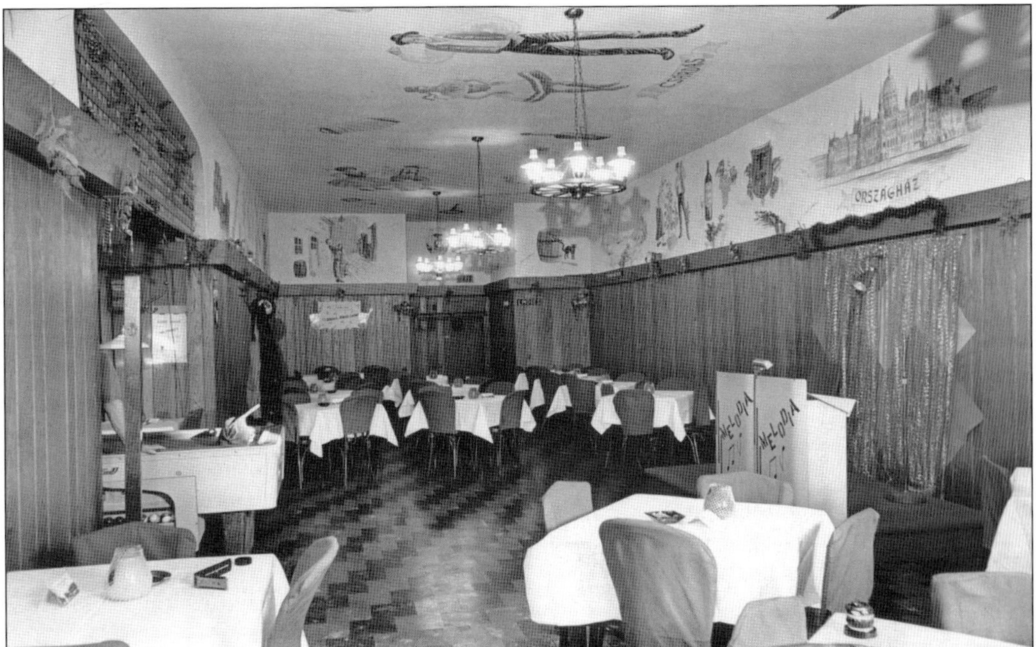

Papp's Hungarian Heritage, 1968. This interior view of Papp's Bar and Restaurant at West 41st and Lorain Avenue captures a classic ethnic establishment. The space features traditional Hungarian murals above wood paneling, with tables arranged around a small stage, reflecting the neighborhood's strong cultural connections. (Michael Schwartz Library Special Collections, Cleveland State University.)

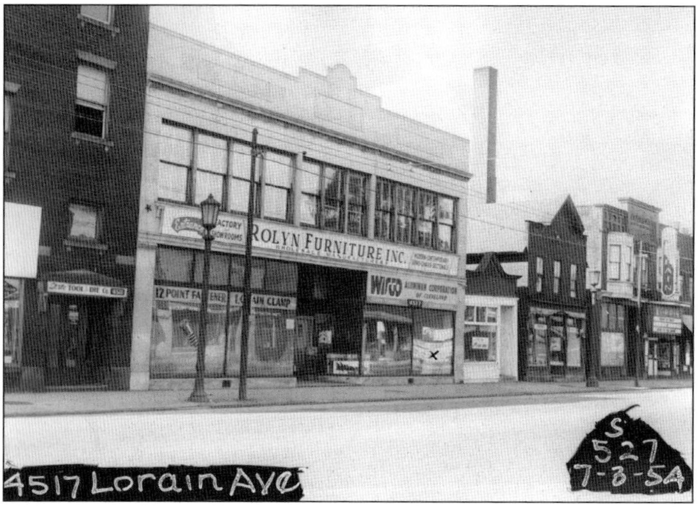

Lorain Avenue's Business Corridor, 1954. This view of 4517 Lorain Avenue, near Ohio City's boundary with the Detroit-Shoreway neighborhood, shows how the commercial district extended well beyond West Twenty-Fifth Street. Small businesses lined this stretch of Lorain, creating a continuous shopping corridor that served residents from multiple west side communities. (Cleveland Public Library Photograph Collection.)

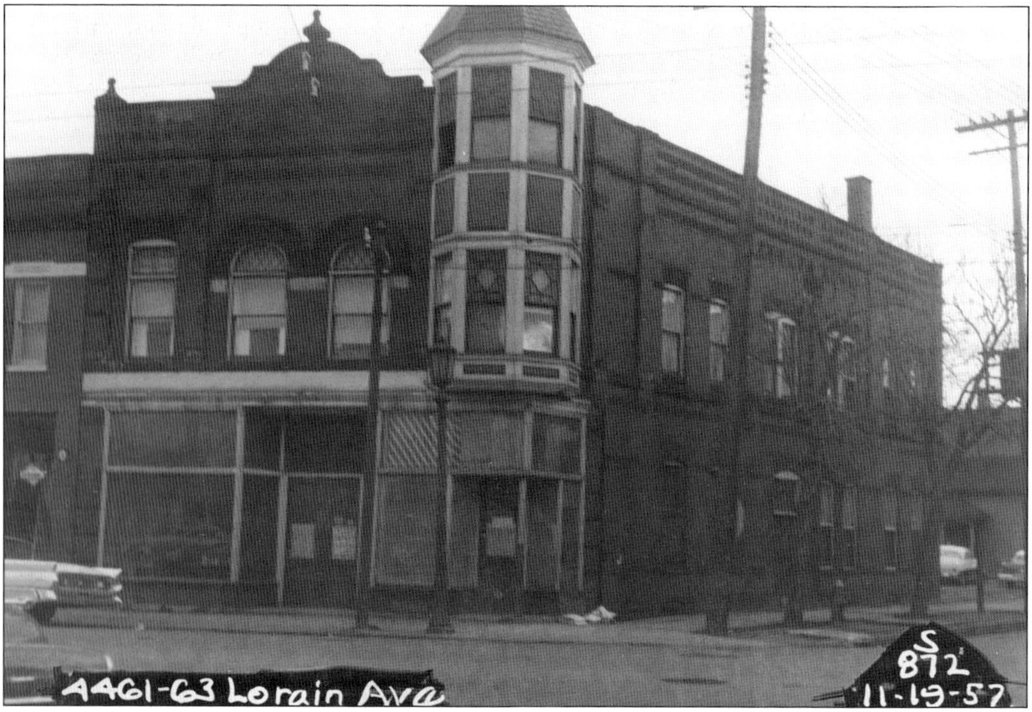

Lorain Avenue's Transformation. This 1957 view of 4461-4463 Lorain Avenue shows a weathered storefront with residential units above. The building's successful renovation into a modern retail space reflects the ongoing revitalization of Ohio City's historic commercial structures. (Cleveland Public Library Photograph Collection.)

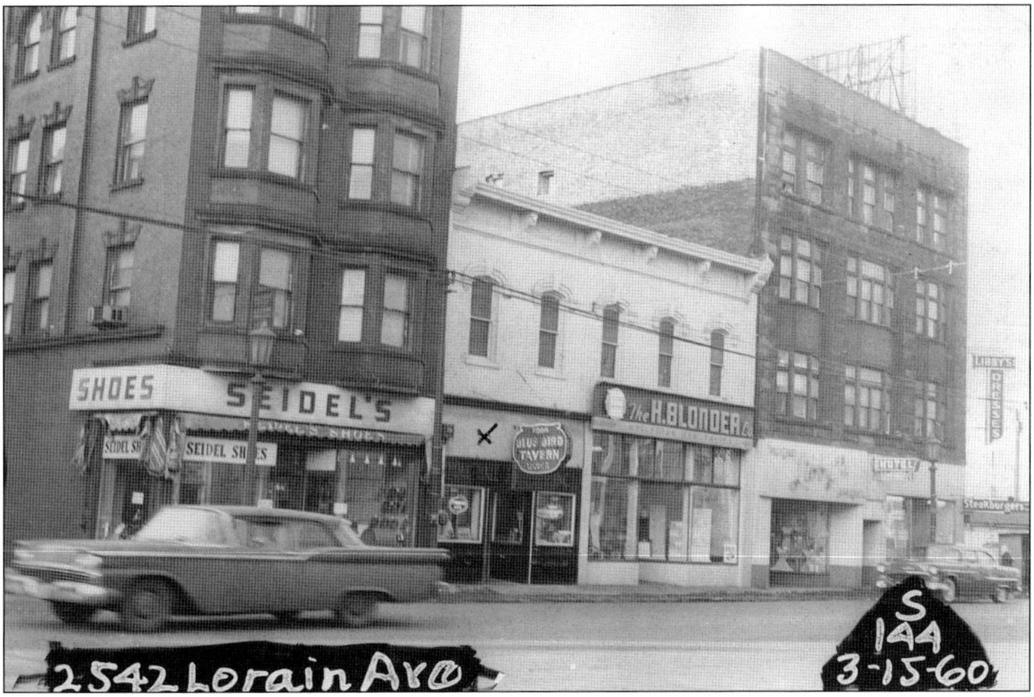

LORAIN AVENUE COMMERCE, 1960. This view west of West Twenty-Fifth Street shows the continuation of Ohio City's bustling business district along Lorain Avenue. The surviving buildings, with their distinctive storefronts, represent the seamless extension of commercial activity beyond the West Side Market area, serving neighborhood shoppers through generations. (Cleveland Public Library Photograph Collection.)

LORAIN AVENUE'S VITALITY, 1963. This stretch of Lorain Avenue captures the thriving business district that extends through Ohio City. Storefronts and sidewalks buzz with activity, showing how neighborhood commerce flourished well beyond the West Side Market area during the early 1960s. (Cleveland Public Library Photograph Collection.)

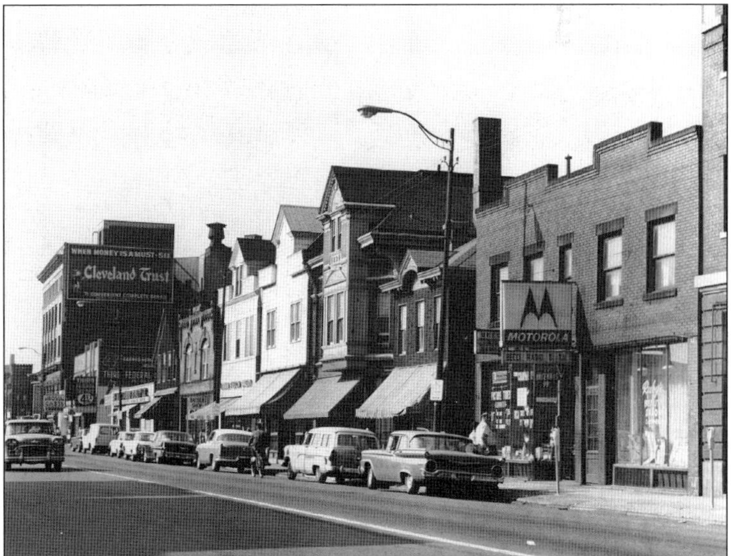

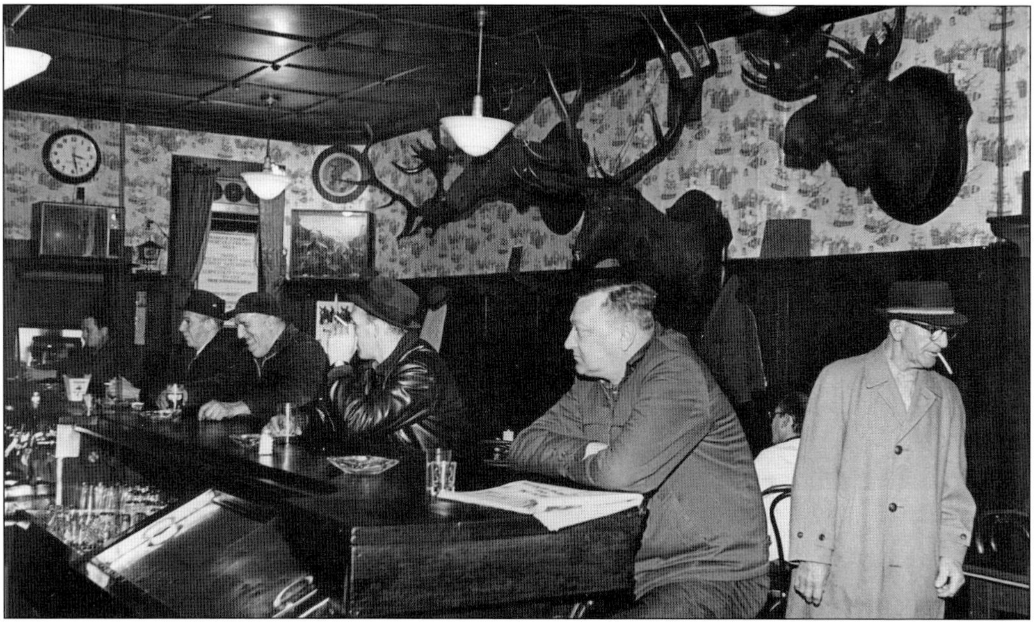

Market Street's Historic Bar, 1968. These February 1968 photographs capture the Market Tavern at 2516 Market Street, now part of Great Lakes Brewing Company. The first image shows workers enjoying an after-shift drink at 3:30 p.m., the well-worn bar, and cigarette smoke, capturing a typical afternoon scene. The second features Fred Dietz seated in what was known as "Eliot Ness's chair"—a reminder of the establishment's connection to Cleveland's famous safety director, who frequented the tavern. For well over a century, this building has served as a neighborhood gathering spot, reflecting the close relationship between local bars and nearby industries. Today, its historic bar continues to welcome guests as part of Great Lakes' taproom, maintaining the space's social heritage. (Both, Michael Schwartz Library Special Collections, Cleveland State University.)

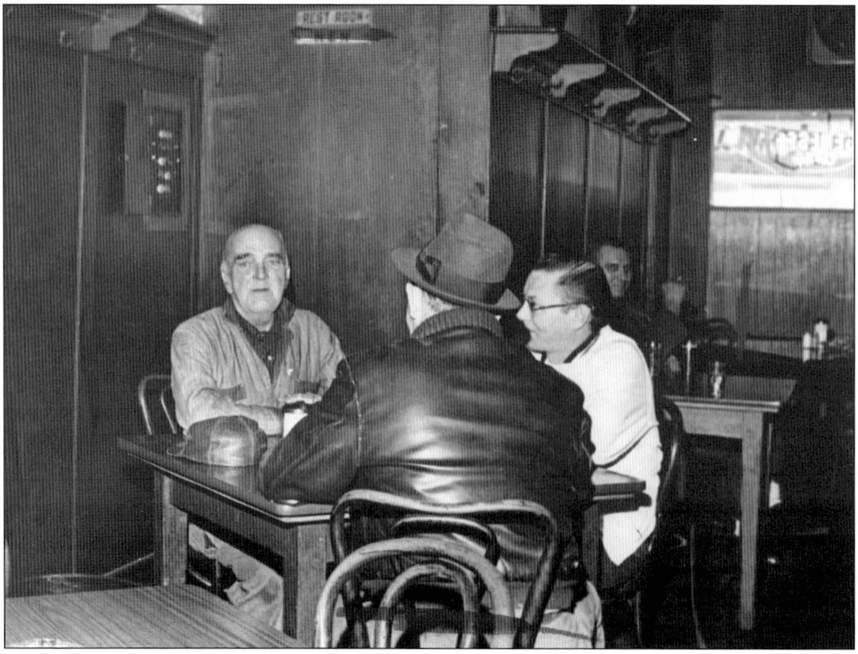

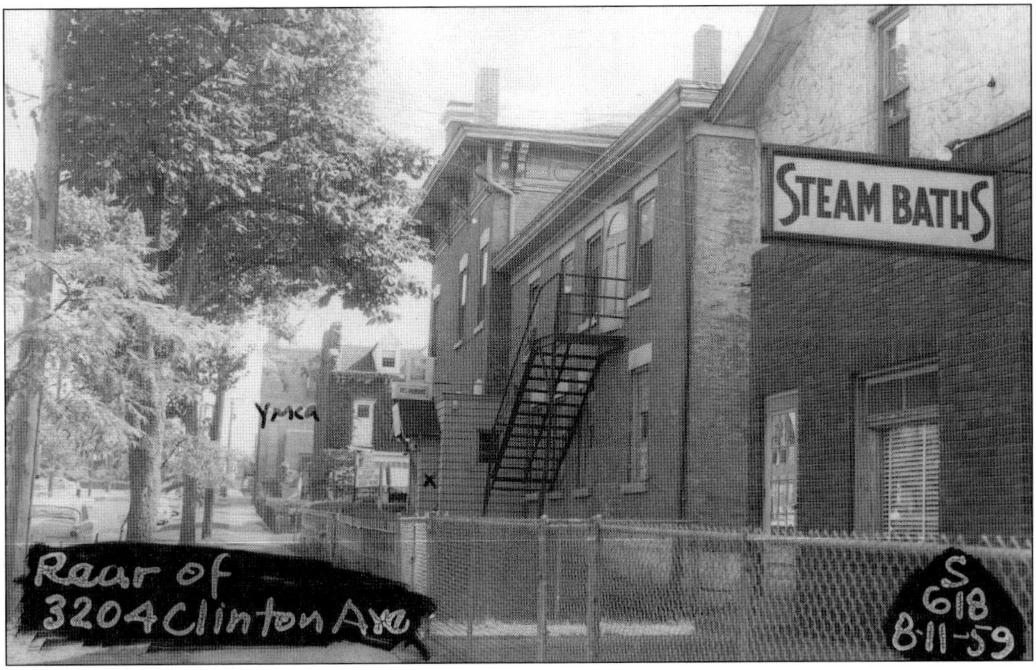

Hidden History, 3204 Clinton Avenue, 1959. While the main house at 3204 Clinton served as Dr. Frederick Taylor's residence in the early 1900s, this rear building on West Thirty-Second Street had its own colorful history. Photographed here as a steam bath establishment, the space would later house the Clinton Bar and eventually become part of the Christian Fellowship Church. (Cleveland Public Library Photograph Collection.)

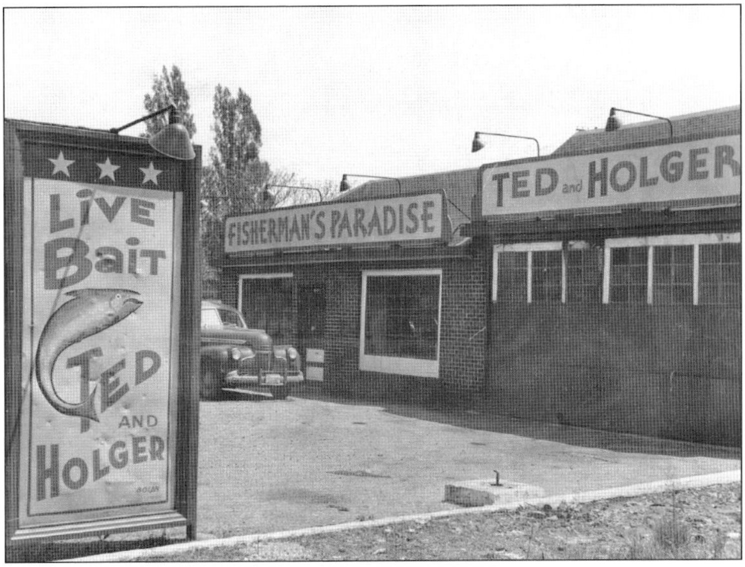

From Fishing to Food Equipment, 1943. This view of 4307 Detroit Avenue captures Ted & Holger's Fisherman Paradise, a neighborhood spot where locals picked up bait before heading to Edgewater Park. Today, the site houses Biro Manufacturing Co., a leading food equipment supplier. (Cleveland Press Collection, Michael Schwartz Library Special Collections, Cleveland State University.)

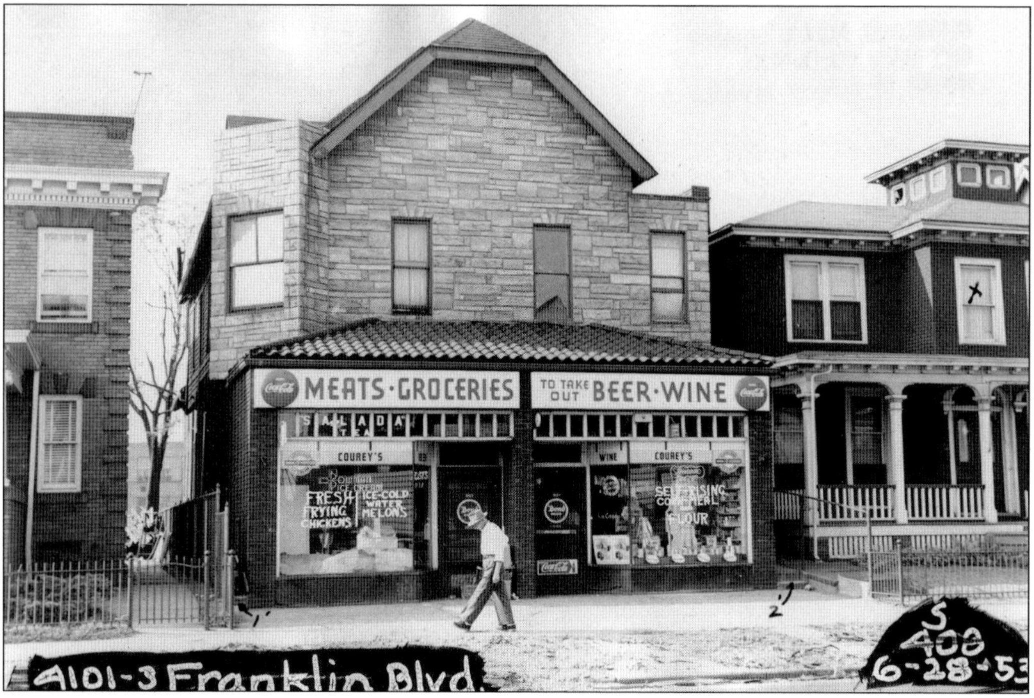

CORNER STORE CONVENIENCE, 1953. This neighborhood grocery at 4101 Franklin Boulevard exemplifies the small shops that served Ohio City's residential areas. Nestled among homes, these local stores provided essential goods within walking distance, creating a seamless blend of commercial and residential life typical of mid-century urban neighborhoods. (Cleveland Public Library Photograph Collection.)

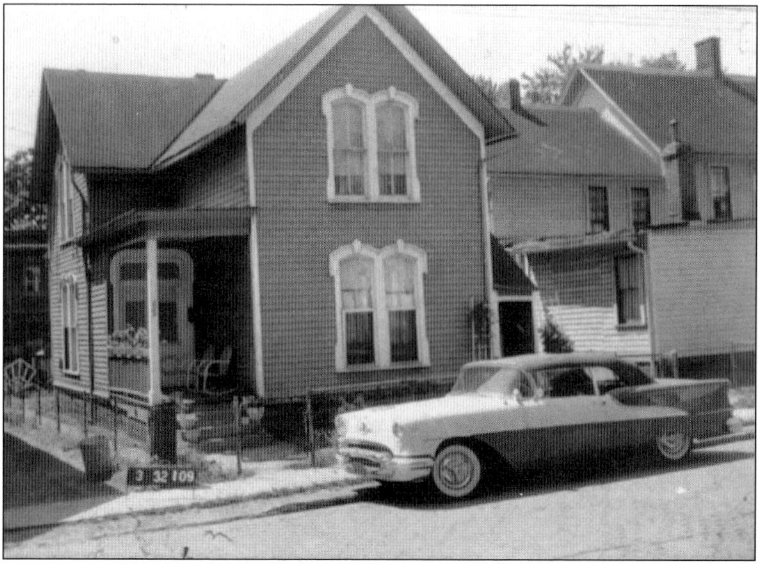

THE KIDD HOUSE, 1957. This modest home south of Franklin Boulevard at 3059 Mabel Court was the birthplace of Rear Adm. Isaac Campbell Kidd, who died heroically on the USS Arizona's bridge during the Pearl Harbor attack. The highest-ranking casualty that day, Kidd became the first US Navy flag officer killed in World War II. (The Cuyahoga County Archives)

Seven

CHALLENGES AND CHANGE 1940s–1970s

The Great Depression deeply affected Ohio City, with institutions like the Martin de Porres House of Hospitality providing crucial support to residents across social classes. The neighborhood's recovery from economic hardship was soon disrupted by World War II, which strained families and reshaped local industry. In the post-war decades, Ohio City's traditional fabric began to fray as housing conditions deteriorated, crime rates surged, and demographic patterns shifted.

Many of the neighborhood's 19th-century homes, already subdivided into multiple units during harder times, faced mounting maintenance challenges. Some properties fell into neglect as original owners aged or moved away, while others were poorly maintained by absentee landlords. The deteriorating housing stock became symbolic of the broader urban challenges facing many American cities. Rising crime—ranging from property theft and vandalism to assaults and robberies—instilled fear in the community. Concerns about personal safety became a daily reality, contributing to the neighborhood's declining reputation and further accelerating the flight of middle-class families to the suburbs.

The 1950s and 1960s brought dramatic changes as suburban development drew families away from urban neighborhoods. Local businesses felt the impact, with some relocating to the suburbs while others adapted to serve the changing demographics. The West Side Market remained a commercial anchor, though it too faced challenges as supermarkets and shopping centers pulled customers away from traditional vendors.

New arrivals brought both opportunities and tensions. Working-class families, including Appalachian and Puerto Rican immigrants, found affordable housing in Ohio City's aging buildings. However, rising crime rates and deteriorating infrastructure fueled tensions between longtime residents and newcomers. By the 1970s, early signs of gentrification appeared as young professionals and artists, drawn by the neighborhood's historic architecture and proximity to downtown, began to move in. While some residents welcomed the neighborhood's gradual revival, others feared displacement and the erosion of Ohio City's close-knit character. This clash of perspectives marked the beginning of a complex transformation that would shape the neighborhood's future for decades to come.

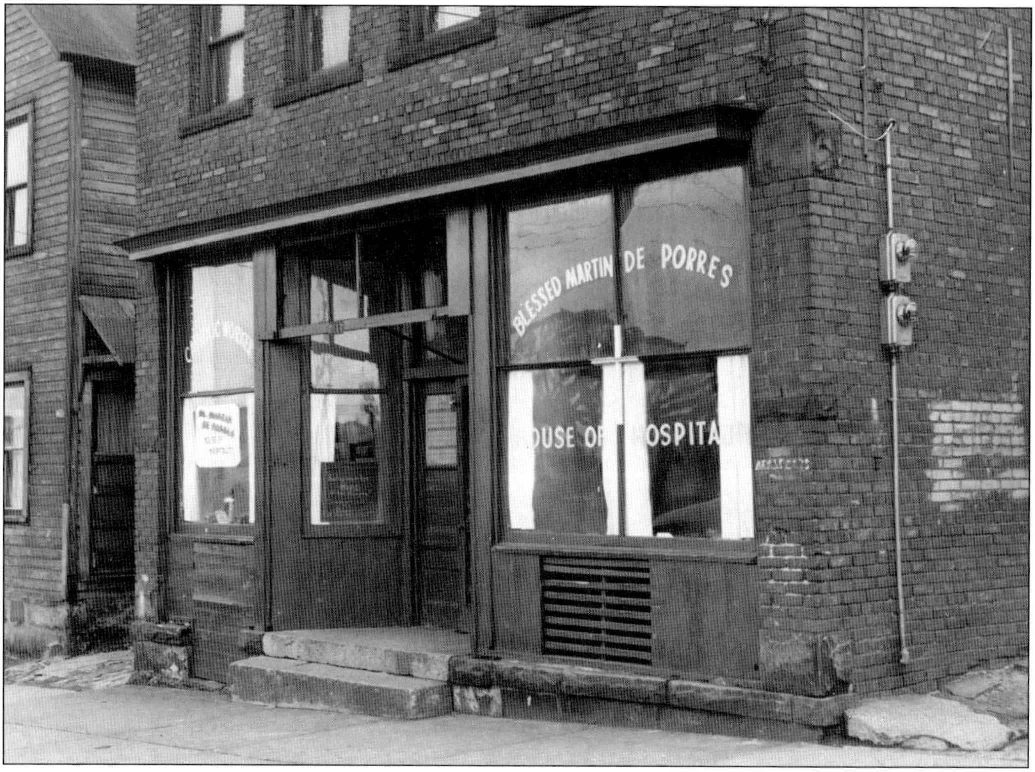

SERVING HOPE DURING HARD TIMES, 1938. These photographs document the Martin de Porres House of Hospitality at 2305 Franklin Boulevard, which provided meals to those in need during the Great Depression. The exterior view shows the modest building that served as a beacon of hope for struggling families. Inside, the second image captures a diverse group gathered at long tables for dinner—both young and old, some surprisingly well-dressed, reflecting how the Depression affected people across social classes. Named for Martin de Porres, a Dominican brother known for his work with the poor, the facility represented Ohio City's tradition of community support during difficult times. Though the building is no longer standing, it symbolizes the neighborhood's history of caring for its most vulnerable residents. (Both, Cleveland Press Collection, Michael Schwartz Library Special Collections, Cleveland State University.)

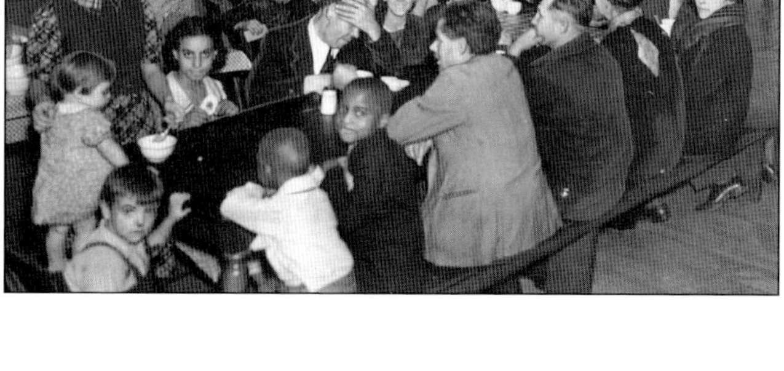

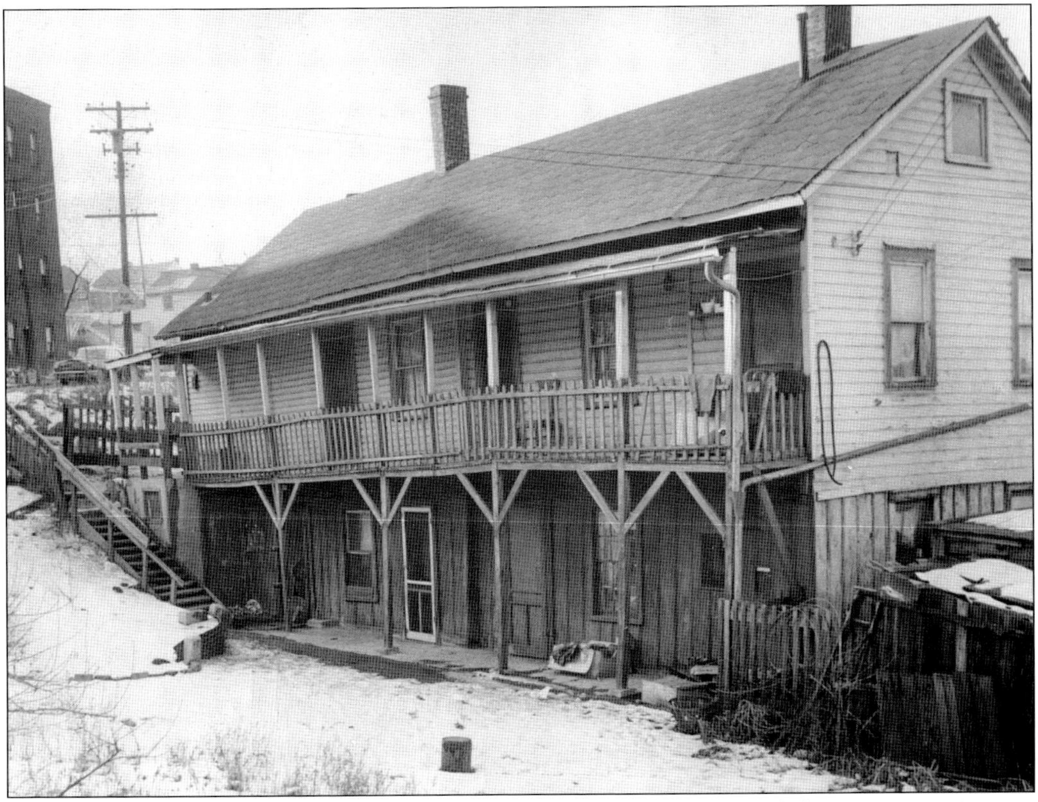

URBAN DECLINE ON FRANKLIN HILL, 1958. This deteriorating multi-family home at West Twenty-Second and Franklin Hill exemplifies the housing challenges Ohio City faced in the postwar era. Once-grand houses, subdivided into multiple units during harder times, often fell into disrepair as original owners moved to the suburbs and maintenance declined. (Cleveland Press Collection, Michael Schwartz Library Special Collections, Cleveland State University.)

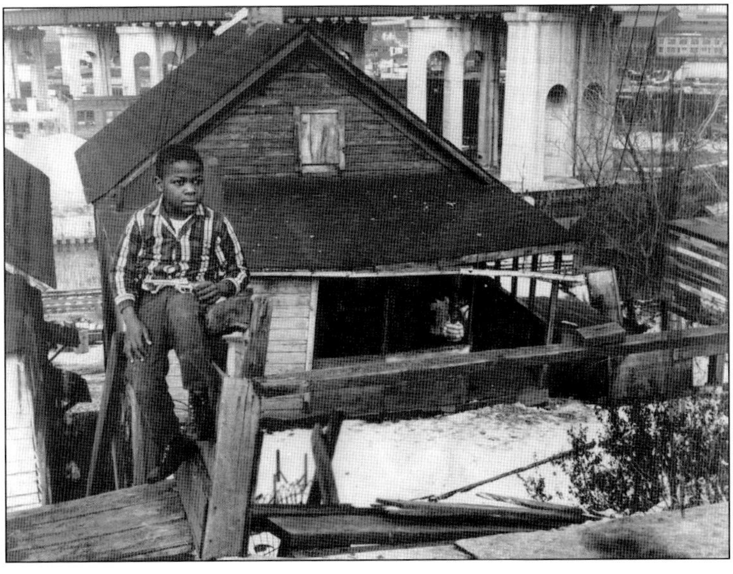

CHILDHOOD AMID CHANGE, 1959. A child sits on a railing outside a deteriorating home, with the Cuyahoga River visible in the background. This poignant scene captures both the human dimension of Ohio City's housing challenges and the neighborhood's enduring connection to the industrial valley below. (Michael Schwartz Library Special Collections, Cleveland State University.)

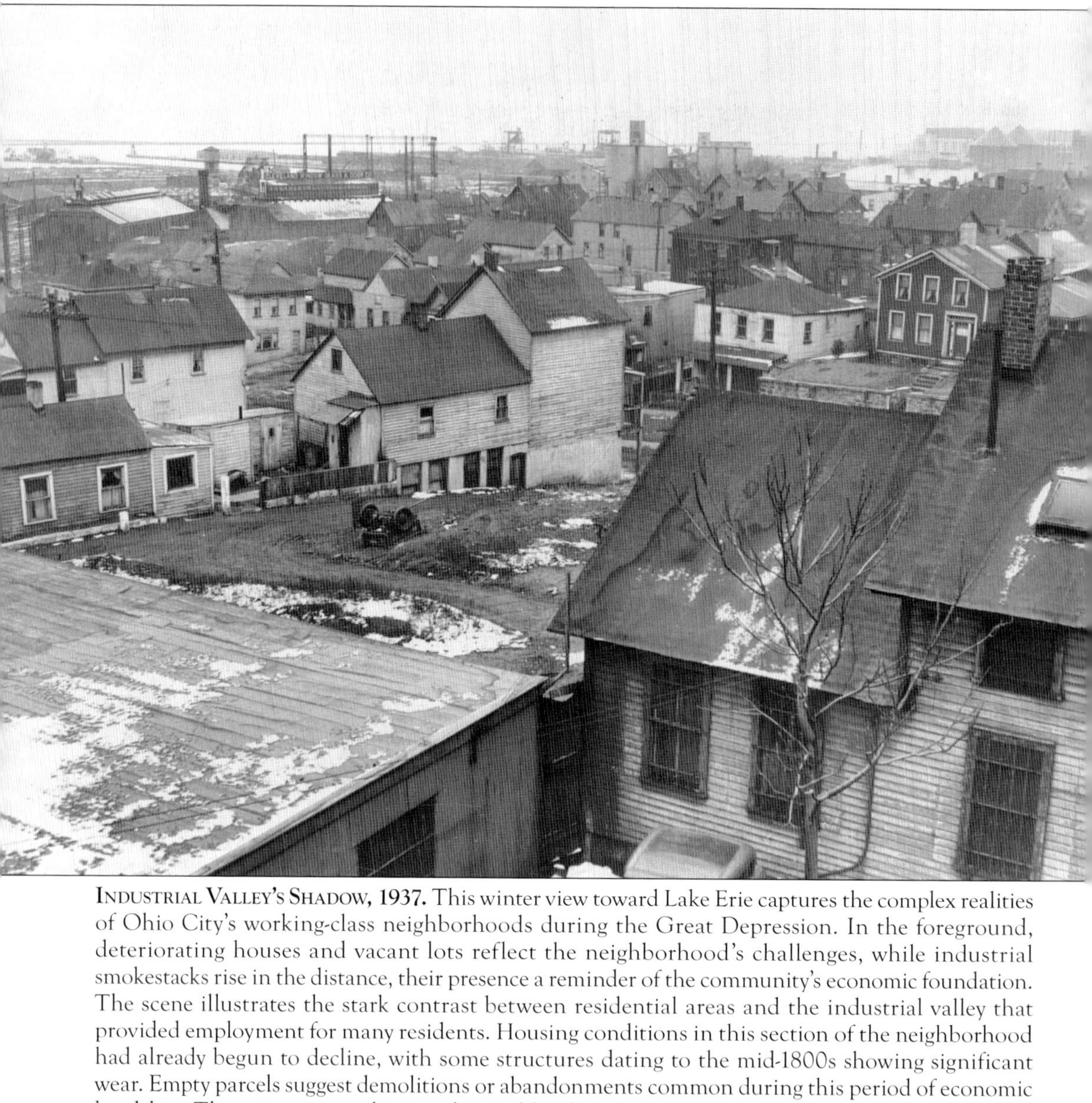

INDUSTRIAL VALLEY'S SHADOW, 1937. This winter view toward Lake Erie captures the complex realities of Ohio City's working-class neighborhoods during the Great Depression. In the foreground, deteriorating houses and vacant lots reflect the neighborhood's challenges, while industrial smokestacks rise in the distance, their presence a reminder of the community's economic foundation. The scene illustrates the stark contrast between residential areas and the industrial valley that provided employment for many residents. Housing conditions in this section of the neighborhood had already begun to decline, with some structures dating to the mid-1800s showing significant wear. Empty parcels suggest demolitions or abandonments common during this period of economic hardship. The gritty atmosphere, enhanced by the winter setting, provides a vivid snapshot of urban conditions that would persist and worsen in the coming decades, eventually spurring both demolition and preservation efforts. (Michael Schwartz Library Special Collections, Cleveland State University.)

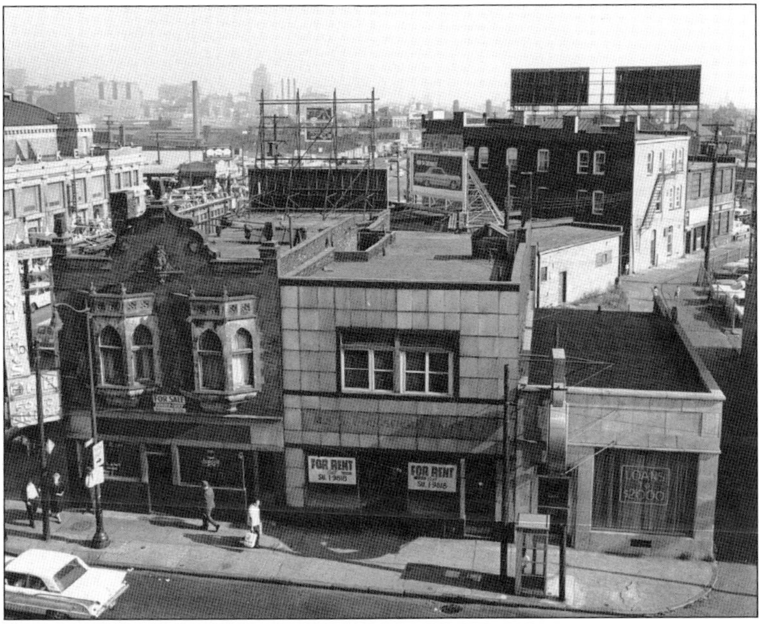

Signs of Change on West Twenty-Fifth, 1963. This elevated view of the 2000 block of West Twenty-Fifth Street shows the commercial district in transition. "For Rent" and "For Sale" signs reflect the challenges facing urban retailers as customers increasingly moved to suburban shopping areas. (Cleveland Public Library Photograph Collection.)

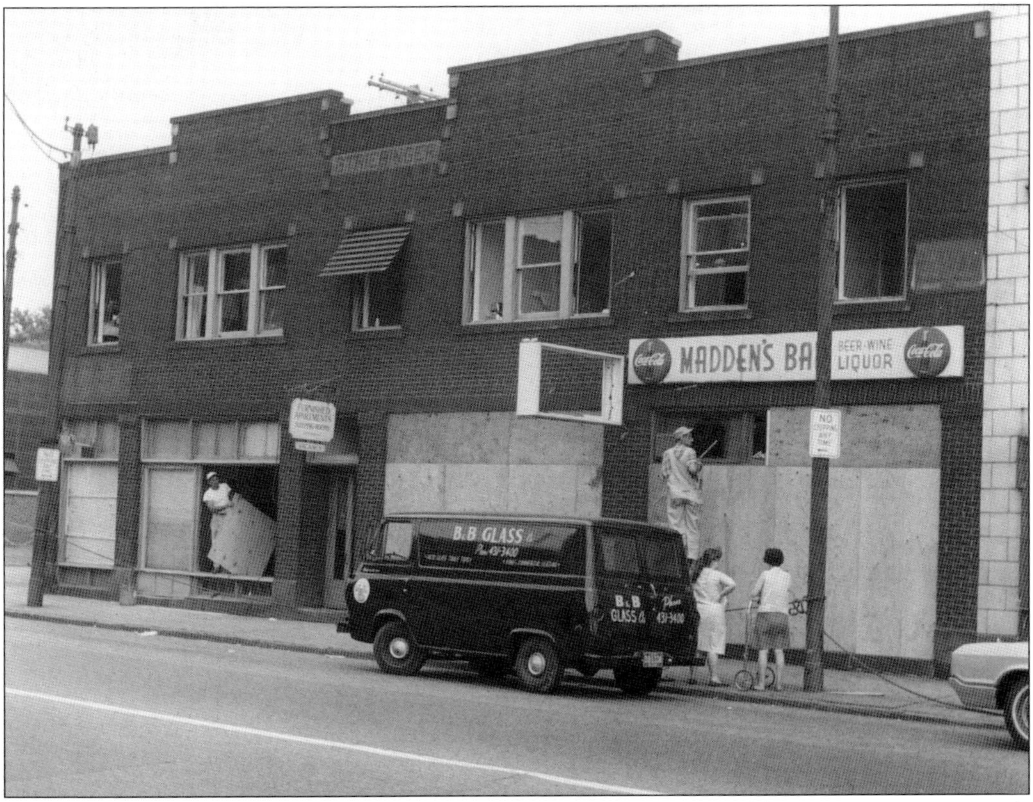

Detroit Avenue Decline, 1967. This view captures the Striebinger Building at West Twenty-Ninth and Detroit Avenue during its days as a run-down rooming house, with the adjacent Madden's Bar being boarded up. The scene reflects the deterioration of once-vital commercial buildings that defined Ohio City's street corners. (Cleveland Public Library Photograph Collection.)

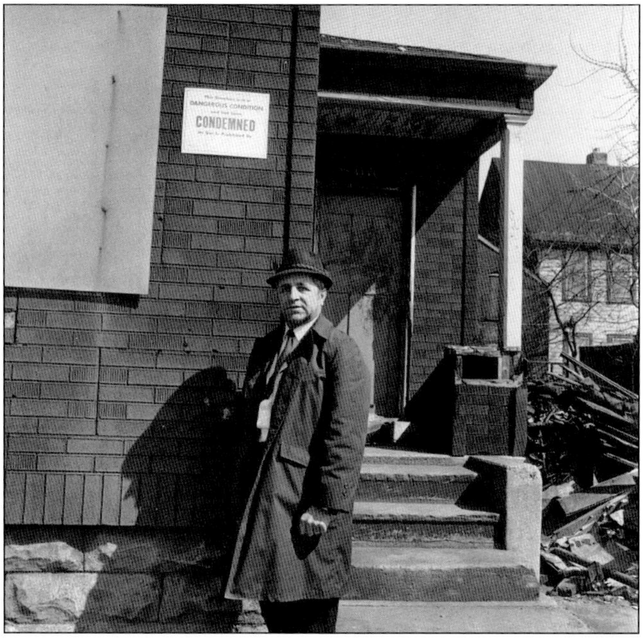

A Home's Final Days. This condemned house at 2025 West Nineteenth Street exemplifies the housing crisis facing Ohio City in the 1960s–1970s. This structure was ultimately demolished, and more than 40 years later, a new home was finally constructed on the site. (Cleveland Public Library Photograph Collection.)

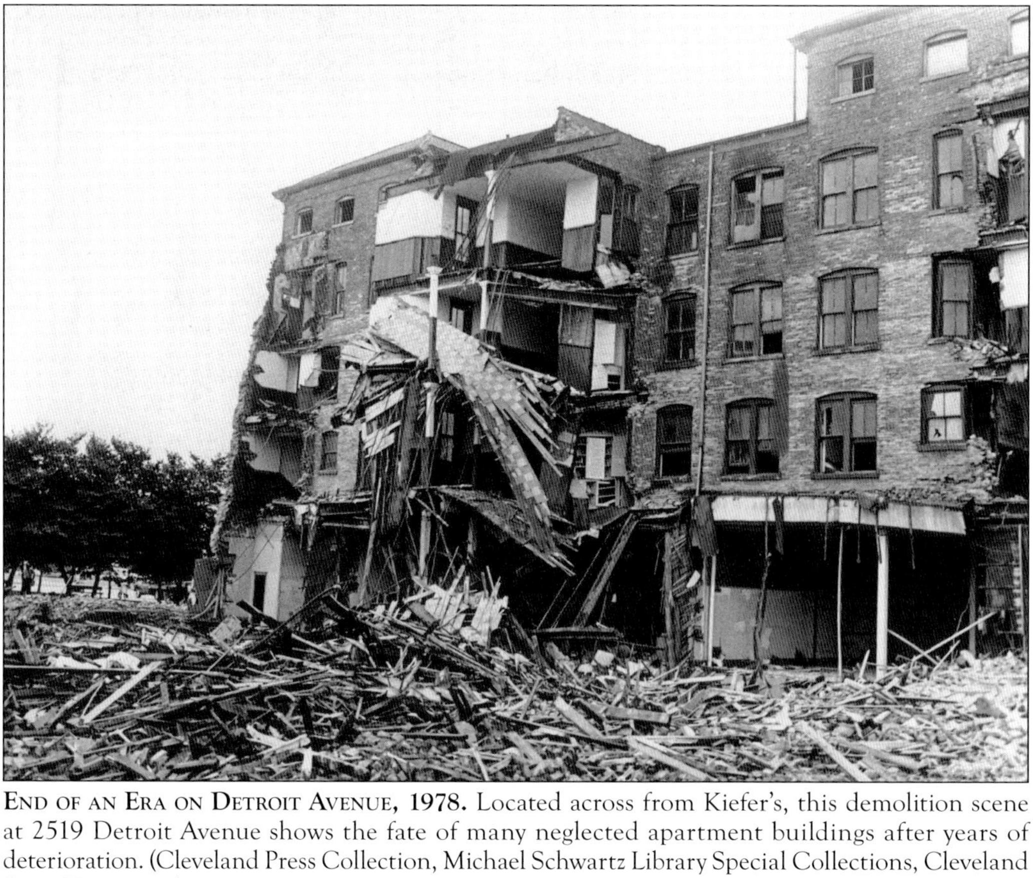

End of an Era on Detroit Avenue, 1978. Located across from Kiefer's, this demolition scene at 2519 Detroit Avenue shows the fate of many neglected apartment buildings after years of deterioration. (Cleveland Press Collection, Michael Schwartz Library Special Collections, Cleveland State University.)

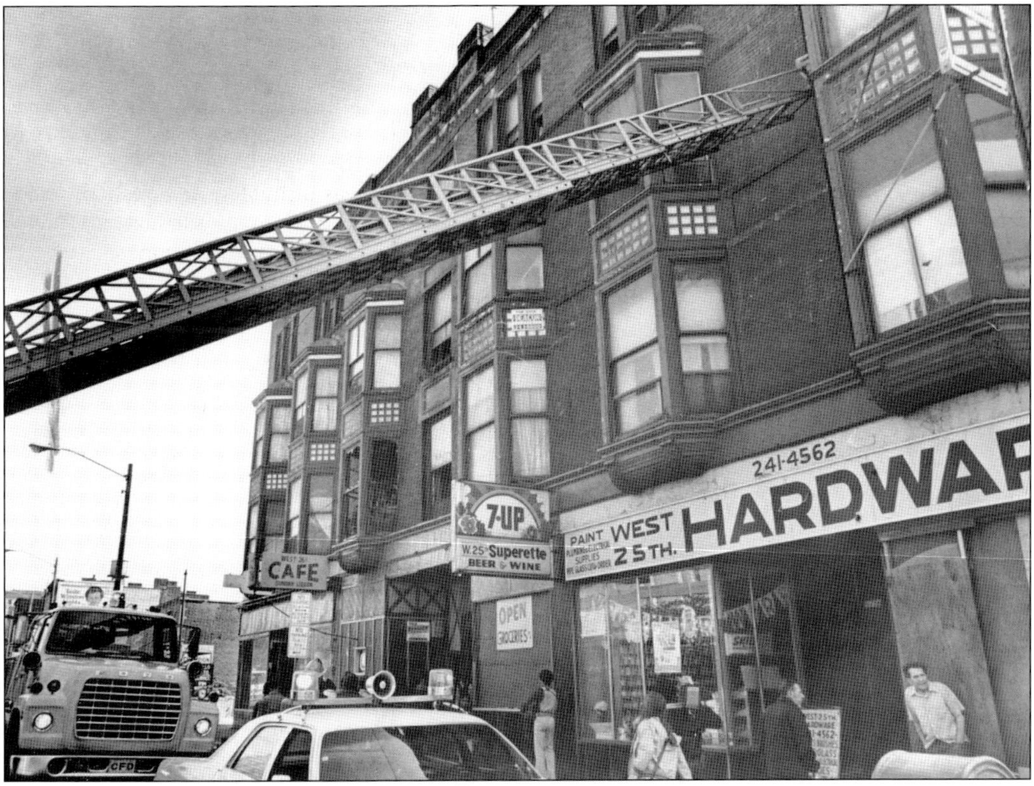

TROUBLED TIMES AT THE FRANKLIN HOTEL, 1979. Fire trucks respond to a blaze at 1762 West Twenty-Fifth Street's Franklin Hotel, a building long associated with neighborhood problems. The incident, coming just three months after a murder on the premises, highlighted the ongoing challenges faced by this deteriorating rooming house. (Cleveland Press Collection, Michael Schwartz Library Special Collections, Cleveland State University.)

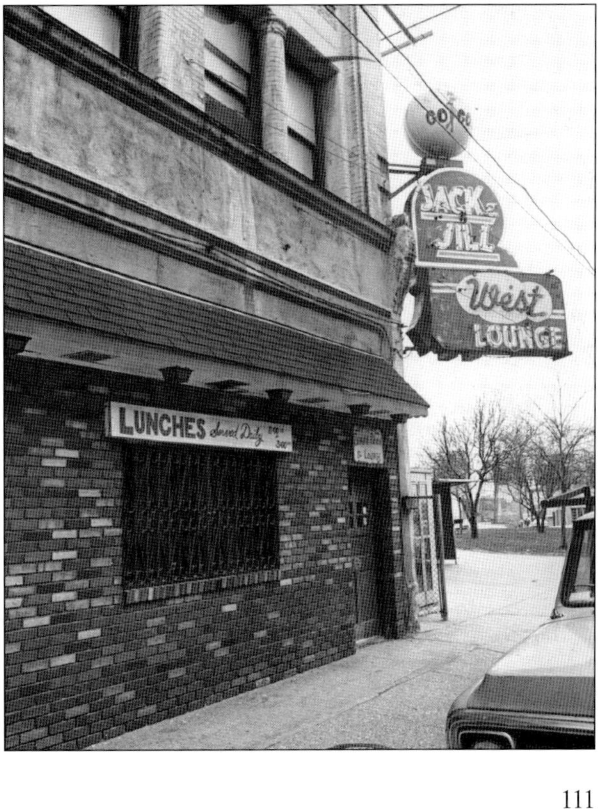

DEATH AT CHRISTY'S LOUNGE, 1975. This view shows the former Jack & Jill Lounge at 2516 Detroit Avenue, later renamed Christy's. The go-go bar, located near St. Malachi's Church, gained notoriety as mobster Shondor Birns's regular haunt before his death in a car bombing outside the establishment on March 29, 1975. (Cleveland Press Collection, Michael Schwartz Library Special Collections, Cleveland State University.)

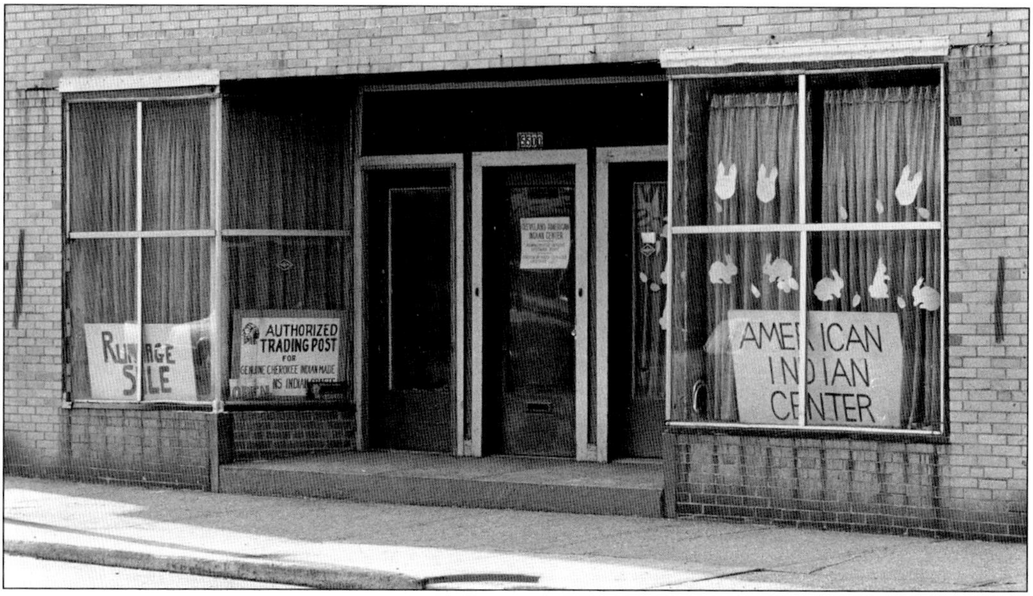

CLEVELAND'S AMERICAN INDIAN CENTER, 1969. The first photograph features the American Indian Center's building at 5500 Lorain Avenue, established to support a growing urban Native American population that had relocated from reservations. Facing widespread discrimination in housing and employment, many sought support through the West Side Development Corporation (WSDC), which coordinated resources to help families adapt to city life. The movement found early support at Ohio City's St. John's Episcopal Church, where the community first gathered to organize. The second image captures activist Russell Means during a protest at Cleveland's "Super Sesqui" reenactment of Moses Cleaveland's landing. Means was instrumental in establishing the Cleveland American Indian Center and challenged historical narratives glorifying colonization while helping create vital resources for Native Americans facing discrimination in housing and employment. (Both, Cleveland Press Collection, Michael Schwartz Library Special Collections, Cleveland State University.)

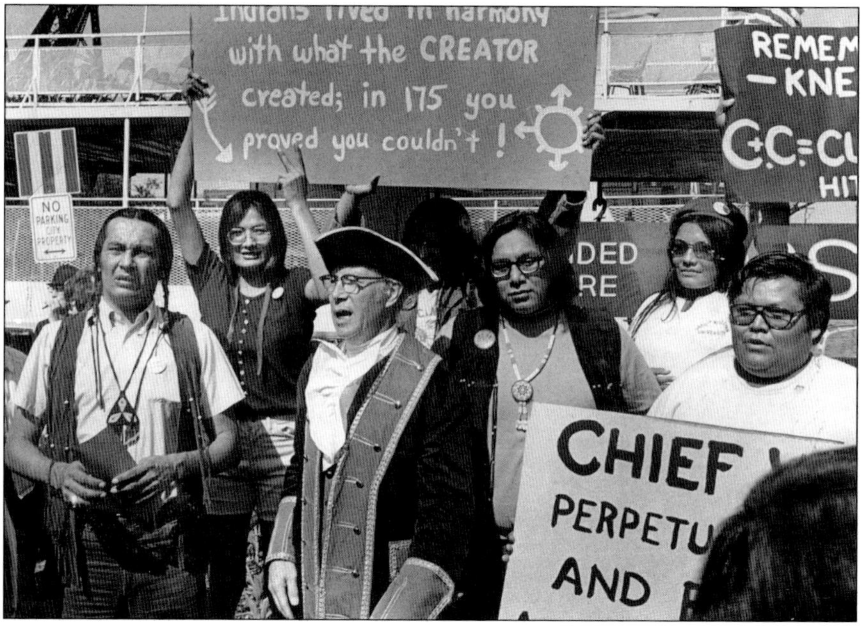

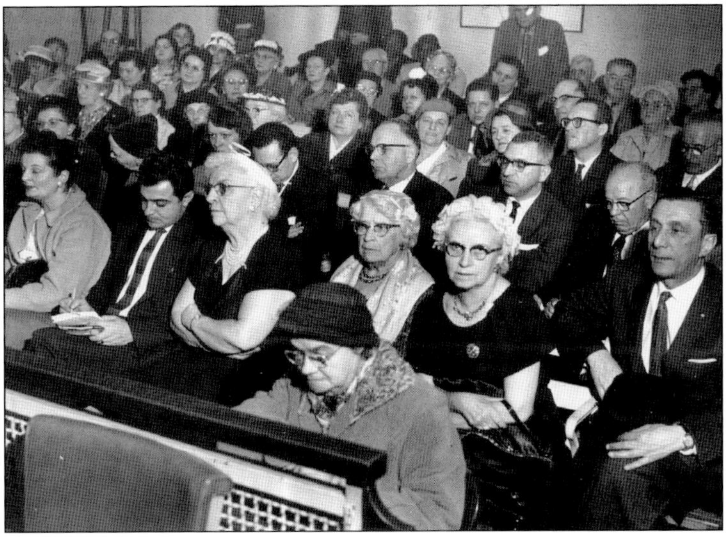

Community Voices, April 1961. This image captures Ohio City residents participating in a public hearing about the Lakeview Housing Project. The meeting reflected growing tensions between residents and housing authorities as the neighborhood grappled with changing demographics and urban policies. (Cleveland Press Collection, Michael Schwartz Library Special Collections, Cleveland State University.)

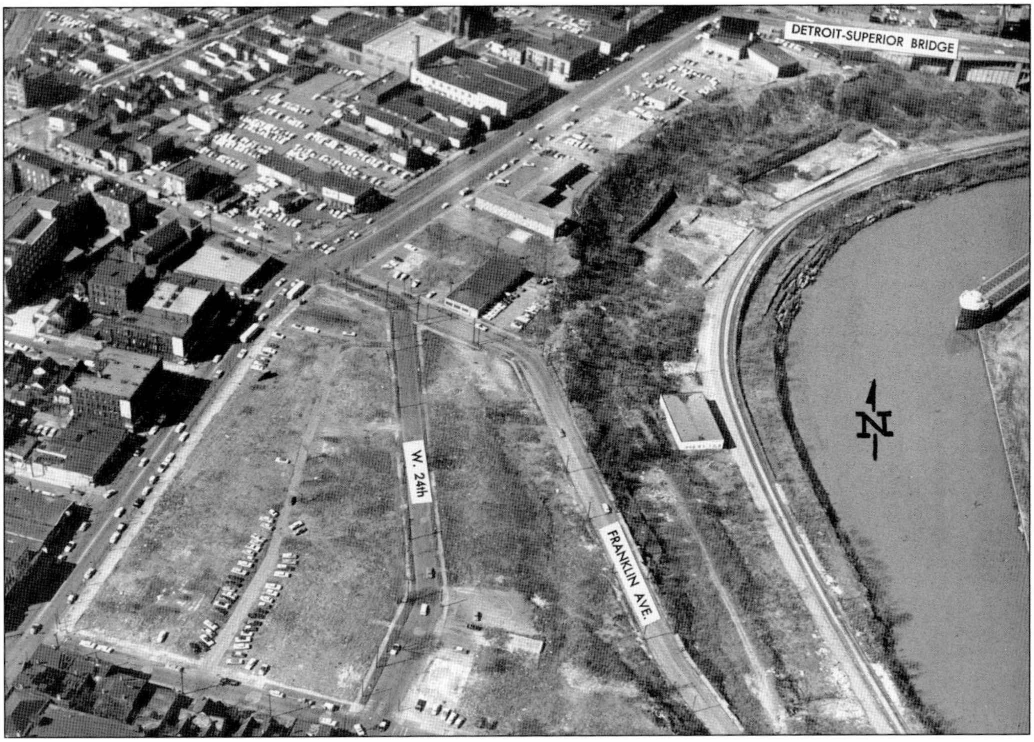

Urban Vantage Point. This aerial view shows the Lakeview Terrace site and surrounding vacant land, illustrating both the public housing complex's prominent position overlooking the Cuyahoga Valley and the neighborhood's shifting development patterns. The cleared parcels reflect the era's impact on Ohio City's urban fabric. (Cleveland Press Collection, Michael Schwartz Library Special Collections, Cleveland State University.)

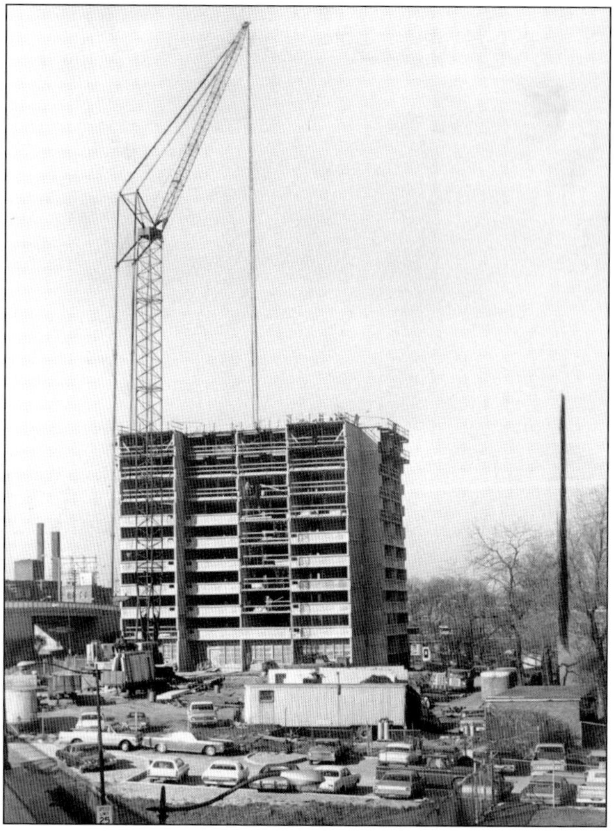

Lakeview Terrace Expands, 1972. Construction is underway on the high-rise addition to the Lakeview Terrace public housing complex. The expansion marked a significant change to the original 1930s development, adding vertical density to the historic hillside site overlooking the Cuyahoga River. (Cleveland Press Collection, Michael Schwartz Library Special Collections, Cleveland State University.)

Tenants Demand Safety, 1974. Residents of Cleveland Metropolitan Housing Authority properties protest at West Twenty-Fifth Street, calling attention to security concerns and rising crime in their communities. The demonstration highlighted growing tensions between public housing tenants and management over safety and living conditions. (Cleveland Press Collection, Michael Schwartz Library Special Collections, Cleveland State University.)

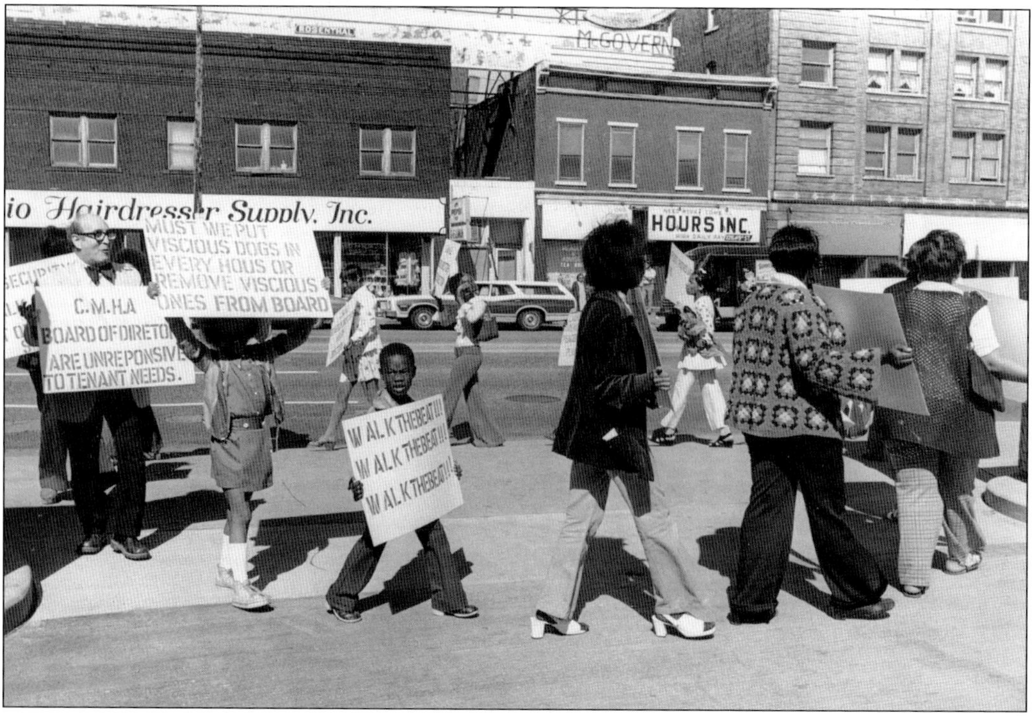

Eight

Renaissance and Revival

1970s–Present

Ohio City's renaissance began in the late 1960s when residents and community leaders recognized the value of its historic architecture and unique urban character. The 1968 formation of the Ohio City Community Development Association marked a turning point, as preservationists began working to protect and restore the neighborhood's architectural heritage. Early pioneers like Bruce Hedderson and Bruce Wade demonstrated how 19th-century homes could be successfully renovated, inspiring others to invest in the area's historic properties.

The 1970s brought new energy to the commercial district. The transformation of Market Street's historic buildings set the tone, with restaurants like Heck's and Ohio City Tavern drawing suburban diners back to the neighborhood. The 1988 opening of Great Lakes Brewing Company in the former Schlather bottling plant sparked a craft brewing renaissance that would eventually make Ohio City a destination for beer enthusiasts. Meanwhile, the neighborhood's historic churches maintained their architectural grandeur and spiritual presence, with their spires still defining the skyline. St. Ignatius High School continues its tradition of academic and athletic excellence, remaining a prestigious Catholic institution and sports powerhouse.

The area around West Twenty-Ninth Street, now known as Hingetown, played a significant role in Cleveland's LGBTQ+ history. From the 1970s through the 1990s, it served as a haven for the gay community, hosting the city's first Pride parade in 1989 and housing important community organizations. This legacy is now commemorated with an Ohio Historical Marker, while the district continues to evolve with new businesses and housing.

Recent decades have brought dramatic changes through both preservation and new development. Historic homes have been carefully restored, while contemporary apartment buildings have risen near the Market District. The neighborhood has attracted young professionals, artists, and entrepreneurs while maintaining its diverse character through various community organizations. Today, Ohio City exemplifies how historic preservation can work alongside new development to create a vibrant urban community that honors its past while embracing the future.

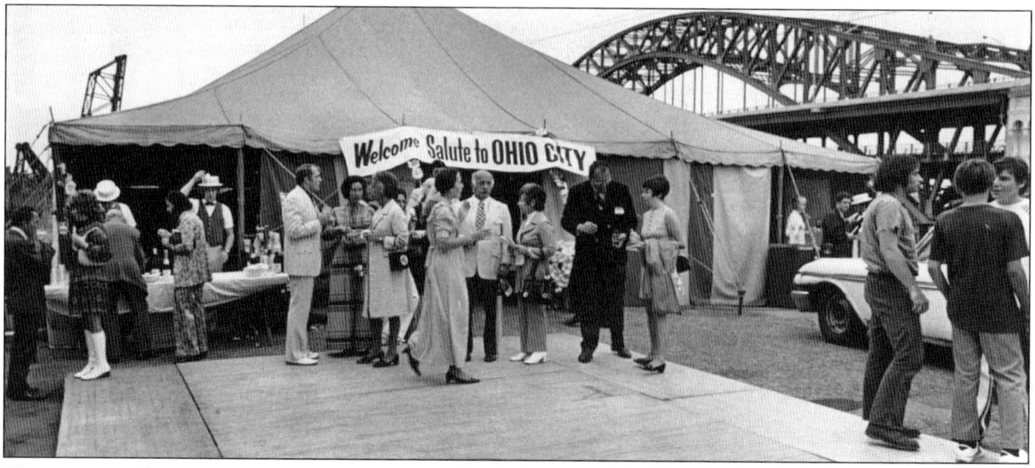

Community Pride on Display, 1971. This view from the Superior Viaduct captures a "Salute to Ohio City" celebration where 400 tour participants gathered under tents on September 12, 1971. The event demonstrated growing neighborhood pride and public interest in Ohio City's preservation movement. (Cleveland Press Collection, Michael Schwartz Library Special Collections, Cleveland State University.)

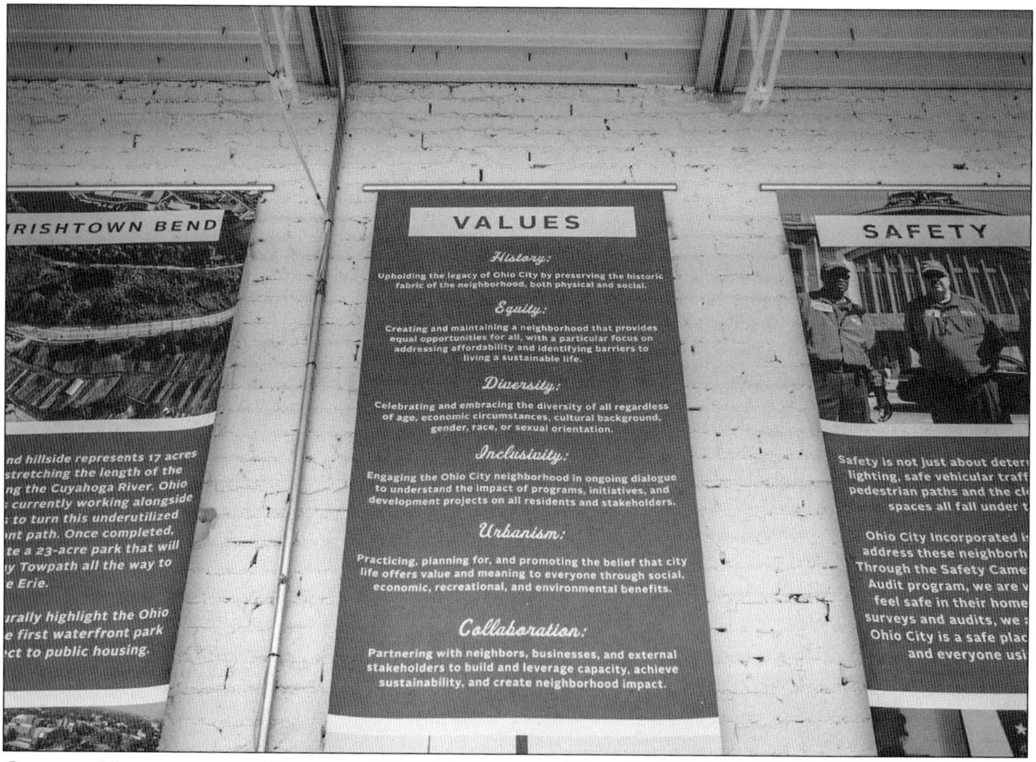

Guiding Neighborhood Growth. These banners at Ohio City Incorporated offices (OCI) reflect the organization's mission to balance preservation with development. As the area's community development corporation since 1978, OCI promotes housing assistance, business attraction, and cultural events to enhance the neighborhood's vitality, serving as stewards of Ohio City's ongoing renaissance. This image was captured in 2020. (Photograph by Adam Jaenke, Cleveland Public Library Photograph Collection.)

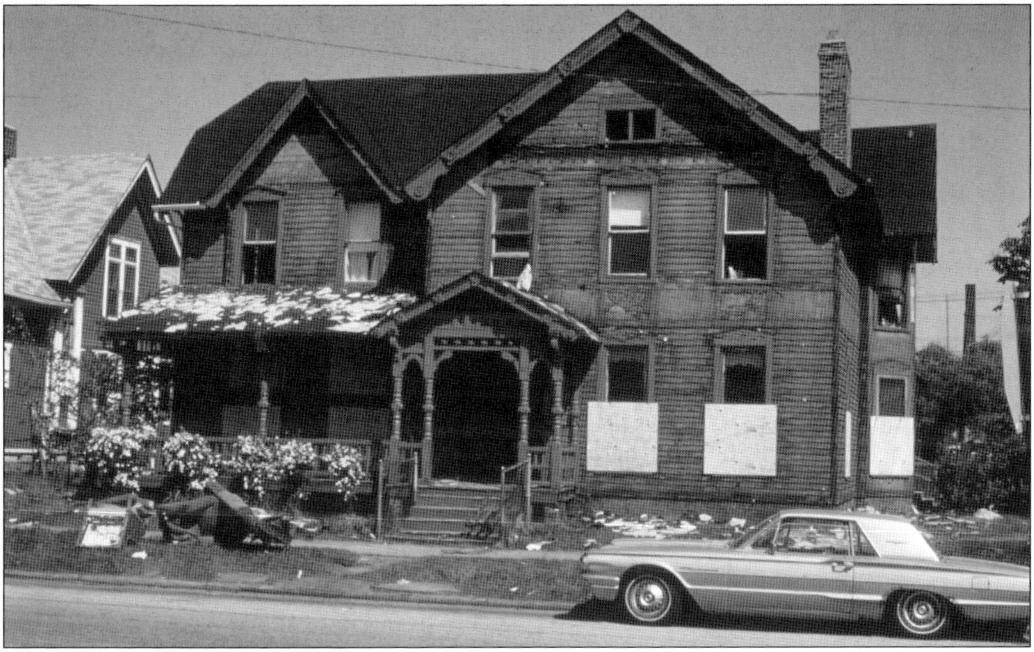

PRESERVATION IN ACTION, 1973. These two renovation projects represent different approaches to Ohio City's preservation movement. At 2904 Clinton Avenue, a Victorian-era home undergoes restoration as part of the official Ohio City Renewal Project, demonstrating public investment in neighborhood revitalization. Meanwhile, a few blocks away on Jay Avenue, private financing supports the renovation of another historic residence. Together, these 1973 photographs capture a pivotal moment when both institutional and grassroots efforts began reversing decades of decline, proving that Ohio City's architectural heritage could be saved through varied preservation strategies. Fifty years later, preservation efforts continue throughout Ohio City. (Both, National Archives Collection.)

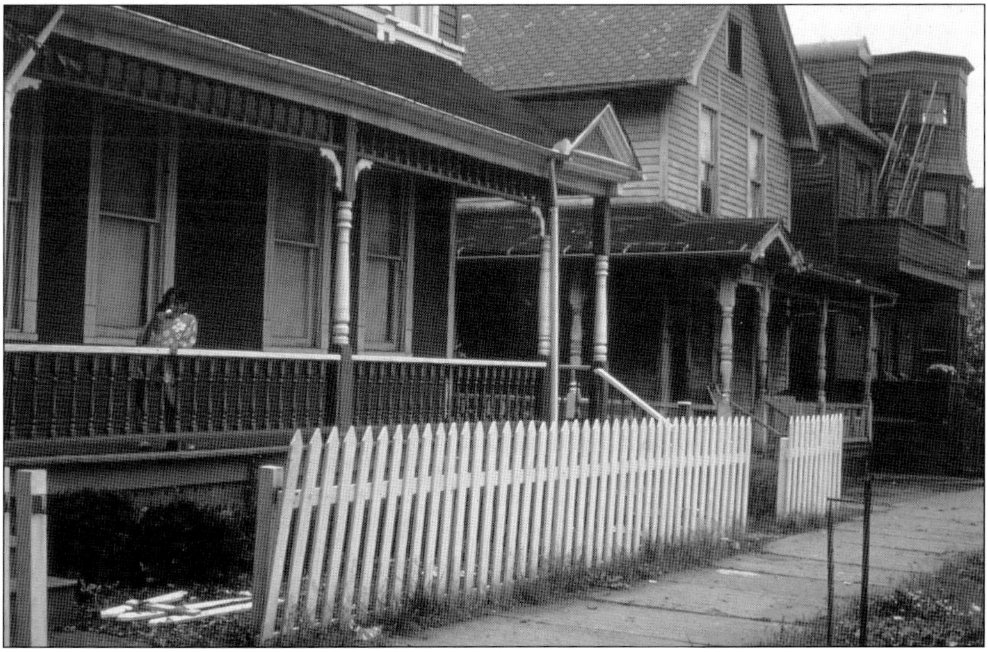

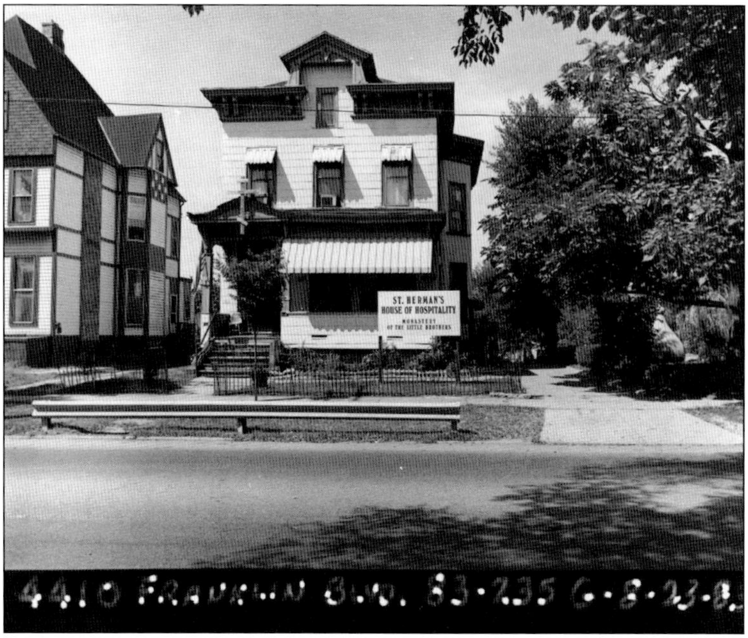

A MISSION OF HOPE ON FRANKLIN, 1983. St. Herman's House of Hospitality, established at 4410 Franklin Boulevard in 1977, has provided shelter and assistance to men in need for over four decades. Founded by the Orthodox Christian community, this historic building continues its mission of service today, offering food, shelter, and hope. (Cleveland Public Library Photograph Collection.)

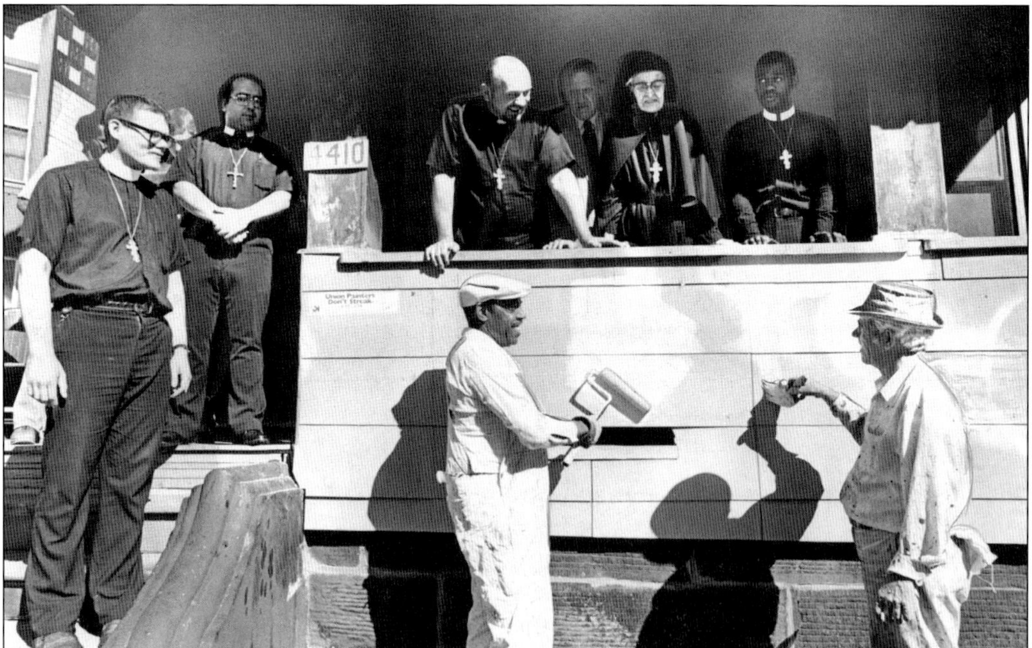

SERVICE MEETS PRESERVATION, 1980. This view captures painters refreshing the porch of St. Herman's House of Hospitality while the organization's founders and staff look on. To this day, the front porch is a popular gathering place for the residents. (Cleveland Press Collection, Michael Schwartz Library Special Collections, Cleveland State University.)

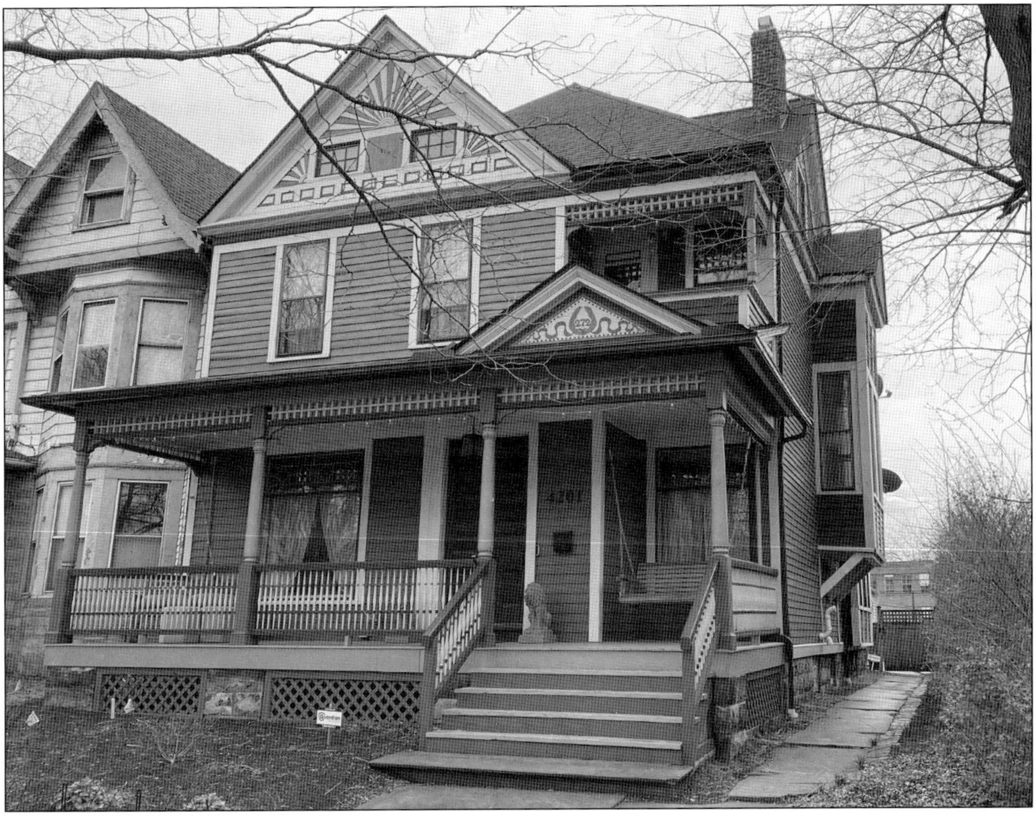

Victorian Row Revival, 2021. This view captures the restored terrace row houses at 4201-4207 Clinton Avenue, built in 1888 by Jesse Brainerd and designed by architect Andrew Mitermiler. After decades as 14 Depression-era apartments and later condemnation, owner Paul Meeker completed a remarkable rehabilitation in 2016, returning the structure to its original four attached dwellings. (Photograph by Adam Jaenke, Cleveland Public Library Photograph Collection.)

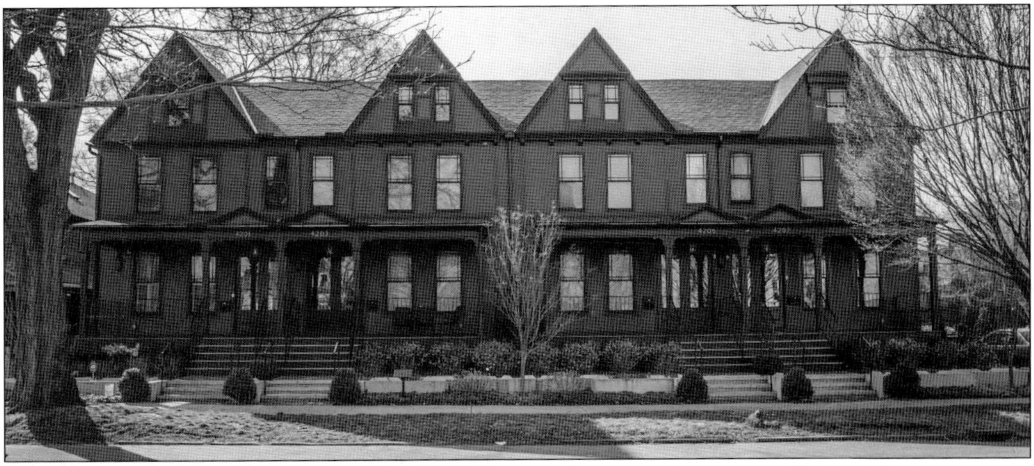

The Ford House. This 2022 view shows the Queen Anne residence at 4201 Franklin Boulevard, built in 1891 for William and Ella Day Ford on her family's property. Following a meticulous 2014–2017 restoration guided by the Cleveland Restoration Society, the home stands as one of Franklin Boulevard's finest preserved Victorian treasures. (Jim Dubelko.)

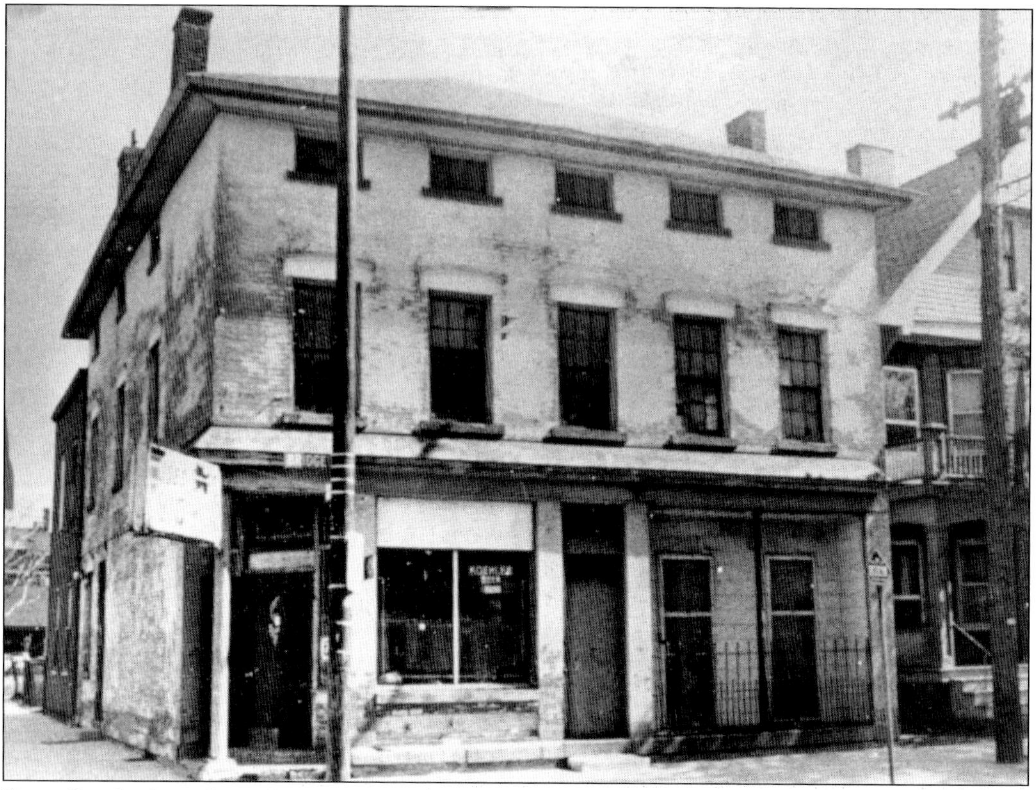

From Old Joe's to Ohio City Tavern. These two images showcase the remarkable transformation of 2801 Bridge Avenue. The first shows Old Joe's Café (previously Dorko's Café until 1965), a typical neighborhood tavern. The second captures the same building after Paul Martoccia's 1973 renovation into Ohio City Tavern—one of the area's first fine dining establishments. Martoccia's vision included salvaging stained glass windows from the demolished St. Mary's Church to create dramatic ceiling decorations, helping establish the restaurant as a destination that drew diners from across Cleveland. The building's evolution continued through the decades, housing Parker's Restaurant (1992), the Black Pig, and eventually Harper and Ivory Bridal Boutique—mirroring Ohio City's broader renaissance. (Both, Cleveland Press Collection, Michael Schwartz Library Special Collections, Cleveland State University.)

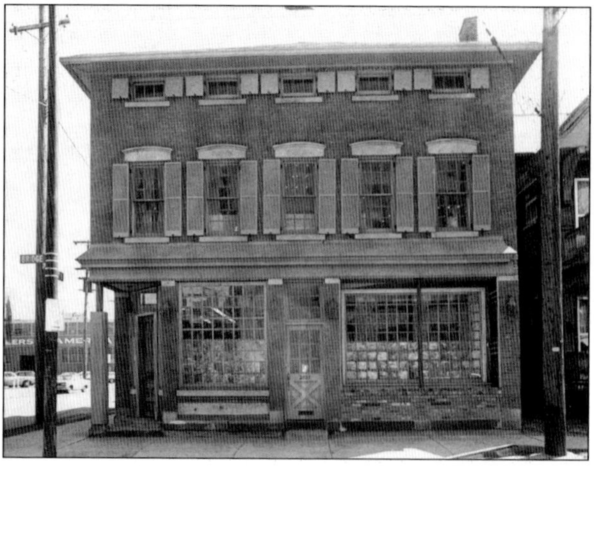

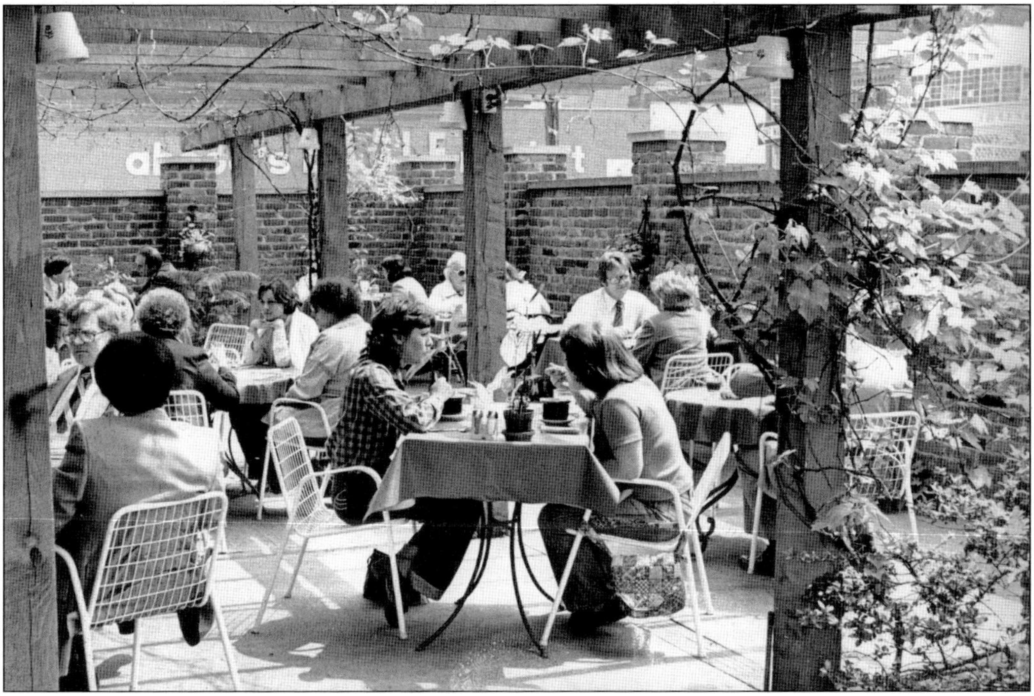

Summer Dining in Ohio City, 1980. This lunchtime scene captures the popular patio at Ohio City Tavern. The restaurant's outdoor space exemplified the neighborhood's growing appeal to visitors from across Cleveland. (Cleveland Press Collection, Michael Schwartz Library Special Collections, Cleveland State University.)

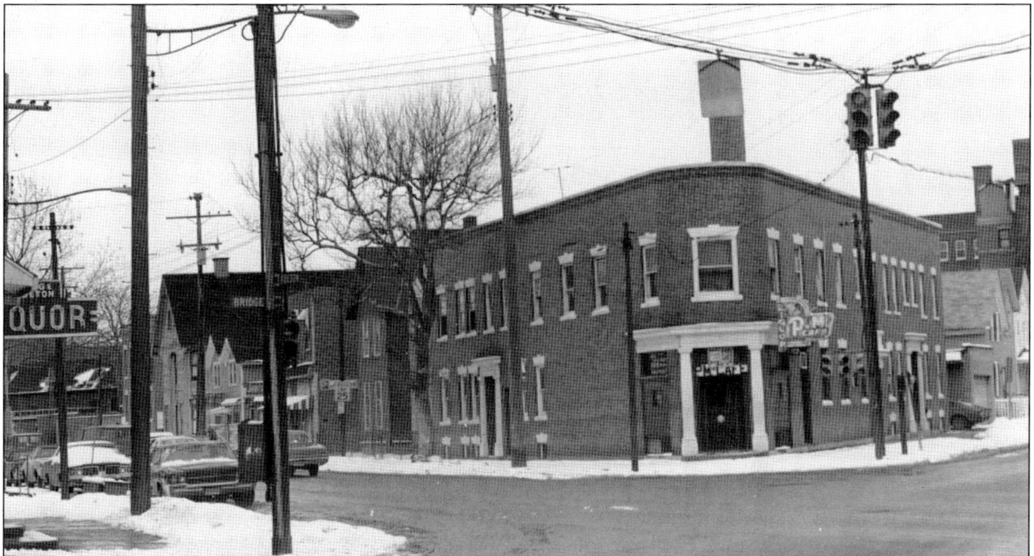

Bridge Avenue's Culinary Evolution. This 1977 view shows the P.M. Café at the corner of Bridge and Fulton, a site with a long history as both a bar and, earlier, delicatessen. Today, the building houses Johnny Mango World Café, a vibrant restaurant offering global cuisine with Mexican, Thai, and Caribbean influences in a tropical-inspired setting. (Cleveland Public Library Photograph Collection.)

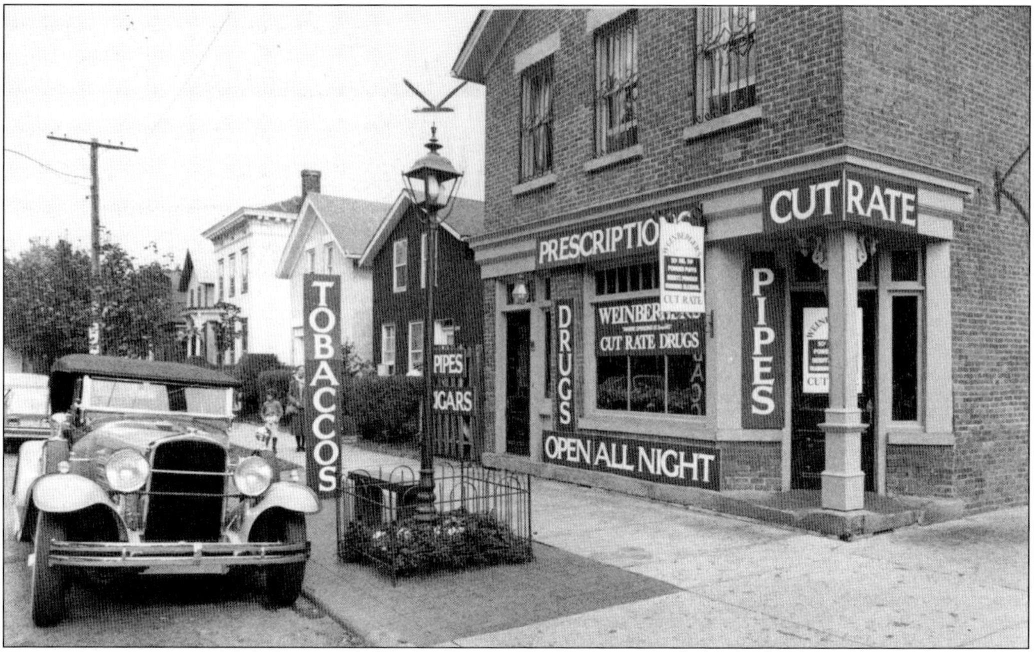

Heck's, From Pioneer to Film Set. The first image shows Heck's Restaurant at 2927 Bridge Avenue temporarily transformed into a Weinberger's Cut Rate drugstore for a 1978 Gray Drug Stores commercial, complete with a 1929 Jordan automobile parked outside. One of Ohio City's earliest revival businesses, Heck's opened in the early 1970s when few establishments were willing to invest in the neighborhood. The second image captures the restaurant's lush interior from 1974, where hanging plants created a garden-like atmosphere for diners. Known for 15 distinctive burger variations, Heck's continues to draw customers from across Greater Cleveland, proving historic Ohio City could become a dining destination and encouraging other entrepreneurs to invest in the area. (Both, Cleveland Press Collection, Michael Schwartz Library Special Collections, Cleveland State University.)

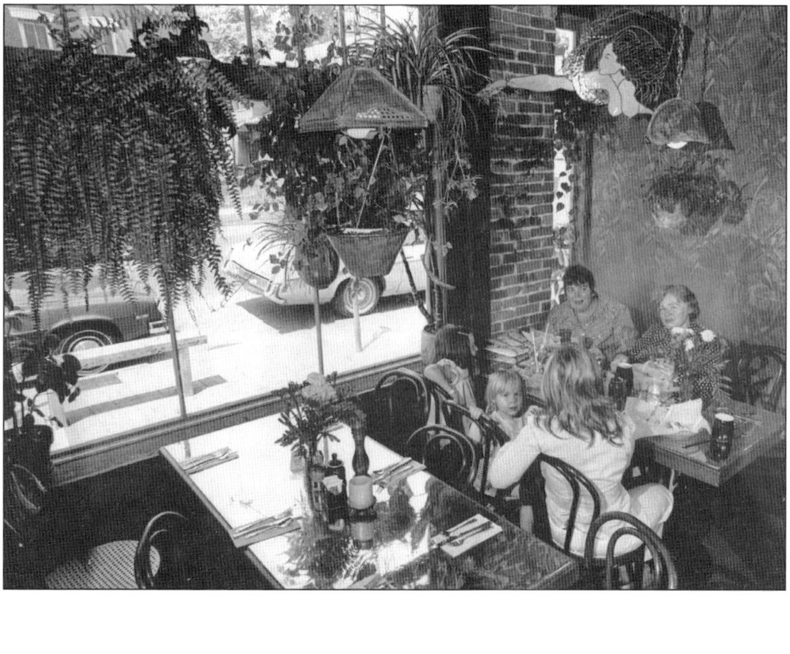

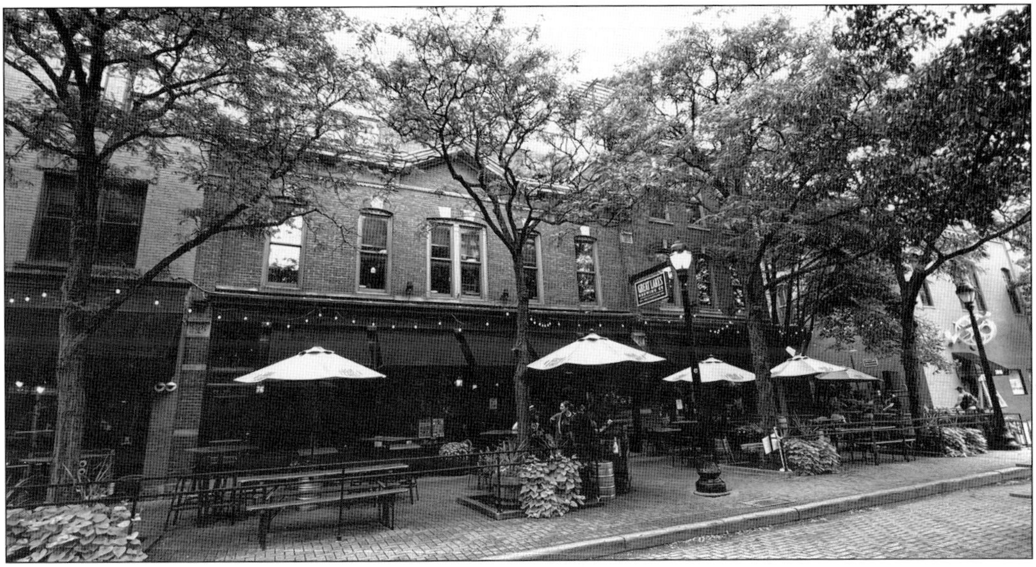

Birthplace of Cleveland's Craft Beer Revolution. This 2024 view shows Great Lakes Brewing Company at 2516 Market Avenue, where Patrick and Daniel Conway established Cleveland's first craft brewery in 1988. Originally the Market Tavern, this historic building underwent preservation by James and Jane Bowers in the 1970s, who saved its original brick walls, heavy beams, and historic bar. Now a national craft beer brand, Great Lakes helped spark Ohio City's revival. (Author's collection.)

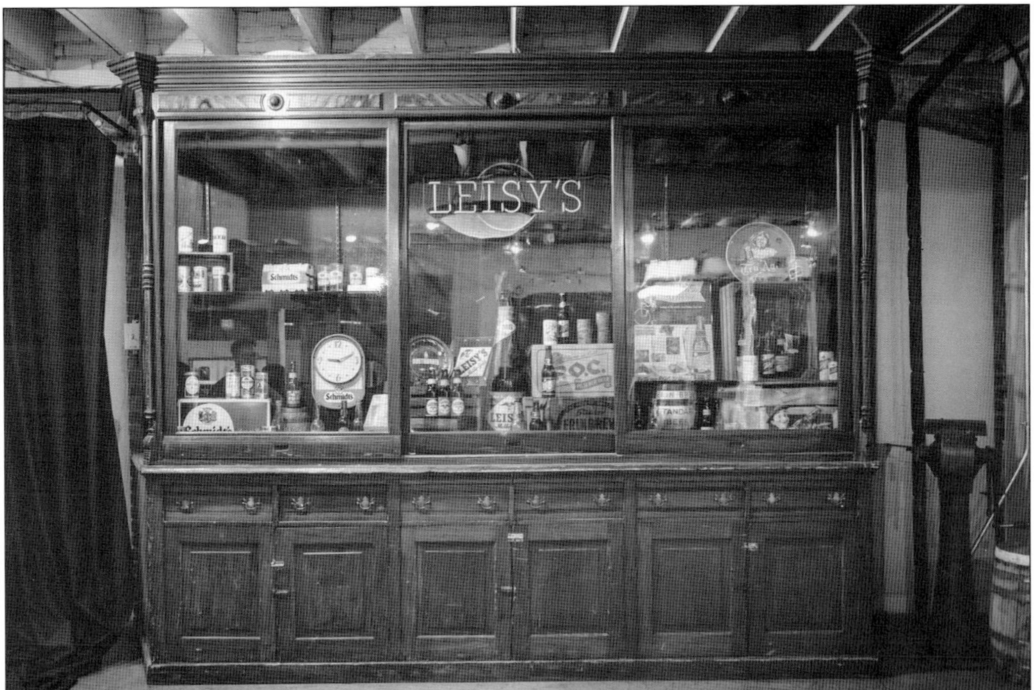

Brewing History Reimagined, 2024. This view inside Great Lakes Brewing Company showcases the brewery's homage to Cleveland's rich brewing heritage through historic memorabilia. Great Lakes has honored the neighborhood's brewing traditions while revitalizing them for a new era of craft beer enthusiasts. (Photograph by Adam Jaenke, Cleveland Public Library Photograph Collection.)

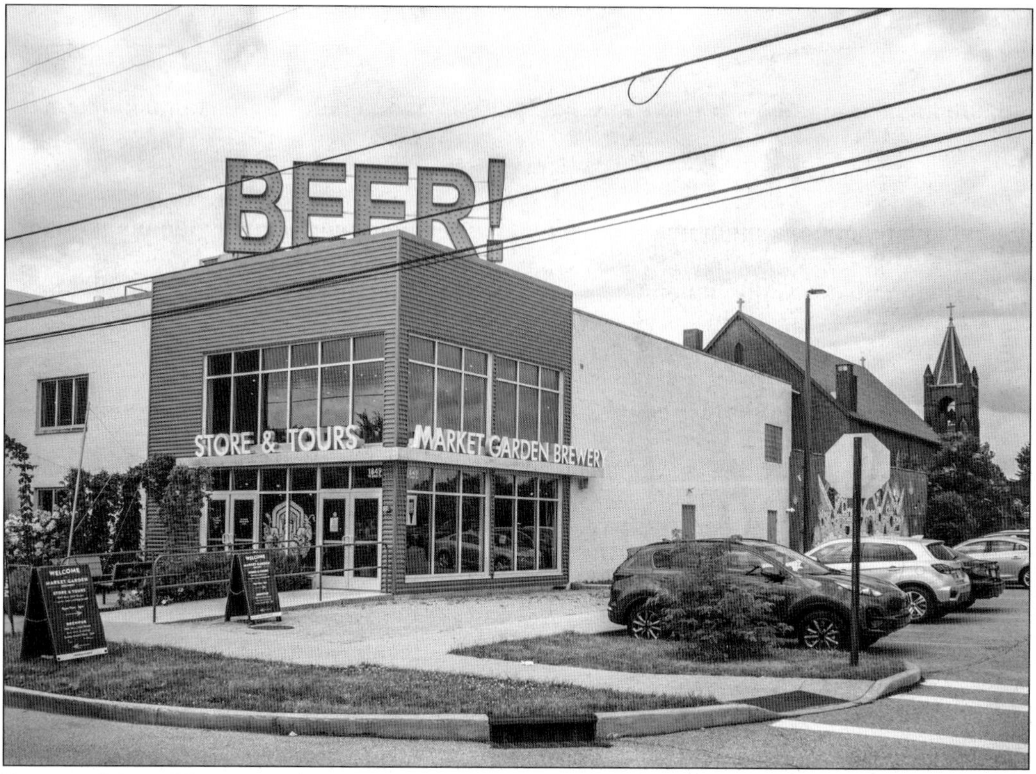

Brewing Meets Heritage. This 2021 view captures Market Garden Brewery's production facility and retail store located behind the Brewpub on West Twenty-Fifth Street. St. Emeric's Roman Catholic Church is visible in the background, symbolizing how Ohio City's brewing renaissance coexists with its historic landmarks. Established in 2011, Market Garden has contributed significantly to the neighborhood's rebirth as a craft brewing destination. (Photograph by Adam Jaenke, Cleveland Public Library Photograph Collection.)

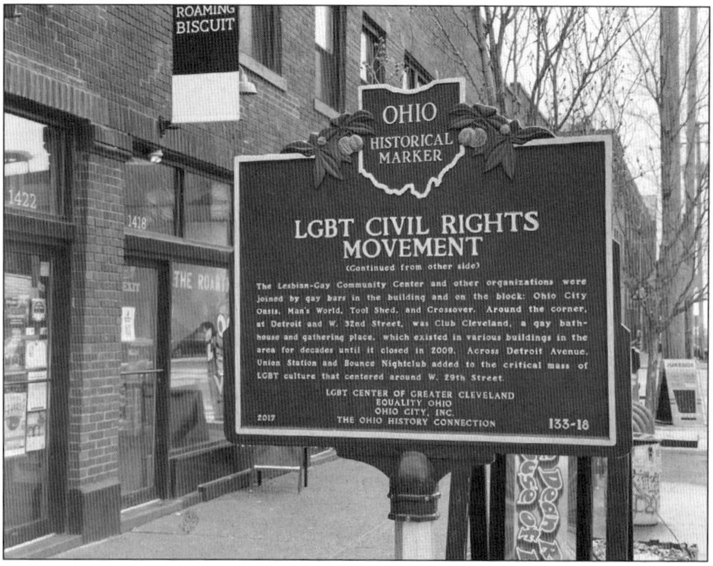

Honoring LGBTQ+ Heritage. This historical marker commemorates Ohio City's significant role in Cleveland's LGBTQ+ civil rights movement. The area around West Twenty-Ninth Street, now known as Hingetown, served as a haven for the gay community from the 1970s through the 1990s, hosting Cleveland's first Pride parade in 1989 and housing essential community organizations. (Author's collection.)

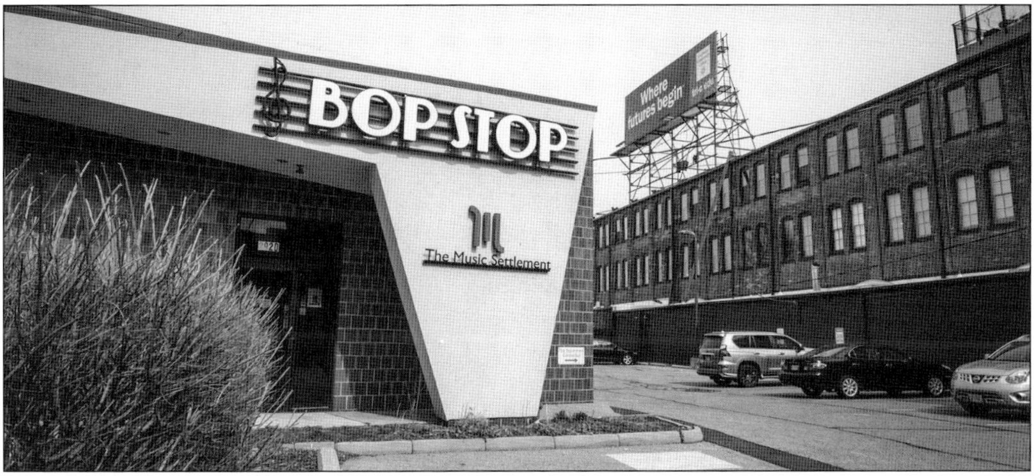

NURTURING ARTS IN OHIO CITY, 2021. This 2021 view shows Bop Stop at the Music Settlement, located at 2920 Detroit Avenue. Established in 2003, this intimate venue has become a cornerstone of Ohio City's vibrant arts scene. The modern performance space reflects the neighborhood's cultural renaissance, complementing its commercial revival with live music, education, and community programming. (Photograph by Adam Jaenke, Cleveland Public Library Photograph Collection.)

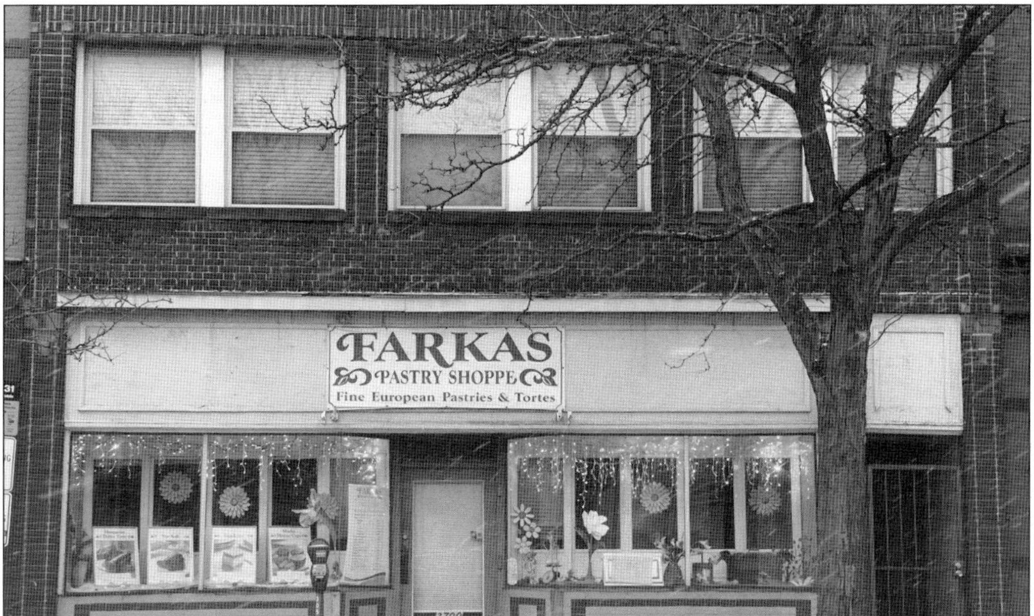

FARKAS PASTRY SHOPPE. This 2025 view captures Farkas Pastry Shoppe, a beloved Ohio City institution preserving Hungarian culinary traditions since 1966. Founded by master pastry chef Sandor Farkas and his son Attila, the shop began with simple krémes (napoleons) and grew into a regional destination for authentic European pastries. Located just two blocks from the West Side Market, it exemplifies the neighborhood's enduring ethnic heritage. (Author's collection.)

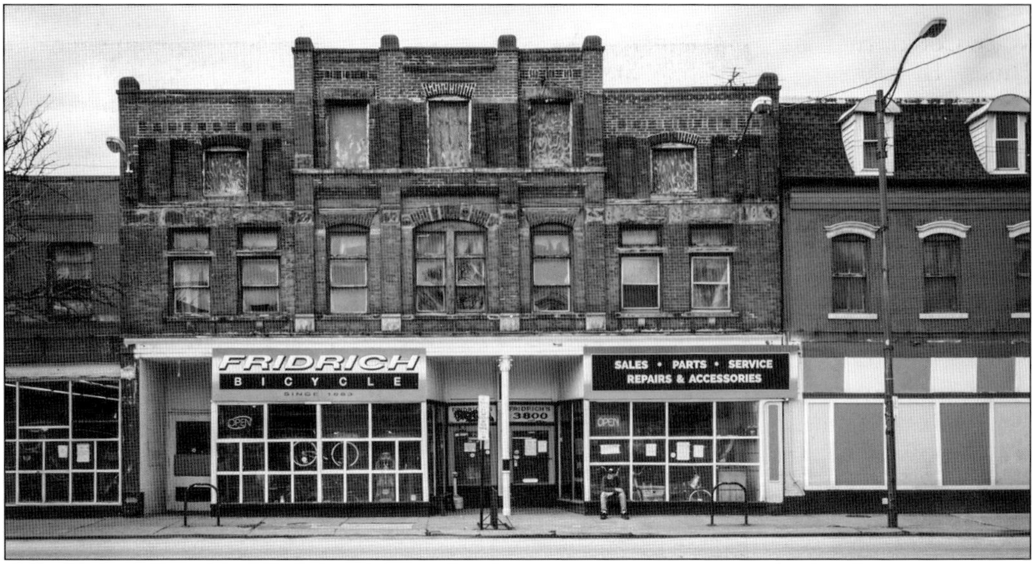

Fridrich Bicycle, Cleveland's Oldest. This view shows Fridrich Bicycle Shop at 3800 Lorain Avenue, Cleveland's oldest bicycle business, established in 1883. Originally a coal and feed store, the shop converted to bicycles around 1900, remaining in the same family for three generations. After 141 years in business, the historic shop closed in August 2024 when third-generation owner Chuck Fridrich retired. (Photograph by Adam Jaenke, Cleveland Public Library Photograph Collection.)

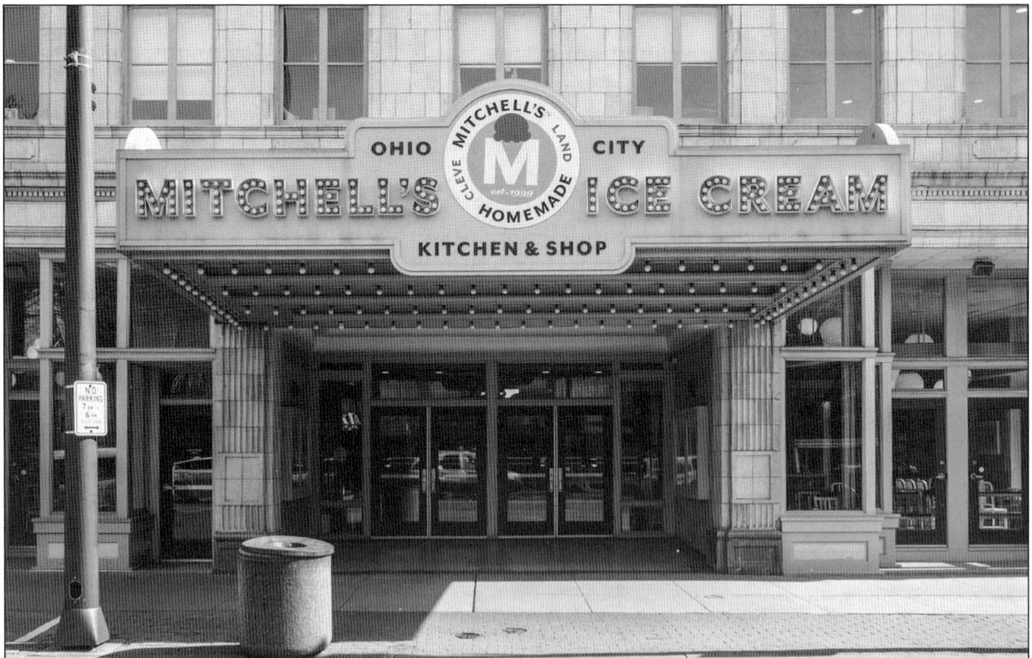

Sweet Transformations on West Twenty-Fifth. This 2020 view shows Mitchell's Ice Cream in Ohio City, a theater-turned-flagship store featuring both retail space and a 6,000-square-foot production kitchen. Founded in 1999, the local company transformed this historic building into a popular destination where visitors can watch ice cream being made while enjoying handcrafted flavors. (Photograph by Adam Jaenke, Cleveland Public Library Photograph Collection.)

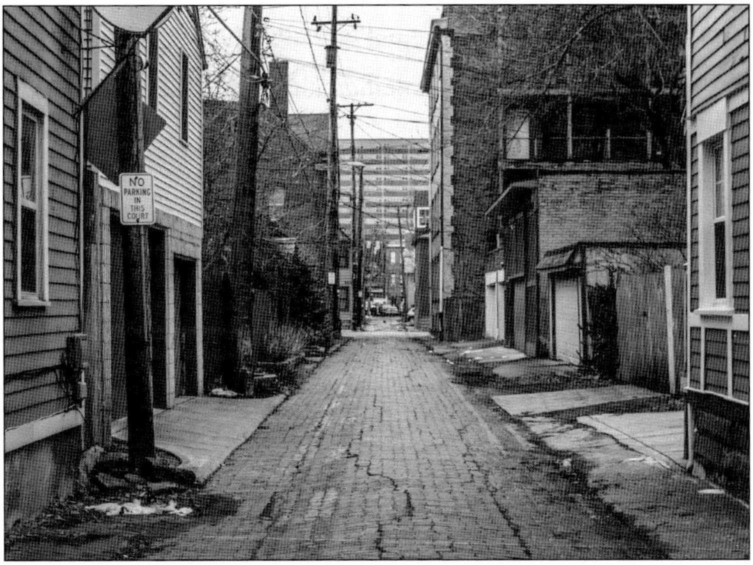

WACO COURT, THE HIDDEN HISTORIC ENCLAVE. This 2020 view looking northeast toward West Twenty-Eighth Street captures Waco Court, running parallel to and north of Bridge Avenue. The brick-paved court, accessible through a narrow alley, creates the sensation of stepping back in time. (Photograph by Adam Jaenke, Cleveland Public Library Photograph Collection.)

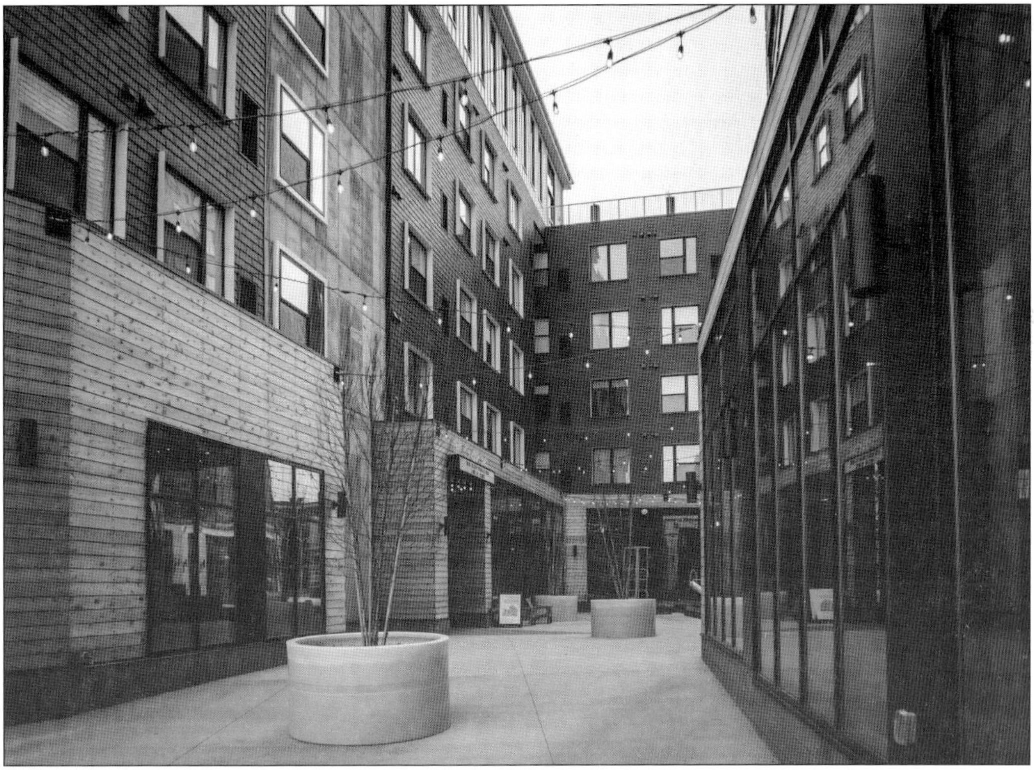

MODERN LIVING MEETS HISTORIC DISTRICT, 2021. This view shows Church + State Apartments at Church Avenue and West Twenty-Ninth Street. Completed in 2020, the development blends contemporary architecture with the neighborhood's historic fabric. Its name reflects its location—West Twenty-Ninth Street was formerly known as State Street. (Photograph by Adam Jaenke, Cleveland Public Library Photograph Collection.)